INTERNET USERS' RESEARCH GUIDE

We work with leading authors to develop the
strongest educational materials in Internet training
and education, bringing cutting-edge thinking
and best learning practice to a global market.

Under a range of well-known imprints, including
Prentice Hall, we craft high quality print and
electronic publications which help readers to understand
and apply their content, whether studying or at work.

To find out more about the complete range of our
publishing, please visit us on the World Wide Web at:
www.pearsoned.co.uk

INTERNET USERS' RESEARCH GUIDE

Fourth edition

TERENA

Trans-European Research and Education
Networking Association

Harlow, England • London • New York • Boston • San Francisco • Toronto
Sydney • Tokyo • Singapore • Hong Kong • Seoul • Taipei • New Delhi
Cape Town • Madrid • Mexico City • Amsterdam • Munich • Paris • Milan

Pearson Education Limited
Edinburgh Gate
Harlow
Essex CM20 2JE
England

and Associated Companies throughout the world

Visit us on the World Wide Web at:
www.pearsoned.co.uk

———————————

First published 1998
Fourth edition published 2006

© TERENA 1998, 2006

ISBN-13: 978-0-13-196429-7

ISBN-10: 0-13-196429-1

British Library Cataloguing-in-Publication Data
A catalogue record for this book is available from the British Library

Library of Congress Cataloging-in-Publication Data
A catalog record for this book is available from the Library of Congress

10 9 8 7 6 5 4 3 2 1
10 09 08 07 06 05

Typeset in 9½/13 Frutiger Light by 30
Printed and bound in Great Britain by Henry Ling Ltd, Dorchester

The publisher's policy is to use paper manufactured from sustainable forests.

CONTENTS

Preface xi
Publisher's Acknowledgements xiii

1   SEARCHING FOR INFORMATION 1

1.1   Web search tools 1

    1.1.1   Choosing a search tool 2
    1.1.2   Search engines 5
    1.1.3   Meta-search engines 9
    1.1.4   Classified directories 13
    1.1.5   Portal services 17
    1.1.6   Searching for images 18
    1.1.7   Other search tools 19

1.2.   Directory services 20

    1.2.1   Directory service tools 20
    1.2.2   Finding contact details for people and businesses 22

1.3   Search systems for non-web information 24

    1.3.1   Mailing lists 24
    1.3.2   Databases 25

2   WEB TOOLS 26

2.1   The World Wide Web 26

2.2   Web browsers 33

    2.2.1   Netscape Communicator 33
    2.2.2   Microsoft Internet Explorer 35
    2.2.3   Opera 36
    2.2.4   Mozilla 36
    2.2.5   Lynx 37

2.3   Caching and caches 38

2.4   Semantic Web 39

2.5   Web services 40

3   **WEB PUBLISHING** 43

3.1   Web authoring 43

3.2   HTML 45

3.3   Web authoring tools 47

3.4   Publishing Web pages 49

3.5   Graphics in Web pages 51

3.6   Graphics software 55

3.7   Multimedia 59

3.8   Multimedia software 61

3.9   Interactive Web pages 64

      3.9.1   Dynamic content and caching 65
      3.9.2   Dynamic HTML 66
      3.9.3   Java 69
      3.9.4   JavaScript 70
      3.9.5   Common Gateway Interface 71
      3.9.6   Active Server Pages 72
      3.9.7   PHP 74
      3.9.8   Application program interface 74
      3.9.9   Server Side Includes 75
      3.9.10 Cookies 76

3.10 Web databases 78

      3.10.1 Web database tools 79

3.11 XML: what is it? 81

      3.11.1 eXtensible Style Language .82
      3.11.2 XML browser compatibility 83

3.12 Metadata 84

3.13 Robots 86

3.14 Accessibility 88

4   PROTECTING USERS AND INFORMATION 90

4.1   Security risks 90

   4.1.1   Maintaining a secure environment 92
   4.1.2   Security requirements 92

4.2   Security for applications 93

   4.2.1   The SSL protocol 94
   4.2.2   E-mail 96
   4.2.3   Remote system connection 98

4.3   Encryption 99

   4.3.1   Methods of encryption 99
   4.3.2   Keys and computational power 101

4.4   Authentication, authorization and accounting .102

   4.4.1   Authentication 103
   4.4.2   Authorization 103
   4.4.3   Accounting 104

4.5   Digital signatures 104

   4.5.1   Creating a digital signature 104
   4.5.2   Certificate authorities 106
   4.5.3   Digital certificates 107

4.6   Public key infrastructure 108

   4.6.1   Public key infrastructure 109
   4.6.2   Obtaining a public key certificate 109
   4.6.3   Signature verification 110

4.7   Smart cards and tokens 111

   4.7.1   Smart card types 111
   4.7.2   Certificates on USB tokens 113

4.8   Firewalls 114

   4.8.1   How firewalls work 114
   4.8.2   Personal firewalls 115

4.9   Hostile code 117

   4.9.1   Viruses 117

4.9.2   Macro and e-mail viruses 118
4.9.3   Trojan horses 119
4.9.4   Worms 120
4.9.5   Defences 120

4.10 Spam 122

4.10.1 Spam from different points of view 123
4.10.2 How to stop spam 123

5   **REAL-TIME COMMUNICATION** 125

5.1   Instant messaging and chat 125

5.1.1   Instant messaging 126
5.1.2   Chat 127
5.1.3   Internet Relay Chat 128
5.1.4   Jabber 129
5.1.5   Resources 131

5.2   Codecs 131

5.2.1   Audio codecs 132
5.2.2   Video codecs 133

5.3   Videoconferencing 134

5.3.1   Overview of videoconferencing 135
5.3.2   Problems with NAT and firewalls 136
5.3.3   Videoconferencing standards 137
5.3.4   Resources 143
5.3.5   Videoconferencing networks 143

5.4   **Streaming** 145

5.4.1   The technology behind streaming 146
5.4.2   Streaming media standards 148
5.4.3   Resources 148

5.5   VoIP and IP telephony 149

5.5.1   VoIP: the forerunner of Internet telephony 150
5.5.2   IP telephony: a possible replacement for PSTN 152
5.5.3   IP network for the support of VoIP/IP telephony 153
5.5.4   Standards 153
5.5.5   H.323 154

5.5.6   SIP 156
5.5.7   H.323 or SIP? 158
5.5.8   Links 158

5.6   GRID 159

6   **MAIL, NEWS AND FTP** 160

6.1   E-mail 160

6.1.1   Becoming an e-mail user 162
6.1.2   E-mail addresses 163
6.1.3   Finding other people's e-mail addresses 163
6.1.4   Mailbox forwarding 164
6.1.5   Configuration parameters in MUA 164
6.1.6   Message composition 166
6.1.7   Sending e-mail 167
6.1.8   Receiving e-mail 167
6.1.9   Transmission of files 168
6.1.10   Transmission of viruses 170
6.1.11   Multipurpose Internet Mail Extensions 171

6.2   Mailing lists 172

6.2.1   How do mailing lists work? .173
6.2.2   Setting up a mailing list 174
6.2.3   MLM commands 176
6.2.4   Handling mailing list correspondence 176
6.2.5   Mailing list managers 177

6.3   Usenet News 184

6.3.1   Accessing Usenet News 185
6.3.2   News coverage 185
6.3.3   Newsreader programs 187

6.4   Transferring files 188

6.4.1   FTP software 188
6.4.2   Using FTP software 188
6.4.3   General aspects of using FTP 190
6.4.4   Further information about FTP 193

7   **NETWORK TOOLS FOR USERS** 194

7.1 Basic networking concepts 194

    7.1.1 Network components and structure 195
    7.1.2 Protocols and standards 197
    7.1.3 Client/server and peer-to-peer model 197
    7.1.4 Addressing and routing 198
    7.1.5 Routing 200
    7.1.6 NAT 200
    7.1.7 DHCP 203
    7.1.8 IPv6 204
    7.1.9 Network performance and problems 205
    7.1.10 Naming systems 205

7.2 Network tools 211

    7.2.1 Troubleshooting a network problem 211
    7.2.2 Command line interface 212
    7.2.3 Connectivity testing tools 213
    7.2.4 Tools for host network configuration 220
    7.2.5 DNS lookup tools 224
    7.2.6 Finding contact network managers 231
    7.2.7 Whois 232

Glossary 239

Index 255

PREFACE

The *Internet Users' Research Guide* has been published to provide an introduction to the basic tools and services available on the network. The 2006 edition provides a comprehensive guide of a wide spectrum of Internet services, from basic network tools, simple e-mail and Web tools to multimedia collaboration tools, searching for information, Web publishing and security. This edition, which is based on the previous editions of the *Guide to Network Resource Tools* (GNRT), also explores the fields of streaming, videoconferencing and networking.

Who is responsible for the guide

The *Internet Users' Research Guide* was produced by TERENA (Trans-European Research and Education Networking Association) for the members of the academic and research networking community. Primarily intended for Internet users and user support staff in this community, an online version is available at **http://gnrt.terena.nl/**.

Background

The *Internet Users' Research Guide* is an evolution of the GNRT which was originally produced as a small booklet by EARN (European Academic and Research Network). The original GNRT was published in the Internet Engineering Task Force's Request for Comments (RFC 1580) in 1994. The guide became very well-known and popular with end-users and support staff. In 1996, TERENA undertook a major update of the publication, which resulted in a completely new version which included many new developments and a wide range of popular tools. In 2000, the second online edition of the guide was produced and simultaneously published as a book, *The Internet Users' Guide to Network Resource Tools* by Addison-Wesley Longman. The third edition was published in 2001.

Acknowledgements

The Internet Users' Research Guide was edited by Miroslav Milinović, University Computing Centre, University of Zagreb with individual sections written by:

- Corrado Derenale (Italy)
- Dave Hartland (Netskills UCS, Newcastle University, United Kingdom)
- Debra Hiom (SOSIG ILRT, University of Bristol, United Kingdom)
- Dan Mønster (UNI•C, Denmark)
- Saverio Niccolini (University of Pisa, Italy)
- Maria Verina (Italy)

Thanks to Egon Verharen (SURFnet) and Päl Axelsson (University of Uppsala) for acting as reviewers and Ann Pocklington of UKERNA.

Jeroen Houben (TERENA) developed the online version of the publication. John Dyer (TERENA) undertook the final review and corrections. The project was managed by Licia Florio (TERENA).

PUBLISHER'S ACKNOWLEDGEMENTS

We are grateful to the following for permission to reproduce copyright material:

Figure 3.1 screenshot, Netscape and the 'N' Logo are registered trademarks of Netscape Communications Corporation. Netscape content © 2005 Netscape Communications Corporation. Used with permission; Section 3.14 extracts from Supporting Web Developers and Managers TechDis website, from http://www.techdis.ac.uk, reprinted by permission of TechDis; Figure 4.1 screenshots from TORSEC private site reprinted by permission of TORSEC Group; Figure 4.1 (right) screenshot frame reprinted with permission from Microsoft Corporation. Figure 5.1 screenshot, America Online, AOL, AIM and the Running Man icon are registered trademarks of America Online, Inc. AOL content © 2005 by America Online, Inc. The America Online content, name, icons and trademarks are used with permission.

In some instances we have been unable to trace the owners of copyright material, and we would appreciate any information that would enable us to do so.

1

SEARCHING FOR INFORMATION

The Internet makes available a huge and heterogeneous amount of data and specialized tools are required to perform searches. Business sectors have developed new services for finding information in a way which is pertinent to their requirements.

This chapter will describe how to find information:

- in non-specific Web-based systems like databases, mailing lists etc;
- in directory services;
- using specific Web searching tools, such as search engines, portal services, meta-search engines etc.

1.1 WEB SEARCH TOOLS

Web search tools gather, index, classify and search for information on the Web. These tools are constantly being developed and improved to meet the challenge of the ever-increasing size of the Web. The starting point is knowing what they can do and where to find them. In this section, we take a detailed look at some of the current tools. There are various classes of Web search tools and a selection of the most popular has been described below.

The main types of search tools are:

- **search engines** enable users to search for specific subjects or keywords in automatically generated indexes of Internet resources;
- **meta-search engines** enable users to search across more than one search engine simultaneously;

- **classified directories and subject gateways** select and list resources within a subject hierarchy and enable users to browse or search these listings;
- **portal services** aim to offer an all-round entry point to the Internet and generally mix both search engine and classified directory approaches and a variety of other services.

1.1.1 Choosing a search tool

Criteria for choosing an appropriate search tool include:

- control over the search;
- assessment of relevance;
- presentation of results;
- quality of content;
- comprehensiveness;
- presentation of results.

Control over the search

Web search tools generally provide a simple entry point, via a single window, for input of the search term(s). Most search tools take the search terms and check for documents in which those terms are found.

They provide ways of allowing users to control and refine their searches and some of the common ways are listed below. However, they often differ in the way they allow users to search, so for best results always consult the help files of the service.

Multiple search terms

If the search tool retrieves documents containing any of the search terms, this is different from retrieving documents that contain all of the terms, especially if relevance is based on a straight count of occurrences. In a search for

> *training guide dogs blind*

a search tool looking for documents containing any of the terms, i.e.

> *training* OR *guide* OR *dogs* OR *blind,*

could give a higher ranking to a document containing the word 'training' 15 times than a document that was actually on the topic of `Training Schools for Guide Dogs for the Blind' but contained this phrase only three times. Most search tools usually allow the user to specify how search terms are combined, either by typing the search string using the Boolean terms AND, OR and NOT into the search window, or giving equivalent functionality via drop-down menus. The use of parentheses in nesting Boolean search combinations provides a further level of control, for example

(*cricket* AND (*pitch* OR *ground*)).

Other ways of including or excluding search terms

Words that must be in the document can often be indicated with a plus sign, "+", and those to be excluded by a minus sign, "–".

Phrase searching

Commonly, the syntax for phrase searching, where it is provided for, is to enclose the phrase in inverted commas, for example "formula one". This will ensure that pages where these words appear together are returned.

Proximity searching

Proximity searching will allow the user to specify the order and closeness of search terms using operators such as NEAR or FBY (followed by).

Special operators

Some search tools support the use of other search operators, such as:

- `title` will search for pages that contain the specified term(s) in the title tags, e.g. *title:*sports news;
- `link` will search for pages that link to a particular Web address, e.g. *link:* **www.sosig.ac.uk**;
- `url` will search for pages that contain the specified term(s) in the *url*, e.g. url: terena;
- `domain` will search for pages from a particular domain e.g. *domain:*gov.

There are many more of these special operators so check the help pages of particular search engines to see if they are supported.

Truncation and stemming

Some search tools automatically truncate words. For example, a search using `anthropologist` is interpreted as a search for `anthropolog`. Other ways include word stemming – for example, `anthropolog*` will cover anthropology, anthropological, anthropologist, and so on.

Case sensitive searching

Case sensitive searching is often useful when searching for acronyms, for example, UN. Also, some search tools interpret adjacent search terms starting with capital letters as proper names.

Assessment of relevance

Search tools have different mechanisms for ranking and displaying results. Some services will rank first those documents in which all the search terms were found, in others the ranking is based on a raw score of occurrences of any search words in the document. The position of search terms in the document count is also frequently a significant factor.

Other factors that influence the ranking of results

Some services sell keywords to site owners (providing a guarantee of being found in the top ten hits for searches on a specified keyword). Also, if a search engine does not protect itself from index spamming, users may find irrelevant matches in their results lists.

Presentation of results

Many search engines provide the user with different ways of presenting the results. Most will provide some portion of the text on the site to allow the user to decide if it is worth following the link. Some services provide alternative criteria for ranking results, for example location or date. A number of search tools give the option of treating all pages from a site as a single entry.

Quality of content

More attention is being given by search tools to techniques that address the issue of quality of content. Where, previously, speed and size were the goals, getting relevant quality search results now ranks high on the agenda of all enlightened information services. Additional processing, be it human or machine, is used to sift, sort and add value to search results. Examples of such processing are:

● subjective evaluation and rating by a human classifier;

● automatic checking of how often a resource is linked to by others;

● automatic processing of data on previous accesses to the resource.

The results of such processing, combined with matching of search terms, generate a relevance score to be used in the ranking of search results. Currency of the information in the database, particularly working links, is another aspect of quality. A number of search engines revisit Uniform Resource Locators (URLs) at a variable rate depending on how often changes are made to the page.

Comprehensiveness

Many of the well-established search tools index hundreds of millions of Web documents. However, no service can index anything like all the information on the Web and as information increases, the proportion indexed decreases rather than increases. Currently, the maximum coverage by any one service is estimated at around 20–30 per cent.

Index spamming

Index spamming is the practice of inappropriately stacking Web pages with words likely to be used as search terms, hence boosting the chances of being found and accessed through a search. Index terms may be incorporated into the metadata in the head of the document, or placed in an area of the document, body not normally seen by the user. Some search engines have built-in safeguards against index spamming and may block offending sites.

Finding more information

To keep up to date with general search tool developments, look at the following sites.

- Search Engine Watch **http://www.searchenginewatch.com/**
- Search Engine Showdown **http://www.searchengineshowdown.com/**

1.1.2 Search engines

Search engines are generally the most popular starting point when looking for information on the Web. They create massive indexes of Web pages by using software programs that start with a single Web page, follow all the links it contains and index the data found, then all the subsequent links and so on. There are two types of search engine:

- spiders or robots (See Section 3.13);
- crawlers.

A user's search keywords are matched against the indexes using relevance ranking techniques that aim to retrieve and rank the pages that best match the user's query, and to allocate a numeric score accordingly. Although these indexes are impressive, the rate of growth at which new Web sites are appearing makes indexing difficult. There is an ever-increasing amount of material to index, and all of it is uncontrolled text. So while search engines can index millions of Web pages, it is still estimated that any one search engine covers only between 20 and 30 per cent of the Web at best. Because of differing gathering techniques or coverage policies, the content of search engines can differ – so if a really comprehensive search is required it is worth using a variety of search engines.

The search engine market is complicated by the fact that many of the services are created using combinations of Web indexes that are licensed by a few big companies, some of which themselves do not offer end-user services but act simply as information providers to search engines, for example, Inktomi®.

AllTheWeb.com

AllTheWeb.com (formerly known as FAST™ and powered by FAST™ Search) was launched in May 1999 and has quickly become one of the most popular search engines on the Web.

Access

http://www.alltheWeb.com

Coverage

It is one of the largest indexes of the Web searching over 2.1 billion Web documents, pictures, videos, Motion Picture Experts Group Audio Layer 3 (MP3) and File Transfer Protocol (FTP) files. The strengths of this service are the size of the database, currency of content and the speed of retrieval. It also recently included Portable Document Format (PDF) documents in its index. The FAST technology is being used by a number of other search services, including Terra Lycos®, Scirus and FirstGov™.

Use

It has a default AND search and can also use "   " for phrase searching. It uses + before terms which must be included and – before terms which must be excluded.

It provides an option to search by language, and a tabbed search box affords an easy method of switching between the types of information searched (Web, news, pictures, video, audio and FTP files). The advanced search options allow users to restrict by domain and IP address. It offers an option for users to customize the default search settings, including a filter for offensive content.

AltaVista™

AltaVista is one of the older search engines and is still popular, although it has lost some of its lead to other services such as Google and AllTheWeb in the last few years. It recently underwent a redesign that has streamlined its look and feel.

Access

http://www.altavista.com
AltaVista has many regional sites around the world including Canada, France, Germany, Netherlands, Sweden, the UK and the US. The service generally detects the browser's country and language header (or infers the location from the IP address) and offers options that allow the user to search worldwide or limit the search to the user's own country.

Coverage

It provides a search of Web pages, images, MP3/audio, video and news items. In addition to the main database it also offers search centres around specific topics such as finance, jobs, shopping etc.

Use

It supports default AND searching, all Boolean search features and phrase searching. It provides searching by fields and can limit searches on date and language. It offers a very useful translation service for foreign language Web pages.

Google™

Originally developed by two students at the University of Stanford as a research project, Google now ranks amongst the most popular search engines. Its popularity is due to its very effective ranking algorithm (PageRank™), which is based on how many other sites link to a particular Web page as well as where the search words appear in the document.

Access

http://www.google.com

Coverage

Google currently indexes over four billion documents. As well as a search of Web pages, it also provides access to images, news, Usenet groups and a directory of Web pages (using the Open Directory). The advanced search features allow phrase searching and restricted Boolean searching, language, file format (including PDF documents), and domain searching. The site also offers specialized searches in a number of topics such as Microsoft® and other software related sites, US government and US university sites. Google offers its search interface in 77 languages with more translations on the way.

Use

Google has a very clear interface, the focal point being the search box. Simply enter a term in the search box and press the Google search button. The default search is to combine terms. The Boolean operator OR can be used to search for either term. The search engine also supports the +/− convention for including and excluding terms.

For all the pages that Google has indexed there is a cached link that provides a copy of the page as it was when it was indexed. This can be useful if a particular site is unavailable or if the information has changed on the existing page.

HotBot®

HotBot has been providing a search service since 1996, although it no longer runs its own index and is now owned by Terra Lycos.

Access

http://www.hotbot.com

Coverage

The index makes use of several sources and providers including Overture™ for sponsored listings, Inktomi and Direct HitSM for Web listings and the Open Directory Project for directory listings.

Use

Quick search provides default AND searching and also supports phrase searching. Advanced search offers a variety of ways to refine searches including by language, date, domain and file type.

MSN® Search

As the search service for the Microsoft Network, it is in the top five of the most-used search engines.

Access

http://search.msn.com

Coverage

The MSN Search Network does not maintain its own index of Web sites but uses a combination of sources including, Overture™,Inktomi and LookSmart.

Use

It supports default AND searching and phrase searching. Search results highlight featured sites that have been chosen by MSN Search editors, sponsored sites (paid listings) and those that appear in the Web Directory.

1.1.3 Meta-search engines

As a rule, meta-search services (or meta-crawlers) do not have their own databases but offer simultaneous searching of a number of search engines from a single starting point. When the user keys in some search terms, the meta-searcher runs the search request on various associated search engines and collects the results. It may then select from the results, process them and generate a composite list of hits representing, in theory, the best matches from a range of search engines. It may then carry out some further processing of the results, for example allocating an overall relevance score, sorting by relevance or other criteria, formatting in a consistent manner, verifying availability and removing duplicate URLs. The final list of results will be a combined list that usually indicates which search engine, generated which entries.

Pros and cons

In a situation where there are many different search engines to choose from, none of which are comprehensive, meta-search services would appear to provide the ideal all-purpose solution. They have developed sophisticated searching and processing operations in order to monitor the performance and results of multiple simultaneous searches. But the task of generating and post-processing searches from a number of search engines returning results within an acceptable time is an ambitious undertaking. Because each of the services they incorporate has slightly different search parameters, they can generally offer only a fairly basic search across the different search engines. Also, many of the meta-search engines carry paid listings that may appear as the top search results, and this is not always made clear to users of the sites.

Ask Jeeves®

Ask Jeeves is a strange hybrid of a meta-search engine and a natural language search based on a database of set answers.

Access

http://www.askjeeves.com

Coverage

The Ask Jeeves service is underpinned by a knowledge base of over 7 million set answers to questions submitted to the service since 1997.

Use

The unique selling point of Ask Jeeves® is that it uses context-sensitive natural language processing to let users ask questions in plain English. It then presents one or more closely related questions to which the service knows the answer. It also provides results from a meta-search of Teoma^{SM}, Direct Hit^{SM} and Mirago®

Dogpile®

Launched in 1996, Dogpile is a popular meta-search engine that also offers a number of additional services such as a browsable Web directory, marketplace and yellow pages directory. The service does carry paid listings and these are not identified in the search results. It is now owned by InfoSpace™.

Access

http://www.dogpile.com

Coverage

Dogpile consults the following search engines as part of its meta-search: About™, Ask Jeeves, Dogpile Web Catalog, Fast, FindWhat®, Google, Inktomi, LookSmart, Open Directory and Overture. Users can choose to search for images, audio, files, news, multimedia, shopping or message boards.

Use

Dogpile searches four search engines simultaneously and results from the four are displayed on a page. If a search does not result in at least 10 matches then Dogpile will automatically search the next four engines, and so on until all are searched or at least 10 matches are found.

Excite^{SM}

Excite was one of the early search engines and is a good example of how these services keep changing to stay in the market. It is now owned by InfoSpace, and relaunched itself as a meta-search engine in 2002.

Access

http://www.excite.com/

Coverage

It combines results from several databases including FindWhat, Overture, Sprinks, AltaVista, FAST, Inktomi and LookSmart.

Use

The Excite meta-search allows users to search either the Web, a directory with people and business information or photos. One disadvantage of this meta-search is that it does not give any indication as to which database the results came from and this includes paid results.

Ixquick

Ixquick submits a search to 12 of the major search engines. It carries paid listings from Go.To and others, although these are not identified in the search results.

Access

http://www.ixquick.com/

Coverage

It provides a meta-search of Web pages, MP3 files, news and pictures. The results are ranked according to the number of search engines that refer to the site. Sites that appear in the top ten of the search engines are starred. It also offers a domain name finder that looks for available domain names by mixing and matching words chosen by the user.

Use

Ixquick offers 'power search techniques' that allow the user to search for phrases, include or exclude particular terms, and use proximity and fielded searching.

KartOO

KartOO is a relatively new meta-search engine (launched in April 2002) with an interesting twist – search results are shown graphically using Flash (although there is also an HTML interface for non-Flash users).

Access

http://www.kartoo.com

Coverage

It conducts a simultaneous search using a number of popular Web search tools including AllTheWeb, AltaVista, Yahoo! and MSN, and repackages the results graphically.

Use

KartOO analyzes a user's search term and sends it to a number of relevant search engines. The results are displayed on a clickable map. Web sites are depicted as spheres and as the user moves the mouse over a sphere a description of the site is displayed. Related topics are also displayed on the map. When the user moves over these a plus or a minus sign appears. Clicking on a plus sign adds the topic to the search and clicking on a minus sign excludes sites with this term. Depending on how many sites are found, users then have the option of moving on to the next map. It also offers an advanced search option.

Vivísimo

Research computer scientists at the Computer Science Department at Carnegie Mellon University founded Vivísimo in June 2000. The service was intended to be a showcase for the organization's automatic classification software; nevertheless, it also won the best meta-search engine award in the 2001 Search Engine Watch Awards.

Access

http://vivisimo.com/

Coverage

Vivísimo does a concurrent search of six of the most popular search engines as well as more specialized search engines such as CNN™, BBC and eBAY™.

Use

It can use Boolean search syntax and field searching including domain, title, sitename and URL. Search results are automatically organized into hierarchical folders using the Vivísimo Clustering Engine™ technology. It shows which of the search engines found the results and in which position they appear on that search engine. The advanced search features allow users to choose which sources are searched, the language of the search and how the results are displayed.

1.1.4 Classified directories

Classified directories, unlike search engines, are created and maintained by human editors. The editors of the directories select and review sites for inclusion using specific selection criteria. Records are usually created for resources that sometimes contain a description and keywords. The resources are then organized to allow structured browsing and searching.

Classified, or subject, directories offer a selection of broad subject divisions at the top level, from which to begin a search. Making increasingly specific choices takes the user down through the subject hierarchy. Classified directories offer the benefit of grouping like with like, enabling the user to see individual resources in their broader subject context. Because the resources are human-selected, there is likely to be a better chance of locating high quality information than with a search engine. The disadvantage of this approach is that the user cannot always predict how a subject will be classified. When searching a classified directory, it is important to remember that the user is searching the 'catalogue record' created for that resource, not the full text of the resource itself. Some classified directories also include abstracts or reviews, which can be very useful in sifting through long lists of resources.

Subject gateways are simply classified directories that are devoted to one specific subject. In looking for the appropriate tool for a search, it may be useful to note that classified directories usually have the following features:

- **context-based searching** items are arranged with like items as in a library arranged by subject, and lateral browsing may offer fruitful possibilities;
- **selected resources** selectivity may well compensate for lack of comprehensiveness in some cases, for instance in searching for a standard or classic work in a subject area;
- **improved chance of finding high quality resources** even though many items may be self-selected by their authors, many will also have been selected for inclusion because they have been found useful by others;

- **low risk of duplication and redundancy** in contrast to automatic index searching, selective human-compiled lists will not normally throw up multiple hits for the same work.

About.com™

About.com (formerly known as The Mining Company) is a classified directory organized by human guides who select and present sites in their specialist subject areas. Biographies of the guides outline each one's experience in that subject area and provide a contact e-mail address. The site makes heavy use of pop-up adverts on the subject pages, which can impede usage after a time.

Access

http://www.about.com
It also has international sites in Australia, Canada, India, Ireland, Japan and the UK.

Coverage

The directory is organized into 24 top-level subjects such as Arts & Entertainment, Health & Fitness, House & Home, Industry & Business and Money. The sites cover more than 50 000 subjects with over a million links and each guide area has site reviews, feature articles and discussion areas.

Use

Users can browse the hierarchical subject headings for their particular area of interest. A keyword search will result in both a search of the directory subject areas and a more general Web search.

Open Directory

The Open Directory is the largest human-edited directory with over 50 000 volunteer editors and 3.8 million sites listed. It is used by a number of the most popular search engines and portals, including Netscape® Search, AOL® Search, Google, Lycos® and many others.

Access

http://dmoz.org

Coverage

There are over 460 000 categories of information listed under 16 top-level headings such as Arts, Reference, Shopping, Recreation and Sports. The Open

Directory makes use of volunteer editors who can sign up to edit any subject area in which they are interested. Categories tend to be more popular subjects, although academic subject areas are also represented.

Use

Users can browse or search the directory. The browse listings are presented hierarchically with lots of cross-references between subject categories. The number of listings within the headings is shown in brackets.

LookSmart

LookSmart is a human-compiled directory of Web sites that accept paid submissions and sponsored listings (these are marked as such on the site). The service provides directory results to MSN Search, Excite and other partners. It contains paid listings, similar to Yellow Pages.

Access

http://www.looksmart.com

Coverage

It provides a browsable and searchable directory of over 700 000 categories. If a search fails to find a match from among LookSmart's reviews, it uses the Inktomi database to provide results.

Use

Users can choose to browse the topic headings or submit a keyword search.

Resource Discovery Network

The Resource Discovery Network (RDN) is a federation of subject gateways in the UK providing selected and organized Internet resources to support education and research. Subject gateways select, classify and describe high quality resources in a specified subject area.

Access

http://www.rdn.ac.uk

Coverage

RDN is targeted at learning, teaching and research communities (primarily in further and higher education). Currently it is made up of five subject services:

- BIOME (Health and Life Sciences) **http://biome.ac.uk**
- EEVL (Engineering, Maths and Computing) **http://www.eevl.ac.uk**
- Humbul (Humanities) **http://www.humbul.ac.uk**
- PSIgate (Physical Sciences) **http://www.psigate.ac.uk**
- SOSIG (Social Sciences, Business and Law) **http://www.sosig.ac.uk/**

A number of other services are planned for release in the near future.

Use

Users are directed to the appropriate subject service through the hierarchical browse listings. Alternatively users can choose to search across all of the services using the 'resource finder'.

Yahoo!®

Yahoo! is one of the oldest human-edited directories and is still one of the most popular Internet services. Over the years the directory has been supplemented with a variety of portal-like services such as e-mail accounts, news, shopping and chat facilities. However it is listed under Classified Directories, as it was for this that it was first renowned, and this still accounts for its massive popularity.

Access

http://www.yahoo.com
There are a number of European sites including Denmark, France, Germany, Italy, Norway, Spain, Sweden and the UK. There are also sites around the world in Asia and the Pacific.

Coverage

The Yahoo! directory lists many thousands of resources within its hierarchy of subject categories. At the top of the hierarchy are 14 broad headings such as Arts & Humanities, Business & Economy, Computers & Internet, Education, Science and Society & Culture. Underneath each of these is a hierarchy of subject subdivisions, and within these are the entries for resources classed under the subject. The hyperlinked entries may consist of a title only, or a title and a brief description.

Use

Users can browse or search the directory. Browsing starts at one of the 14 broad topics at the top level, then proceeds down through the subject hierarchy to reach the desired topic. For example, a user might select the top-level category of Business & Economy, then proceed to the next level where there are links to general works on the subject such as Directories and Economics, to further sub-categories, and to any actual titles in this category. The number of entries within each subcategory is shown in brackets beside it. Following a subcategory link leads to a further similar listing.

Other subject-based services

A further listing of other subject gateways can be found through PINAKES that provides a subject launch pad at
http://www.hw.ac.uk/libWWW/irn/pinakes/pinakes.html

1.1.5 Portal services

An increasing trend is to host a whole collection of services under one umbrella and present it as a 'total' information solution. In addition to the basic search engine and classified directory functions, such umbrella services offer facilities such as finding e-mail and postal addresses, finding telephone and fax numbers, locating details of companies, getting share prices, reading current news and weather reports, online shopping, free e-mail accounts and home pages. Many portals offer 'personalized' services. These allow the user to tailor their personal start page, delivering information that is directly of interest to that individual. The driving force of the portal is to make them as 'sticky' as possible, i.e. to have enough interesting content to keep them in the portal as long as possible to maximize the service's ability to attract advertising revenue and online sales. There are several types of portals:

- general portals are aimed at being a starting point for Internet users;
- national portals bring together information of interest to a geographically based audience;
- subject portals are a starting point for an audience with particular subject interests.

Community portals bring together information for audiences with common geographical, social or political interests.

Some of the major general portals are:

- AOL.com one of the biggest Internet Service Provider (ISP) sites, although much of the information here is accessible only by AOL® subscribers.
  http://www.aol.com
- Lycos® one of the original portal sites, offering a typical portal interface with a wide variety of services offered from the home page. **http://www.lycos.com**

- MSN run by Microsoft this acts as the default home page for MSN subscribers.
  http://www.msn.com

- Netscape the default home page for Netscape browser users.
  http://www.netscape.com

1.1.6 Searching for images

Ditto.com

Ditto.com is described as a visual search engine that retrieves both a picture and the Web page in which it is found. Web sites containing images are identified through an automated crawler. Ditto.com then selects, ranks, weighs, filters and rates the images. Offensive material is blocked from the search results.

Access

http://www.ditto.com

Use

Searches open up a new window to display the results and also have pop-up advertising, which can be tiring after a while. The default is to search for images but the user can also select a general Web search.

ImageFinder

ImageFinder is provided by the Berkeley Digital Library SunSITE and brings together a number of (mostly academic) image catalogues and databases including collections from the Smithsonian Institute, the National Library of Australia and the Library of Congress.

Access

http://sunsite.berkeley.edu/ImageFinder

Use

ImageFinder simply brings different collections together through a single page. Each collection has its own search box and separate search parameters, which the user can use from the start page or link through to the home site.

Other search engines that provide access to images and other multimedia content include Google, AltaVista and AllTheWeb (see entries above for more information about these services).

1.1.7 Other search tools

Encyclopædia Britannica

Based on the classic publication, the site also offers a Web directory listing, full text of magazine articles from selected journals and access to the Merriam-Webster Collegiate Dictionary™ and Thesaurus. The full text of articles from the encyclopædia is restricted to subscribers of the site. Heavy use of pop-up adverts detracts from the otherwise scholarly content.

Access

http://www.britannica.com

Coverage

The Web directory, known as the 'world's best Web sites' contains over 125 000 entries which have been reviewed and indexed by Britannica's editors. Other free services include a search of over 70 magazines, including Time and The Economist.

Use

Options allow users to browse Britannica alphabetically, by subject or through the use of interactive maps. Users can search across all the databases or restrict themselves to a particular type of information. Multiple search terms are processed as an OR operation by default, although Boolean operators are supported for more precise searching.

Scirus

Scirus describes itself as a 'science-specific search engine'. It is run by the academic publisher Elsevier Science. It is a very useful and easy-to-use service that combines Web and traditional print searching through a single interface.

Access

http://www.scirus.com/

Coverage

Scirus combines a Web search engine with journal sources such as MEDLINE, IDEAL (240 000 full-text articles from over 300 journals in the scientific, technical and medical fields), National Aeronautics and Space Administration (NASA) technical reports, and e-print and pre-print archives. The user may need a subscription or online registration to access some of the full text articles.

Use

By default, a basic search will look for journal articles and Web sites and will implicitly AND all of the search terms (i.e. look for all the terms in the results). The advanced search allows users to be much more specific about the types of information they would like to retrieve – abstracts, articles, patents, conferences etc. – as well as which sources are searched. Results are ranked according to relevance by default but these can be re-sorted according to date.

WayBack Machine

Provided by the Internet Archive, a non-profit organization founded to provide permanent access to Web collections, the WayBack Machine provides archived copies of Web pages from 1996 to the present.

Access

http://www.archive.org

Coverage

The search engine contains over 100 terabytes and 10 billion Web pages.

Use

Enter a specific URL or use the browsable directory to find archived Web pages. The advanced search page allows users to retrieve a page from a particular date or over a given time period.

1.2 DIRECTORY SERVICES

Online directory services can be divided into two groups, White Pages and Yellow Pages. White Pages provides a means of searching for people and computers on the net. Yellow Pages provides for searching for businesses. While there is no comprehensive stand-alone global directory, some of the Web directories are quite large and definitely worth a try.

1.2.1 Directory service tools

This section covers a selection of tools commonly used for providing Internet directory services. Some of the tools, such as Whois, are used mainly for local directories, while others such as Lightweight Directory Access Protocol (LDAP) and

X.500 can be used globally. Though the net cast by these tools collectively catches the contact details of millions of people, there are still many people covered only by local directories, which use tools other than those listed here.

Lightweight Directory Access Protocol

This is a protocol enabling directory services to locate organizations, individuals and other resources on the Internet. It is an open protocol enabling any client program using LDAP to access any Directory Access Protocol (DAP)-compliant (or X.500) directory server. An example of its implementation is the e-mail address lookup facility in an LDAP-enabled e-mail client program. The user can specify the LDAP directory to use, for instance their institution's staff directory. The client and server handle the details of information request and delivery.

The LDAP information model is based on the entry, which contains information about some object (for example, a person). Entries may include a mix of information such as text, Joint Photographic Experts Group (JPEG) images, sounds, URLs and Pretty Good Privacy (PGP) keys. Directory entries are arranged in a hierarchical tree-like structure:

- the root directory;
- countries;
- organizations;
- organizational units (divisions, departments, etc.);
- individuals (including people, files and shared resources such as printers).

All directory implementations have an LDAP interface, e.g. Novell Directory Services® and Active Directory®. In addition, many client applications have an LDAP interface, for example, e-mail agents, browsers or PGP clients.

Access

A list of national directory services is available from the NameFLOW Directory from DANTE:
http://www.dante.net/nameflow/national.html

An Open Source Implementation of LDAP is available from
http://www.openldap.org/

X.500

This is an International Organization for Standardization (ISO) and International Telecommunications Union (ITU) standard for distributed directory services. The standard encompasses both the structure of the X.500 database and also the protocol used in querying it. It can be used for different types of directories. Its most notable implementation is a global White Pages service containing in excess of a million names contributed to by X.500 servers in dozens of countries.

It provides a hierarchical database structure (for example, country/organization/ organizational unit/person). The database consists of entries (one per object) that may describe persons, network resources, organizations and so on, each with its own set of attributes.

Access

It is based on the client–server model. The user with an X.500 client (known in the X.500 world as a Directory User Agent or DUA) can query an X.500 server (Directory System Agent or DSA). The server maintains the local X.500 database, but it can also communicate with other X.500 servers. If a query cannot be answered locally it may be passed on automatically to other X.500 servers and the response passed back to the user. To the user it appears that the entire directory is accessible from the local server. As well as queries, X.500 also supports data management functions (addition, modification and deletion of entries).

A list of national directory services is available from the NameFLOW Directory from DANTE: **http://www.dante.net/nameflow/national.html**

Whois

Whois is both a directory and a protocol. The Whois directory is a searchable database of information about networks, networking organizations, domains, sites and the contacts associated with them. It can be used in the following ways:

- to find information about networks, domains and hosts;
- to locate contact information (people) for networks and domains;
- when registering a domain name, to see if the name is already in use.

Access

Whois can be accessed through the Web-based form at
http://www.internic.net/whois.html

1.2.2 Finding contact details for people and businesses

On the Internet it is possible to locate e-mail addresses, postal addresses, telephone numbers and fax numbers, using searchable online directory services. What is not possible is to give any guarantees about what might or might not be able to be found. There is no universal directory of net users, nor even comprehensive coverage of names within any one country. Coverage is certainly uneven from country to country and from discipline to discipline. On the plus side, the existing directories contain millions of names and corresponding contact details. As well as the White Pages and Yellow Pages services, there are specialized directories such as directories of professional groups, databases of subscribers to mailing lists, campus and organizational directories, and a directory of people who have posted articles to Usenet newsgroups. Almost universally, these services are available via the Web.

The information contained in the directories on the net may be sourced from commercial directory publishers who use phone books and public records to obtain data. Alternatively, it may be generated by a robot that collects data from Web sites. E-mail addresses may be extracted from Usenet postings, submitted by ISPs, and/or a range of manually collected sources such as organizational staff listings, or self-submitted details from users. Internet directory services may use a variety of technologies. The service may rely on a database held in a single location and interrogated from a single point using some sort of index searcher, or it may use a distributed database accessed through a common protocol such as LDAP, Whois or X.500. Information on popular tools for building and accessing directory services can be found in Section 1.2.1.

Portal services

Some of the leading people-finding services are now to be found under the umbrella of portal services.

InfoSpace

This offers searching for e-mail addresses, telephone and fax numbers, businesses, company Web sites, and other material. Yellow Pages offers multiple search options for US companies, plus links to directories and information for a selection of other countries. White Pages offers searching to locate residential phone numbers and e-mail addresses of individuals. A lot of the information has a strong US bias.
http://www.infospace.com

Directory services

There are also major sites dedicated exclusively to directory services.

Infobel.com

This provides access to people, businesses, classified directories etc. from a number of countries including Canada, Denmark, France, Italy, Netherlands, Spain, the UK and the US.
http://www.infobel.com/world/default.asp

BigFoot™

This is a US centric e-mail directory; however, a general search will pick up e-mail addresses not based there.
http://www.bigfoot.com

World E-mail Directory (WED)

This has access to millions of e-mail addresses, business phone numbers and addresses worldwide.
http://worlde-mail.com

Global Yellow Pages™

This is a simple, but very useful, listing of national residential telephone and business directories from all over the world.
http://www.globalyp.com/world.htm

Searching phone numbers is generally patchy, nevertheless there are a number of searchable national telephone directory services available on the Internet.

1.3 SEARCH SYSTEMS FOR NON-WEB INFORMATION

While most of the information available on the Internet can be retrieved using search engines, there are a few cases where different tools may be needed. Specific examples are obtaining information about mailing lists and obtaining information from databases.

1.3.1 Mailing lists

The Internet is very effective for making contact with people who share common interests through discussion lists and newsgroups. These give such groups of people the opportunity to exchange ideas and news on their subject of interest easily, and may also generate further one-to-one dialogues between like-minded individuals. To find others who share an interest in a particular subject, the most useful starting point is to identify mailing lists (discussion lists) or newsgroups that cover the topic. There are several services that offer searching by topic.

- JISCmail a UK-based mailing list service that administers a large number of lists primarily for the UK academic and research community (although membership of the public lists is open to anyone).
  http://www.jiscmail.ac.uk

- TILE.NET lists discussion groups, and is browsable by name or subject.
  http://tile.net/lists

- CataList the official catalogue of ListServ.
  http://www.lsoft.com/lists/listref.html

- TOPICA is a searchable and browsable database of mailing lists.
  http://www.topica.com/

1.3.2 Databases

Some of the most valuable resources accessible via the Internet are the many specialist databases used as everyday working tools by librarians, scientists, and other professionals. For instance, online bibliographic databases are the stock-in-trade of librarians, and scientific datasets figure prominently in many scientific disciplines. They are sometimes referred to as the 'deep web' as the content of the databases is not available through traditional search engines. Many, though not all, online databases are subscription or fee-based and are accessed with a user-id and password. There are several services through which you can locate online databases for a given subject.

- CompletePlanet™ directory of over 103 000 searchable databases and specialty search engines organized into more than 5 000 subject headings. CompletePlanet estimates that collectively this provides access to over 4 billion documents.
  http://www.completeplanet.com/

- InvisibleWeb™ a directory of over 10 000 databases, archives and search engines that contain information that traditional search engines have been unable to access.
  http://www.invisibleWeb.com

- Ingenta provides access to over 27 000 full-text online publications.
  http://www.ingenta.com

- Northern Light® searches over 7 000 sources including newspapers, broadcast news transcripts, academic and scientific journals, analyst reports etc.
  http://www.northernlight.com/search.html

2

WEB TOOLS

Above all other network tools, the World Wide Web has helped to advance the ongoing revolution in the use and application of networked information. It has fired the enthusiasm of users as well as the imagination of software developers generating rapid uptake and development of new functions and capabilities. The Web has colonized most other network tools and integrated their functionality into its own all-enveloping interface to such an extent that the only essential network tool for many users is a Web browser.

Tools entries here include:

- The World Wide Web
- Web browsers
- Caching and caches
- Semantic Web.

Entries on Web search engines and other tools are included in Section 2.2.

2.1 THE WORLD WIDE WEB

The WWW is a hypermedia information system providing seamless access to distributed information on the Internet and a flexible means of publishing information.

Hypermedia

Hypermedia (or hypertext, if it is text only) documents are those that contain embedded links (hyperlinks) to other related documents in any media. The presence of a link may be indicated to the reader by special formatting of the linked item, or some change in its appearance when the mouse is dragged over it. The information contained in the link includes the unique Internet address of the referenced document, that is, its URL (Uniform Resource Locator). The format that makes it possible to embed this information invisibly is HTML (HyperText Markup Language), the standard format for Web documents.

When a hyperlink is selected, the document to which it refers is immediately fetched and displayed for the user. This document may contain links to further documents. Thus the user can track related concepts from one document to another, traversing the net in a seamless fashion, regardless of the physical location of the documents or the type of computers on which they are held.

Hyperlinking offers advantages to Web authors as well as readers. By offering optional levels of enrichment and enhancement of document content through links to related documents, it adds value and context to Web documents with an immediacy seldom possible with traditional forms of information.

Links in Web documents span not only the universe of networked information but also the range of media because the Web is a multimedia system encompassing text, audio, video, graphics and other types of information.

Distributed information

Through the Web, the user can access documents distributed across millions of linked computers all over the world. The Web interface makes it appear that there is one integrated corpus of documents, one massive file system, when in fact the files are held on many separate computers.

Publishing information

The Web provides an easy, platform-independent, supremely flexible means of making information available. It is easy because Web documents are normally written in HTML, the rudiments of which are easily learnt, and for which there are many editing and conversion programs available. Documents in standard HTML can be read by any Web browser on any platform. Distribution of the information worldwide becomes just a matter of making potential users aware of it, and revision and updating of the information are managed by maintaining the files at the source of distribution, namely on the server.

Access

Access with a client

Users access the Web with client software, normally referred to as a Web browser. There are other types of Internet client–server systems in which the client (the browser) interacts with a remote server. The server stores the information to give out, or 'publish'. The browser has the task of requesting, fetching and displaying the information on behalf of the user. Many Web browsers for different platforms are available. At the no-frills end of the spectrum are plain text browsers such as Lynx which runs under Unix and VMS. The most popular browsers are high-end graphical browsers such as Netscape Navigator/Communicator and Internet Explorer (Microsoft), both of which are available for PC Windows and Apple Mac. Versions of these browsers are also available for Unix.

Mosaic was the first graphical browser to gain widespread usage, but currently the bulk of Web users use either Netscape or Internet Explorer. While these two browsers are developing into massive all-encompassing Internet tools trailing plug-in and add-on programs in their wake, there is a reverse trend in certain areas, such as the development of trimmed-down browsers for hand-held devices.

Standard functions of browsers

With a graphical Web browser, the user can expect to be able to:

- open requested HTML documents;
- follow links to other Web documents;
- follow links to other Internet information systems, such as ftp;
- open local documents;
- save retrieved documents;
- print the current document;
- maintain a history of visited URLs;
- move back and forward between URLs visited in the current session;
- trigger programs on the server side and review the results;
- view the source (the HTML) of the current document;
- keep a note of URLs required for future reference;
- search for a term in the current document;
- handle forms;
- view images (GIF, JPEG, PNG formats) inline;
- follow links from imagemaps;
- maintain a store (cache) of visited pages for reuse where appropriate;
- configure preferences for:
  - the home (starting) page;
  - the appearance of documents;

- whether or not to automatically display images;
- how particular file types should be handled;
- use of a proxy server;
- security safeguards;
- character set;
- language;
- screening access according to content rating.

Accessing a specific URL

Following embedded links in Web documents offers a convenient ready-made exploration trail. But it is also possible to tell the browser to go to a specific URL by typing it directly into the address bar (or use the GO command with Lynx).

Additional functions of browsers

As the leading Web browsers have developed, they have absorbed more and more functions until they have reached a point where they effectively fill the role of all-purpose Internet tools. E-mail and Usenet news functionality are commonly included, plus options for chat, calendaring, Web authoring and FTP.

Offline reading of Web pages

Offline reading of Web pages enables a user to download pages, directories or even whole Web sites for reading at leisure without the expense or inconvenience of staying connected. Internet Explorer 5.0 has a facility for downloading Web pages for offline browsing.

Programs such as Webwhacker
http://www.bluesquirrel.com/products/whacker/whacker.html
will also download pages which may be viewed offline.

Accessing the Web with telnet

The W3 Consortium has a line-mode Web browser at **telnet://telnet.w3.org/** that, by default, points to its own Web server. To access other Web addresses, at the prompt type the command 'go' followed by the URL you wish to access. This facility is useful when investigating accessibility issues since it will establish a Web site's dependency on images and graphics.

The Web protocol

A protocol in this context is a set of rules that govern the exchange of data between two computers. It is important to understand that several different protocols may be used in order to access different computers on the Internet.

Different types of client software use different protocols. The main protocol of the Web is the Hypertext Transfer Protocol (HTTP) – hence the familiar `http://`prefix for Web addresses. (Note: you can normally omit this prefix if you are using a reasonably up-to-date browser.)

Other Internet protocols are ftp, telnet and news, and at one time you needed different client software in order to use each different protocol. However, modern Web browsers generally have all these different functions built-in and the user may not be aware that different protocols are being used.

Using

At a basic level, the Web offers the point-and-click interface for viewing documents and following hyperlinks. Viewing documents may mean reading, playing or listening, depending on which media are included in the document and which facilities are available at the user end through the browser. Documents may include one or more files of different file types. Documents may also contain scripts or small programs which are run in response to user actions. Alternatively, scripts or programs on the server may be activated through Web forms. In order to make the Web useful in a wide range of environments, it supports a range of security features. These are described in Chapter 4.

Handling additional file types

The standard role of Web browsers is to access and display HTML documents. Browsers interpret the HTML tags and display the document accordingly. They can also retrieve and display other types of files if they recognize the Internet media type (MIME type) and have the software to handle it. The software may be built into the browser, for example, certain image file types (GIF, JPEG and PNG) are displayed by graphical browsers as an integral part of the document. Other file types may require some extra software. These are commonly programs designed to work in conjunction with a browser for the display of a specific file type (plug-ins), or possibly stand-alone programs that the browser can launch to handle certain file types (helper and viewer applications).

Interactivity

A Web form is a page where the user is asked to enter some data, for example keyword/s on which to perform a search. Web forms provide a basic level of interactivity on the Web. Through forms, input can be taken from the user, then processed in some way, and the output of the process delivered back to them. In a search engine search, for example, the Web form is used to collect search terms from the user – the data from the form is transmitted to the Web server, where a script is run which sends a query to a database of index data from thousands of Web sites. The results of the database search are passed back via the server and output as a freshly generated HTML page containing the search results. The actual processing took place at the server end in this case.

In other cases, the interactivity is generated by the user's Web browser as it interprets scripts embedded in Web pages. These scripts, or programs, contain instructions for the browser on how to respond to user actions such as loading a new Web page or moving the mouse over some object on the Web page, just for visual effect. They can also be used in conjunction with forms. These 'local' scripts are more limited in what they can do, but usually the response is instantaneous – much more desirable for the user.

There are also many competing proprietary technologies used for creating multimedia/interactive Web pages. These products usually require extra plug-in software to be installed on the user's computer, to run in conjunction with the Web browser. For more detailed information, see Section 3.9.

Keeping track of useful resources

With millions of resources available, identifying and finding useful material can be a problem. One important information management tool for the Web is the 'bookmark' facility provided by Web browsers (also known as 'Favorites' (in Internet Explorer). Bookmarks are a way of saving and organizing URLs, enabling users to keep track of Web resources that they find useful. Most browsers provide a facility for hierarchical organization of annotated bookmarks.

EXAMPLES

The Web is now a densely populated place and new sites proliferate at a dramatic rate. The Web has a presence in most corners of human activity, ranging from recreation to education, from scientific research to commercial transactions, and most areas in between. On the Web you can buy a house, find a job, book a cruise, check out weather maps, browse a local newspaper, look at a medieval manuscript or take a tour of the solar system. The most interesting sites are, of course, those which contain information pertinent to the user's interests or concerns – sites which offer solutions to problems, commercial advantage, information which is otherwise unavailable, or just plain convenience. For instance, the Web might be used to look up a list of local medical practitioners, which movies are showing in town this evening, the price of a company's shares, whether the parcel you sent yesterday has reached its destination.

If you are interested in the techniques being used, you can see examples of the Web as a front-end to a database using forms and technologies such as CGI and

Active Server Pages, Flash animation, streaming audio, video and 3-D graphics. There are journals online with the look of conventionally published journals (viewed with Adobe Acrobat), interactive graphical effects produced with scripting, animated images, Java applets enhancing the interactivity of Web pages, and the use of agent technology to find a job. There is an increasing trend to relate the information on the Web to the interests and preferences of the individual.

One important and increasing trend is the use of the Web as a collaborative tool. Mailing lists and newsgroups are standard sources, but computer-supported collaborative work via the Web is also possible.

Finding more information

World Wide Web Consortium

The World Wide Web Consortium (W3C) is an international industry consortium that seeks to develop common standards for the evolution of the World Wide Web. These standards are issued as W3C recommendations and supported for industry-wide adoption by consortium members. W3C also develops applications for demonstrating use of new technology, and a reference code implementation to embody and promote standards. It maintains a repository of information about the World Wide Web for developers and users.

Requests for Comments

RFCs are the standards developed by the working groups of the IETF (Internet Engineering Task Force). They define the protocols on which the Internet operates and constitute a primary reference source on any technical aspect of the Internet, including the Web.

WWW FAQ

Maintained by Thomas Boutell and mirrored at a number of sites, the WWW FAQ (frequently asked questions) answers basic questions about the Web, including information on obtaining browsers for a number of platforms such as Amiga, NeXT, VM/CMS, Acorn and others.

Web discussion lists

W3C mailing lists can be found at
http://www.w3.org/Mail/Lists.html

2.2 WEB BROWSERS

The browsers covered here are:

- Netscape Communicator
- Microsoft Internet Explorer
- Opera
- Mozilla
- Lynx.

Information on other Web browsers can be found at the Yahoo! Web browsers page: **http://dir.yahoo.com/Computers_and_Internet/Software/Internet/ World_Wide_Web/Browsers**

2.2.1 Netscape Communicator

Netscape Communicator is really a suite of software applications based around the Netscape Navigator browser. The Netscape Navigator browser supports additional technologies such as Java, JavaScript, Cascading Style Sheets and common multimedia formats.

The suite also includes an e-mail program (Netscape Messenger), newsreader (Netscape Newsgroup), chat client (Netscape AOL Instant Messenger) and Web authoring tool (Netscape Composer). The browser includes a Flash animation viewer and optional extras such as Netscape Media Player. There are facilities for filing useful URLs (bookmarks), caching retrieved files, specification of proxies, encrypted communications and transactions (via SSL 3.0) and customizing the appearance and operation of the browser.

With recent versions, the Navigator browser incorporates a 'what's related' feature, which recommends Web sites related to the current document. Internet searches can be initiated by typing search terms into the location window. The home page of a corporation can be located by simply typing its name into the location window, e.g. `'ibm'`. Offensive content can be screened out using NetWatch.

Netscape Communicator is available in other European languages including Danish, Italian, Portuguese, Spanish and Swedish.

New features in Netscape 7.1 include:

- ability to control pop-up windows;
- tabbed browsing through multiple windows;
- viewing large images in their entirety with zoom control;
- powerful searching within Web pages;
- full screen mode;
- ability to download and manage multiple files and sites;
- web searching from within the browser.

Access

http://channels.netscape.com/ns/browsers/default.jsp

Platform

Windows 98/98SE/ME/NT4/2000/XP
Minimum hardware:

- Pentium 233 MHz;
- 64 MB RAM;
- 52 MB hard drive space.

Mac OSX 10.1/2
Minimum hardware:

- PowerPC 604e 266 MHz;
- G3, G4, 64 MB RAM;
- 72 MB hard drive space.

Linux 2.2.14
With the following libraries or packages minimums:

- # glibc 2.2.4
- gtk+ – 1.2.0 (1.2.5 or greater preferred)
- XFree86-3.3.6.

Supported platforms: Netscape has been certified and is supported on Red Hat Linux 7.0 and greater. Minimum hardware:

- Pentium 233 MHz;
- 64 MB RAM;
- 52 MB hard drive space.

2.2.2 Microsoft Internet Explorer

Like Netscape, Internet Explorer (IE) is a suite of tools based around a Web browser. IE supports other technologies such as Cascading Style Sheets, Java, Javascript and various multimedia formats.

IE also supports Microsoft-specific technologies such as VBScript and ActiveX, a technology for bringing Windows-style applications to the Web. IE6 also supports XML (Extended Markup Language) and its own version of downloadable fonts. Dynamic HTML is supported, and IE 6 contains a facility called 'DHTML behaviours' enabling the storage of dynamic scripts independent of the pages that use them, thus providing reusability.

IE offers a range of optional extras, including Mail and News capabilities (Outlook Express), tools for workgroup collaboration (NetMeeting), a chat client, an ftp client, multimedia components including Windows Media Player and Macromedia Shockwave Flash, Web authoring components including FrontPage Express, and powerful multilanguage support. The appearance and operation of the browser can be customized.

Convenience features introduced with the current version include auto complete assistance with typing in URLs, such as a prompting drop-down list of sites with similar URLs to that being typed in, and automatic correction of typos. IE6 offers added help with searching. Queries can be typed directly into the address bar; there is a search assistant to help in choosing resources to search, and a customizable search bar. There is a 'related links' option (from Alexa) to see sites similar to the one currently being viewed. Local secure cookies save passwords, addresses, e-mail addresses and other details previously typed into Web forms. The data is presented in drop-down lists when a form is being filled in. Download and viewing of Web sites offline is provided for. The 'File/Save as' command downloads all the items that go into displaying a Web page, such as HTML, stylesheets, scripts and images.

IE6 supports P3P privacy policies and is able to import customized privacy settings into Internet Explorer 6 using XML. Other features include a media bar which assists in locating and playing media within the browser window, and a new image bar which allows you to quickly and easily save e-mail, and print pictures that you find on Web pages.

Other language versions of IE6 are available and it also supports different encodings for other alphabets, e.g Cyrillic.

Access

http://www.microsoft.com/windows/ie/default.htm

Platform

Windows 95/98/NT/2000/XP: versions for these platforms may be one step ahead of other platforms, such as **Windows 3.x, Apple Mac and Unix.**

2.2.3 Opera

Like Netscape and Internet Explorer, Opera is a suite of applications based around a graphical Web browser. Opera promotes itself as an 'alternative' browser that is independent of Netscape and Microsoft, and yet offers many of the same features. Opera is a very compact program that makes it quick to download, and it also has the advantage that it can run on older versions of Windows, e.g. Windows 95.

Access

http://www.opera.com

Platform

Opera 6.0:
Windows 95/98/ME/NT/2000/XP, Mac OS, 8.6–10.2, Solaris, FreeBSD.

Opera 7:
Linux.

2.2.4 Mozilla

'Mozilla' was the original code name for the product that came to be known as Netscape Navigator, and later Netscape Communicator. Later, it came to be the name of Netscape Communications Corporation's dinosaur-like mascot.

The name Mozilla is now accepted as the generic term referring to Internet client software developed through the Mozilla.org® open source project. (Mozilla.org is a registered trademark of the Mozilla foundation.)

Mozilla 1.4 is an open source browser that is designed to support open Internet standards across a variety of platforms including Windows, Linux, Mac OS X, OS/2 and Solaris. Mozilla provides users with simple and effective browsing along with more advanced features such as pop-up blocking, junk mail controls and tabbed browsing. Mozilla also provides a sophisticated platform for developing Web and intranet applications using cutting-edge technologies such as XML, SOAP and XSLT. Mozilla offers users high levels of support for existing and emerging Web standards and compatibility with the existing Web. Pages lay out correctly and quickly. In addition, Mozilla supports popular plug-ins like Java, Flash, Acrobat, Windows Media Player, Quicktime and RealPlayer.

For the power user, Mozilla provides advanced JavaScript controls, tabbed browsing, image blocking, multiple mail accounts, privacy management, themes and extensions. Mozilla is also a Web development platform with advanced tools like the DOM Inspector, the JavaScript Debugger, and support for XML, DHTML, XUL, SOAP, XSLT.

Access

http://www.mozilla.org

Platform

Windows, Linux, Mac OS X, OS/2, Solaris and others.

2.2.5 Lynx

Lynx is a plain-text World Wide Web browser for access from character-based terminals. Lynx displays HTML documents as plain text, providing support for most common HTML tags, including plain-text rendering of tables and frames. Its functions include support for forms, menu rendering of imagemaps, caching of pages, a history function and bookmarks.

Access

http://lynx.browser.org/

Platform

Lynx 2.8.2: VMS, Unix, Windows 95/98/NT/2000, DOS via DJGPP and OS/2 EMX, Mac in beta.

2.3 CACHING AND CACHES

Retrieved Web pages may be stored (cached) locally for a time so that they can be conveniently accessed if further requests are made for them. Whether or not the most up-to-date copy of the file is retrieved is handled by the caching program that initially makes a brief check and compares the date of the file at its original location with that of the copy in the cache. If the date of the cached file is the same as the original, then the cached copy is used.

Web browsers maintain a cache of retrieved documents and this is used for retrievals where possible. In addition, the user may configure the browser to point to a caching server. File requests not able to be supplied from the browser cache will then be directed to the caching server. The caching server would supply the files from its cache if they are current, or pass the request on to the originating server if they are not.

Useful Web sites:

- DESIRE project Web caching architecture recommendations: **http://www.desire.org/html/research/deliverables/D4.1/d41-11.htm**

- Cache Now! **http://vancouver-Webpages.com/CacheNow/** is a campaign to raise awareness about Web caching and what individuals and organizations can do to save time, money and bandwidth for themselves and others.

Proxy servers

Where a high level of security is required, a proxy Web server may be used to provide a gateway between a local area network and the Internet. The local network is protected by firewall software installed on the proxy server. This software enables the proxy server to keep the two worlds separate. All outward HTTP requests from the local network pass through the proxy server and similarly all information retrieved comes back in via the proxy server and is then passed back to the client. Using the options or preferences, Web browsers can be configured to point to the proxy server. Proxy servers will normally maintain a cache of retrieved documents.

As well as being closer and keeping Web pages all in one place, a proxy server can often distribute the pages much faster than the original server.

- Proxy servers can be used (to some extent) to anonymize your Web surfing.
- Specialized proxy servers can filter out unwanted content, such as ads or unsuitable material.

- Proxy servers can afford some protection against hacking attacks.
- Some proxy servers can even translate pages into your own language before passing them on to you.

There are potentially thousands of proxy servers to choose from – sophisticated use of proxies might involve choosing a server for accessing a certain part of the Web, or for browsing at a particular time of day. However, like many things on the Internet, they are subject to change, going offline, becoming unreliable or inefficient, etc.

A site that offers some information about proxies is **http://www.proxys4all.com**, although some of the information is dated.

See also Section 3.9.

2.4 SEMANTIC WEB

In recent years, the concept of the Semantic Web has emerged. The Semantic Web can be represented as an enormous global mesh of information linked up in a way that is easily processable by machines. In other words, a more efficient way of representing data on the World Wide Web, in a global database. The Semantic Web was first conceived by Tim Berners-Lee, inventor of the web, URIs, HTTP and HTML. The World Wide Web consortium (W3C) is working to improve, extend and standardize the system, and many languages, publications, tools and so on have already been developed.

The Semantic Web was designed to address the issues of information overload and particularly the problems associated with the majority of data on the web being in a form that it is difficult to use on a large scale – there is no global system for publishing data in such a way that it can be easily processed by anyone.

So the Semantic Web is effectively a re-engineering solution: it will enable easier publishing of data in a number of reusable formats; Semantic Web applications could be used for a variety of different tasks, increasing the modularity of applications on the web.

The Semantic Web is built on syntaxes which use URIs to represent data, usually in triples-based structures – many triples of URI data can be held in databases, or interchanged on the World Wide Web using a set of particular syntaxes developed specially for the task. These syntaxes are called 'Resource Description Framework' syntaxes (RDFs).

Semantic Web applications

There are a number of small scale Semantic Web applications in existence, including:

- Dan Connolly's Arcs and Nodes diagrams experiment:
  http://www.w3.org/2001/02pd/
- The RDFWeb is an RDF database-driven hypermedia blogspace, a site where all information is stored as RDF, that is then used to render XHTML. Plans are underway to incorporate more advanced Semantic Web principles into the site.
  http://rdfweb.org/

Useful links:
http://www.diffuse.org/semantic-web.html
http://www.w3.org/2001/sw/Europe

2.5 WEB SERVICES

Web services are a range of Web applications that are modular, self-contained and self-describing. They can be published, located and invoked across the Web and can perform a range of functions, which could include simple operations and requests to complex business processes. A sample Web service might provide financial quotations or process credit card transactions. Once a Web service is operating, other applications (and other Web services) can discover and use the deployed service.

Web services will impact massively on software development and will impact on the way business will be conducted. Many observers foresee the development of 'dynamic business Webs' – flexible Internet-based applications that will allow companies to create new products and services faster than existing methods, reach new customers, change/add customer relationships, engage in new business models and provide customized experiences. Web services will also undoubtedly impact on the way we purchase and sell software.

Web services are based on XML (eXtensible Markup Language), SOAP (Simple Object Access Protocol) and UDDI (Universal Description Discovery and Integration), a form of Web services Yellow Pages for developers, and on WSDL (Web Services Description Language) which describes the functions provided by a given Web service.

A number of significant companies are pledging to Web service strategies, for example Microsoft's Net strategy, IBM's Web services strategy, Sun's Open Net Environment (ONE), HP's e-speak and NetAction technology, and Novell's One Net initiative.

Useful links:

- **www.CBDIForum.com**
- **http://www-106.ibm.com/developerworks/Webservices**, full of articles, tutorials, and tools;
- **http://e-serv.ebizq.net/obj/hildreth_2.html**
- **http://www3.gartner.com/DisplayDocument?id=320121&acsFlg=accessBought**
- **http://www.Webservicesarchitect.com**

WSDL

The Web Services Description Language is a language in XML format that is used to describe a Web service's capabilities. Specifically, these capabilities are collections of communication endpoints that can exchange messages. WSDL is an integral part of UDDI, an XML-based worldwide business registration process. WSDL is the language that UDDI uses. WSDL was developed jointly by Microsoft and IBM.
Useful link:
http://www.w3.org/TR/wsdl

SOAP

The Simple Object Access Protocol was derived from XML. It is a lightweight and simple XML/HTTP-based protocol that is designed to exchange structured and typed information on the Web. SOAP uses XML messages to invoke remote methods in a platform-independent manner. Although a Web service could interact with remote machines through HTTP's `post` and `get` methods, SOAP is preferred, as it is more robust and flexible.

Two important elements of SOAP are the Service Contract Language and DISCO (Discovery of Web Services) and are included in Visual Studio.Net.

Useful link:
http://www.microsoft.com/mind/0100/soap/soap.asp

UDDI

Universal Description Discovery and Integration provides data on the author, category and the technical means used to request Web services developed and published by companies. UDDI enables companies to discover other businesses worldwide that offer similar products and services. They may also register products and services of their own for others to discover.

Useful link:
http://www.uddi.org/

SAML

The Security Assertion Markup Language is a framework for the exchange of authentication and authorization information, based on XML. It complements protocols such as SOAP by enhancing the security, and it incorporates other protocols such as XML Signature and XML Encryption. It allows the interoperation of services through a single sign-on process, achieving simpler, yet more secure access.

Useful link:
http://www.Webservices.org/index.php/article/articleview/743/

3

WEB PUBLISHING

This section explains how to author Web pages and publish them on the Web. All Web pages are written in a special language called HTML, but there are different ways of producing HTML – either writing it directly, using an authoring tool, or converting it from another format (e.g. a Word document). Whatever method is used, it is helpful to understand something of the basics of the HTML language.

When you have written Web pages, how do you 'publish' them on the Web? To do this, the finished HTML file(s) need to be transferred to a computer which is connected to the Internet and which operates as a Web server.

Some of the topics discussed in this chapter are:

- Web authoring
- HTML
- Publishing Web pages
- Graphics in Web pages
- Multimedia
- Dynamic HTML
- Cookies
- Web databases.

3.1 WEB AUTHORING

All Web authoring tools produce HTML, but authoring tools differ in the range of features and facilities they offer. In addition to HTML generation, Web authoring software commonly includes facilities for managing whole sets of Web documents. Also common are ready-made templates and graphics to enable rapid development, wizards to help get novices going quickly, help with generating scripts, styles, graphics, animation etc. Beginners should probably start with one of the simpler authoring tools and then move on to more advanced software.

Authoring tools

There are literally hundreds of different authoring tools available. Many are freeware or shareware, and so beginners are advised not to buy authoring software unless they are sure it meets their needs. Web authors have different requirements and many will champion a particular product – however, this does not necessarily mean that it will be suitable for everyone, as it may have many advanced features that only confuse. The simplest authoring tools consist of a text-editing tool to write HTML (with shortcut facilities which save some typing) and a viewer to see the finished page. Features of more advanced tools are discussed below.

WYSIWYG authoring tools

WYSIWYG tools behave like a word processor, and they hide the details of the HTML from the user. Many authors use both a WYSIWYG interface and some 'raw' HTML authoring. However, the HTML code produced by some of these tools may not conform to the correct standards. This could mean that your page is not displayed properly. WYSIWYG editors also allow you to insert and position images into a page. You can certainly produce a page much quicker using a WYSIWYG tool than by writing HTML, but you should check that the HTML code produced by the tool is of an acceptable standard.

Automatic navigation

Good authoring tools can automatically create links between the pages in your site, and keep them up to date as you add or remove pages. This is much quicker than manually editing links.

Site mapping

Authoring tools with site mapping features display a graphical representation showing how all your pages are linked and also links to external sites.

Site management features

Facilities to manage your site are very useful. They include link checking, HTML validation, global find and replace, global 'themes' or house style, and a simple method of uploading to the server.

Inclusion of other technologies

Authoring assistance/templates for JavaScript, Cascading Style Sheets, Active Server Pages, inclusion of Java applets are also useful facilities to have.

Finally, some tools also allow you to produce dynamic pages that normally require other programming technologies. For example: database connectivity, password authentication and processing of forms data. However, the important thing to note here is that for the dynamic pages to work, these tools require special software installed on your Web server. Beginners using this type of authoring tool may create dynamic pages only to find that their service provider or institution does not provide the necessary software on the Web server. Examples are ColdFusion, FrontPage ('FrontPage Extensions' needs to be installed on the Web server) and Drumbeat.

Validating HTML

If Web authors wish to provide pages that are accessible to the widest possible audience, they should check that their HTML conforms to current standards. This process is known as HTML validation. Information on the current standard is available on the W3C Web site, **http://www.w3c.org**.

HTML editing programs commonly provide an HTML validation function, and may even enforce conformance to standards as the HTML is generated. Alternatively, documents can be run through an HTML checking program, either locally or by using an online service such as:

- online testing of HTML through the HTML Validation Service **http://validator.w3.org/**
- online testing for broken links, invalid HTML, and server response time through NetMechanic: Online Link Testing, HTML Validation **http://www.netmechanic.com**
- online testing for CSS through the CSS Validation Service **http://jigsaw.w3.org/css-validator**

3.2 HTML

HTML is like a hidden layer behind the document that you see in a Web browser. It is, as its name implies, a markup language. Marking up text is like issuing instructions on how the text should be interpreted and displayed. In the case of HTML, the instructions come in the form of HTML elements, or tags. The Web browser displays a document as instructed by the HTML. HTML tags do a number of things, such as:

- defining the structure of a document, for example, the HEAD (information about the document) and BODY (the main part of the document actually displayed by the browser)

```
<HEAD>
<TITLE>Title of the document</TITLE>
</HEAD>
<BODY>

This is the main body of the document.
</BODY>
```

- indicating features of the appearance, for example, white background and blue text;

```
<BODY BGCOLOR="WHITE" TEXT="BLUE">
```

- indicating formatting of text, for example, text in italics;

```
<I>HTML elements</I>
```

- indicating the presence and position of graphics, for example, show the image file box.gif and place it on the left of the page;

```
<IMG SRC="box.gif" ALIGN="LEFT">
```

HTML files are plain-text (ASCII) files. The filename will have the extension .html or .htm. To see the HTML source of a Web document, select the browser's View/Source menu option. There are many programs that can help in generating HTML, and also a number of programs we are already accustomed to using (such as word-processors) which include a function for automatically generating HTML.

Creating Web pages is not merely a technical exercise. Good style and good practice have an impact on the quality and usability of pages. Check out the information sources below for useful guides for Web authors that cover issues of style, as well as HTML.

For a summary of HTML elements see:

- Bare Bones Guide to HTML by Kevin Werbach **http://werbach.com/barebones**
- Sizzling HTML Jalfrezi a brief reference listing of the most common HTML tags. Available in a number of languages **http://vzone.virgin.net/sizzling.jalfrezi/ iniframe.htm**
- The full HTML standard is available from the WWW Consortium: HTML tags are defined, there is a discussion of techniques, with abundant examples and references **http://www.w3c.org/**

3.3 WEB AUTHORING TOOLS

There are dozens, if not hundreds, of authoring tools available. Many are free but the most expensive can cost several hundred pounds. Beginners are often put off by the bewildering choice of tools. However, the differences between authoring tools at beginner level are relatively unimportant – it is much better to pick one and learn it than waste time and money seeking the 'best' tool. Among professional Web authors there is no widespread agreement on the 'best' tool; as with any type of software, individual preference has a lot to do with it. Practically all the commercial products offer free trial versions – so you should try out software before buying it.

Many Web authors continue to write HTML 'by hand' using a text editor, partly because this offers maximum control, and partly because they are reluctant to spend time learning an unfamiliar tool that may prove unsatisfactory. Whatever tool is chosen, it is helpful, if not essential, to understand a little about the HTML language. Most authoring tools have minor quirks that may require manual viewing or editing of the HTML in order to correct it.

Authoring tools fall into two main types:

- basic HTML tools which require the user to understand HTML;
- WYSIWYG (what you see is what you get) tools which hide the details of the HTML. These behave rather like word processor/desktop publishing software.

More advanced tools may offer features in addition to simple Web page authoring. For example, site management features used to organize, display and create navigation throughout a whole site, image creation/editing software, link checkers, editors for scripting languages such as JavaScript and ASPs. However, this type of tool is very confusing for the beginner, who simply wants to write a few Web pages. A good review site about Web authoring tools is **http://www.Webreview.com**.

Finally, some tools include programming features to create dynamic, complex Web sites that include dynamic features such as live searches, Web form processing and database connectivity. These tools are for large-scale Web sites, typically for ecommerce/Web shop fronts. This kind of 'hybrid' development/Web authoring tool always requires special software to be installed on a Web server otherwise the code produced won't work.

Basic authoring tools

Netscape Composer is built into later versions of Netscape (**http://www.netscape.com/**) and is a basic WYSIWYG editor suitable for beginners. Many other basic tools are available from freeware/shareware sites such as: **http://www.tucows.com/** and **http://www.winsite.com/**. Microsoft FrontPage Express is a basic Web authoring tool that is included with later versions of Internet Explorer.

Popular authoring tools

Name	Available from	Comment
HotDog Professional	**http://www.sausage.com**	
Adobe GoLive	**http://www.adobe.com/ products/golive/main.html**	
Macromedia Homesite	**http://www.macromedia.com/ software/homesite/**	Integrates with other Macromedia products
BBEdit	**http://www.barebones.com/ products/products.html**	Mac only
HoTMetal Pro	**http://www.hotmetalpro.com**	
Dreamweaver	**http://www.macromedia.com/ software/dreamweaver**	Integrates with other Macromedia products
Frontpage 2002	**http://www.microsoft.com/ frontpage/**	Some features depend on special Web server configuration

Complex authoring/site development tools

Visual InterDev **http://msdn.microsoft.com/vinterdev**
ColdFusion **http://www.macromedia.com/software/coldfusion/**

Other types of file

Although HTML is the normal format for Web pages, files in any format can be made available on the Web leaving the user to handle the details of viewing or processing files. Web browsers now contain plug-ins that can automatically display common file formats such as PDF (Portable Document Format). You can also configure your browser to handle other common file formats, such as Microsoft Word .doc files. For other file formats the user can download the file and then run whatever software is necessary outside of the Web browser.

3.4 PUBLISHING WEB PAGES

As a minimum, a Web page consists of a single HTML file. In practice, most Web pages also include some associated image files (.gif, .jpg etc.). To publish a Web page the finished file(s) must be transferred to a Web server. A Web server is a computer which is connected to the Internet, and which has special Web server software installed. How you transfer your files to the Web server depends on local circumstances, but typically this is done in one of four ways.

Directly to a mapped drive

You may be able to connect your computer to the Web server if it is on your local network. For example, on a PC you may be able to set up drive `w:` as a direct connection to the Web server. Ask your network administrator.

File Transfer Protocol

FTP software is used to transfer files between two computers. FTP software is freely available and may be provided by your ISP or network administrator. You 'log on' to the remote computer by entering your user name and password, and then you can transfer files. For more information about FTP see Chapter 6.

Via a Web page

If you have Web space with a commercial ISP, some allow you to upload your files using your Web browser. Their Web site will have an 'upload page' where you enter your login name and password details, and then you are presented with a dialogue box asking for the name(s) of the files to upload.

Web authoring tools

Many Web authoring tools have a built-in facility to transfer files, which connects directly with the Web server.

Announcing your site

There is little point in having a site which no one visits so potential visitors need to be given a way of discovering the existence of the site. The first step is to optimize the site's findability with the popular Internet search services. You do this by registering it with major search engines such as AltaVista, Excite, Infoseek, Lycos,

Hotbot etc. and with directories such as Yahoo!. Also, if there are relevant specialist directories, let them know too. Most search engines and directories provide an obvious and inviting link to their site registration page. Alternatively you can pay a service to do it for you. One such service is Submit It! (**http://submitit.linkexchange.com**).

In either case, search engines will put your URL into a lengthy queue that their spider will eventually visit for the purpose of collecting data for the search engine's index. Once your site is in the index, in theory it can be found by keyword searching. With directories such as Yahoo! the important item in your submission is the description of your site, which will be processed not by a program but by a person, who makes the decision on whether or not to include it in the directory.

Guidelines for optimizing findability with search engines are:

- With each Web page, come straight to the point with concise, descriptive text for the title and headings, and also the first paragraph. Use words directly relevant to the subject of the document. With some search engines, the words used early in the document are more significant for findability than those used later, but repeated occurrences of words and phrases also influence findability (beware of index spamming!).
- Insert meta-tags for keywords and description into the `head` of your documents, particularly pages which are framesets and pages which start with JavaScript.

Maintaining your site

Publishing information on a Web site should not be regarded as a one-off process – if you want people to return you need to put in a lot of time and effort to keep your site up to date. Check hypertext links regularly to make sure that they still work. There are many free tools available for doing such housekeeping tasks automatically. Also read and revise the text if necessary. From time to time, you may wish to review the style too – how impressed are you today by a page of plain black text on a grey background?

Usage statistics are an important aspect of maintenance. They will tell you, for instance, if anyone has accessed the information you are providing or if they encountered errors in finding any of the files you linked to. Some statistics packages also track the route that users follow through the site.

3.5 GRAPHICS IN WEB PAGES

Graphics play an important role in enhancing the appearance of Web pages, aiding navigation through a site, creating a distinctive style or corporate identity, and providing illustration. Some of the issues that Web authors should be aware of when using images include:

- selecting appropriate formats for each image;
- optimization of images for Web delivery;
- use of 'Web-safe' colours to ensure consistent appearance;
- use of animation.

It is also important to consider the accessibility of images to different users and user agents. This section will describe:

- Image formats
- Efficient and effective images
- Imagemaps
- Accessibility.

Image formats

To ensure that Web pages containing images download quickly, the images are compressed. The two main formats that are supported by all graphical Web browsers are:

- GIF (Graphics Interchange Format)
- JPEG (Joint Photographic Experts Group).

In addition, emerging formats include:

- PNG (Portable Network Graphics)
- Vector graphics.

As these formats compress images differently, selecting an appropriate format can have a significant impact on image quality and file size.

Graphics Interchange Format

The GIF format is most suitable for images containing areas of solid colour, such as icons, graphs and line-art logos. Such images will generally be compressed efficiently without deterioration in image quality. However, GIF is not suitable for images containing a large number of colours, such as photographs. Saving such an image as a GIF will result in reduced image quality and increased file size.

Features of the GIF format include:

- **Colours** supports a maximum of 256 colours (8-bit indexed colour);
- **Compression** uses a built-in LZW compression algorithm. This is a lossless form of compression, meaning that the compressed image contains all the information in the original image;
- **Transparency** support allows the background of an image to adopt the same colour as the background of the Web page in which it is displayed;
- **Interlacing** allows for progressive enhancement of the image as it loads, rather like the way in which a view through a window is revealed by a gradually opening Venetian blind;
- **Animation** a compound image consisting of a set of separate images displayed at timed intervals provides the effect of animation.

Joint Photographic Experts Group

JPEG is a particularly effective format for the compression of natural, true-colour images such as photographs or images with subtle colour gradations.

Features of the JPEG format include:

- **Colours** can contain up to 16.7 million colours (24-bit colour) – this enables the display of fine colour gradients that are typically present in photographic images;
- **Compression** uses a lossy method of compression to selectively discard information without reducing image quality – unlike GIF, JPEG allows designers to specify the amount of compression applied to an image;
- **Progressive JPEG** a progressive JPEG is transmitted and displayed in a sequence of overlays, with each overlay becoming progressively higher in quality.

JPEG does not support transparency or animation.

Portable Networks Graphics

The PNG format was created as a non-proprietary alternative to GIF. This format improves on GIF in some regards, such as better compression and control over the level of transparency. However, PNG does not allow animation. PNG is supported in recent versions of Netscape and Internet Explorer.

Features of the PNG format include:

- **Colours** has 8-bit indexed colour support like GIF (256 colours), and 24-bit RGB support like JPEG (16.7 million colours);
- **Compression** is fully lossless;
- **Interlacing** supports two-dimensional interlacing, a sophisticated method of progressive display.

Vector graphics

Vector graphics differ from bitmap formats (GIF, JPEG and PNG) in that they do not store information describing the image as pixels. Instead, mathematical formulae are used to describe properties such as size, shape, and colour. This means that vector-based graphics tend to have a significantly smaller file size than bitmaps. In addition, vector graphics can be resized without any loss in image resolution or increase in file size.

Vector graphics can be produced by a number of packages including Macromedia Flash and Adobe Illustrator. Scalable vector graphics (SVG) is a language for describing two-dimensional graphics in XML. SVG drawings can be interactive, dynamic, animated and interactive.

For more information on the SVG format see **http://www.w3.org/TR/SVG/intro.html**

Efficient and effective images

Images are relatively large files and therefore have the potential to delay the download of content over the Web. Developers intending to use images should use graphics packages to optimize each image for Web delivery by reducing the file size as much as possible without sacrificing image quality. The file size of an image can be reduced by the following methods:

- reducing the physical size of the image;
- selecting an appropriate image format;
- reducing the number of colours used.

The original image can first be cropped to remove any unnecessary detail. The physical size of an image can then be reduced as much as possible. If a full-sized illustration is required, 'thumbnail' images can be created to provide an indication of what the image looks like before the user is required to download the full size version.

Saving an image in an appropriate format can have a significant impact on file size (use GIF for images with areas of solid colour; JPEG for images with fine colour gradients). This also determines the other steps required in the optimization process.

For JPEGs, optimization involves setting the maximum level of compression that will maintain the required image quality. For GIFs, a range of factors should be taken into account. The more colours a GIF contains, the more the file space required to store that colour information. As GIFs can use between 2 and 256 colors, developers can use an image editor to reduce the number of colours and assess the effect on image quality. GIF files store the values of all the colours used in the image as a colour palette. The use of an appropriate colour palette helps maintain a balance between efficiency and image quality. Palettes may be based on the colours occurring most frequently in the image, the colours to which the human eye is most sensitive and, in the context of the Web, the 'Web-safe palette' – the 216 colours that are displayed consistently by most browsers on Macintosh and Windows platforms.

Many Web authoring programs provide an estimate of the download time for graphics. Over a standard modem connection, download rates can be estimated to be approximately 1 kb per second. As a rule of thumb, Web developers generally aim to keep pages below 50 kb.

The use of interlaced GIFs and progressive JPEGs can also increase usability. Although such images do not download any faster than regular image files, they do provide users with an indication of what they are waiting for.

Note that the height and width attributes of the HTML <img> tag only affect how the image is displayed. As the file size of the original image has not been altered, the download time will be the same irrespective of the display size.

Imagemaps/clickable images

Imagemaps, or 'clickable images', are images on a Web page that are used for navigation. When a user clicks on a specific area of an imagemap, the Web browser displays the linked page.

Imagemaps are usually written in HTML by associating hyperlinks with specified coordinates within the image. Although simple imagemaps may be created by hand, defining complex sets of coordinates is more efficiently done using an authoring tool to create the necessary code. Many authoring tools, including freeware/shareware tools such as MapEdit, provide a facility for creating imagemaps.

Server-side imagemapping is an alternative method that relies on a CGI program running the Web server to process the coordinates and deliver the linked page. Because the production of such imagemaps requires programming skills and because most modern browsers support client-side imagemapping, this technique is now less widely used.

Accessibility

Not all users can access the information present within images. For example, blind and visually-impaired users can use helpful technologies, such as a screen reader, to produce spoken or Braille output directly from the HTML source of a page. Other users may have disabled the display of images to speed up page loading. Therefore, each image used should have an appropriate text equivalent provided.

For simple images, this can be provided using the `alt` attribute of the `<img>` tag. For more complex images, the `longdesc` attribute of the `<img>` tag can be used to provide a link to a Web page containing a text description of the image. As `longdesc` is not widely supported at present, many authors also provide a D-link. This is a standard hyperlink to a Web page containing a description of the image that by convention uses the display text [D].

3.6 GRAPHICS SOFTWARE

Adobe Photoshop

This is a professional package for photo design and production. It has a rich array of functionality and a well-established reputation for creation of high quality graphics.

Features:

- professional photography tools, special effects filters and transformations;
- sophisticated painting and drawing tools;
- advanced selection capability;
- transparency;
- weighted optimization of image areas;
- GIF animation, imagemap and cascading style sheet generation;
- support for images with multiple layers;
- task automation and batch processing.

Platforms: Mac 9.1/9.2/OS X; Windows 98/NT/ME/2000/XP
http://www.adobe.com/products/photoshop/main.html

Adobe Photoshop Elements

Photoshop Elements offers a subset of Adobe Photoshop features, including some that are particularly suitable for the Web.

Features:

- batch processing of images;
- optimized colour palette;
- GIF transparency and animation;
- image slicing;
- generation of imagemaps and Javascript actions.

Platforms: Mac 9.1/9.2/OS X; Windows 98/NT/ME/2000/XP
http://www.adobe.com/products/photoshopel/main.html

Paint Shop Pro for Windows

This is a graphics creation, editing and conversion package.

Features:

- support for a wide range of image formats;
- extensive drawing, painting and manipulation tools;
- special effects filters;
- create animated GIFs, rollover images and imagemaps;
- slice and optimize images.

Platforms: Windows 98/NT/2000/ME/XP
http://www.jasc.com/products/paintshoppro/

Adobe Illustrator

This is a vector graphic creation and editing package.

Features:

- symbols to minimize file size for repeating graphics;
- slicing – specify slice-level format and compression;

- editable scalable vector graphics effects;
- selective anti-aliasing to ensure that small text is easy to read;
- save for Web command to optimize file sizes;
- imagemap creation.

Platforms: Mac 9.1/9.2/OS X; Windows 98/NT/ME/2000/XP
http://www.adobe.com/products/illustrator/main.html

Fireworks

This high-end suite of tools from Macromedia aims to provide a single environment for creating and optimizing high-quality graphics for the Web. It includes tools for text, design, illustration, image editing, JavaScript, and animation and is closely integrated with Macromedia's Dreamweaver and Flash packages.

Features:

- import and optimize a range of formats, including vector and bitmap images;
- share files across graphics applications, including Macromedia Flash and Adobe Photoshop;
- control over compression and color palettes, including Web-specific colour features;
- slice images and manipulate each slice separately;
- automatic generation of Web navigation elements such as rollover buttons;
- GIF animation tool.

Platforms: Windows 9X/NT, Apple Mac.
http://www.macromedia.com/software/fireworks/

DeBabelizer Pro

This tool specializes in automating repetitive tasks in high-volume graphics production for Web, print and multimedia delivery.

Features:

- automated file conversion;
- easy creation of scripts for batch processing;
- ready-made scripts for common tasks;
- easy creation of a palette for a group of images;
- compilation of GIF animations.

Platforms: Apple Mac, Windows 9X/NT.
http://www.equilibrium.com/Internet/Equil/Products/DeBabelizer/index.htm

GIF Construction Set for Windows

This is special purpose software (with a shareware option) for creating transparent, interlaced and animated GIF files for Web pages.

Features:

- easy interface for creating transparent GIFs;
- GIF animation wizard;
- create animated transitions and banners;
- flip, rotate, scale and crop all or part of an animated GIF file;
- supercompress GIF files.

Platforms: Windows 95/98/ME/XP/2000/NT.
http://www.mindworkshop.com/alchemy/gifcon.html

Graphic Workshop Classic

This is a shareware graphics package with a range of functionality.

Features:

- support for a range of image formats including PNG, GIF and JPEG;
- batch convert between image formats;
- image manipulation (crop, resize, rotate);
- thumbnail creation;
- image filters.

Platforms: Windows 95/98/ME/XP/2000/NT.
http://www.mindworkshop.com/alchemy/gww.html

MapEdit

This is a graphical editor for imagemaps.

Features:

- easy creation of client-side imagemaps;
- supports GIF, JPEG and PNG formats;
- will also create server-side maps for backwards compatibility with old browsers.

Platforms: Windows 3.x/95/NT, Unix, Apple Mac
http://www.boutell.com/mapedit/

CoffeeCup Image Mapper

This is a graphical editor for imagemaps.

Features:

- map wizard (guides you through creating an imagemap);
- create 'mouseOver text' on link areas;
- supports GIFs, JPGs, and first frame of animated GIFs;
- viewable HTML code;
- allows testing in multiple browsers.

Platforms: Windows 98/ME/XP/2000/NT
http://www.coffeecup.com/image-mapper/

3.7 MULTIMEDIA

The term 'multimedia' is generally used to refer to formats such as audio, video, images and animation. Such formats typically require proprietary authoring software for creation and appropriate plug-in software playing back. There is a wide range of products available for authoring multimedia applications for Web delivery. This section introduces common terminology and tools.

While the use of multimedia is often concerned with attracting and engaging users, a major concern is the download delay that can be associated with such media. Recent developments in the efficiency of media file compression have resulted in the production of smaller files that are delivered more quickly. One example of how successful such a strategy can be is the widespread use of MP3 (MPEG Audio Layer 3) as the format of choice for delivering audio via the Internet. This format offers an efficient compression standard for audio files allowing delivery of CD-quality sound with relatively small files.

Other developments have addressed the ways in which multimedia is delivered and played back. Traditionally, media such as audio and video have had to be downloaded in their entirety before playback could begin. However, media streaming allows players such as RealPlayer, QuickTime and Windows Media player to process and playback the media as it downloads. Therefore, once a minimum amount of data has been delivered, users can begin watching a video or listening to an audio clip while the remainder downloads in the background. Streaming technology also makes live audio and video broadcasts on the Internet feasible.

Changes have also occurred in animation formats. Although animated GIFs continue to be a popular means of delivering simple animation, other formats are now available for more sophisticated animation. One of the most widely used formats is Macromedia Flash, which is based on the use of vector graphics. As vector graphics tend to generate a much smaller file size than bitmaps, such as GIF, they will be delivered more quickly. In addition, Flash animations can be streamed.

Animation and interactivity can also be created using Dynamic HTML, which employs a combination of JavaScript and style sheets. Although still not implemented consistently across browsers, DHTML has the advantage that it does not require the use of plug-ins (unlike Flash).

Providing multimedia

Multimedia content can be incorporated into Web pages with HTML using the following tags:

- **APPLET** used to embed Java applets – now deprecated by the W3C in favour of the OBJECT tag;

- **EMBED** used for any file type using Netscape plug-ins (Navigator 2+, Internet Explorer 3+) – not supported in Internet Explorer 5.5 or above;

- **OBJECT** general solution for a range of media including images, audio, video, Java applets and Flash animations. Use of this tag is recommended in the W3C specification for HTML 4.0. OBJECT is supported in IE5+ and NS6+. For backward compatibility, authors are recommended to enclose an EMBED element within the OBJECT tag;

- **ANCHOR** used to create a hyperlink to a multimedia file outside the current document;

- **IMG** used for static images and animated GIFs.

The APPLET, EMBED, OBJECT and IMG tags automatically initiate the display or playing of the media object when a page containing them is loaded. If the object is a streaming-media type, playing will begin as soon as the required data has been received. If the media is non-streaming, playback cannot begin until it is fully downloaded. For large files, this may introduce a significant delay and lead to the download being aborted by the user.

As an alternative to embedding media objects in the page, Web authors can provide a hyperlink to the media file using the ANCHOR tag. If this is accompanied by descriptive text, such as the file size, required plug-ins and estimated download time, this gives users control over the download process.

A topic related to the use of multimedia is SMIL (Synchronized Multimedia Integration Language). This is a language specification produced by the W3C to allow the temporal synchronization of different multimedia elements. For example, a video clip could be synchronized with a text file to provide captions. SMIL is currently supported by QuickTime and Real Player. A subset of the SMIL specification (XHTML+TIME) is also supported in Internet Explorer 5.5 and above.

Usability and accessibility

It is important to remember that multimedia should be used to enhance the Web experience. Web developers evaluating the use of multimedia should consider a number of usability and accessibility issues:

- **Download time** users are unlikely to spend significant amounts of time waiting for a media file to download. Delays may be reduced by the use of streaming media, but this may require expertise to create and deliver.

- **Software/hardware requirements** for each media file used, a developer should assess what proportion of users will have the required software/hardware. If plug-ins are required, these should ideally be built into standard browsers, or else be freely available and widely distributed. Users should be informed that a plug-in is required and provided with a link to the source of the software. Manual configuration of a plug-in may sometimes be necessary after download.

- **Accessibility** attempts should be made to make media accessible to all users, regardless of ability/disability. This may involve providing text equivalents for images, text transcripts for audio and captions for video.

3.8 MULTIMEDIA SOFTWARE

QuickTime

This supports a wide range of media formats including MPEG-2 and MPEG-4 video, QuickTime VR, AVI and DV. Video compressors and decompressors optimize the quality of streaming video for a wide range of bandwidths. Other formats supported include MP3, Advanced Audio Coding (AAC), JPEG and Macromedia Flash. QuickTime also supports the synchronization of such media through SMIL 1.0. QuickTime player is included with Netscape Navigator 3.0 and higher.

Platforms: Apple Mac, Windows
http://www.apple.com/quicktime/

RealPlayer

This supports a wide range of media formats, including streaming RealVideo, downloaded QuickTime, Windows Media or MPEG audio/video files and audio formats such as MP3. RealPlayer also supports the synchronization of such media through SMIL 2.0. For content providers, RealNetworks offer a range of products for the creation and delivery of streaming media tailored to different bandwidths over multiple simultaneous streams.

Platforms: Macintosh OS 8/9/X, Windows 98/NT/2000/ME/XP, UNIX/Linux
http://www.real.com

Windows Media Player (9 series)

This supports a wide range of media formats including ASF (Advanced Streaming Format – its native format), Windows Media Audio (WMA), Windows Media Video (WMV), WAV, AVI, MPEG, QuickTime and Macromedia Flash. It can be used for playing anything from low-bandwidth audio to full-screen video, including streaming video. At the server end, Windows Media Services provides for creation and streaming of live and on-demand content.

Platforms: Macintosh OS 8/X, Windows 98/2000/ME/XP, PocketPC
http://www.microsoft.com/windows/windowsmedia/default.aspx

Macromedia Flash

This is a tool for creating browser-independent multimedia content for the Web. Flash movies can include text, animation, interactivity, audio and video. As Flash uses efficient compression methods and vector graphics, the files produced tend to be small. Viewing of Flash content requires the Flash player, which includes support for streamed Flash movies. The Flash player is widely distributed and is included with Internet Explorer and Netscape Navigator.

Platforms: Windows 98/NT/2000/ME/XP, Mac OS 7/8/10.
http://www.macromedia.com/software/flash/

Macromedia Shockwave

This player handles Web content created with Macromedia Director. This includes interactive audio, video, bitmaps, 3-D vectors, text and other rich media. The Shockwave player is freely available as a Netscape plug-in or ActiveX control.

Platforms: Shockwave ships with Windows 95/98, MacOS, Internet Explorer and Netscape Navigator.
http://www.macromedia.com/software/shockwaveplayer

Cosmo Player

This is a universal player for content created in the virtual reality modelling language (VRML). Cosmo Player is freely available as a Netscape plug-in or ActiveX control. Cosmo Player requires ActiveMovie 1.0 or later in order to support video and compressed audio within VRML environments. It uses DirectSound3D to provide realistic, spatialized audio.

Platforms: Windows 9x/NT; Mac OS 7.x/8.x
http://www.cai.com/cosmo/

WinAmp

This offers support for audio formats including MP3, WMA, WAV and CD audio, as well as video formats including MPEG, AVI, WMV and ASF (Windows Media streaming format). The player provides a console with a range of controls, a playlist editor and a media library.

Platform: Windows
http://www.winamp.com

Further sources of multimedia plug-ins and helper applications

- Netscape Netcenter **http://wp.netscape.com/plug-ins/index.html**
- 3-D Graphics Software **http://www.Webreference.com/authoring/graphics/ software/3d.html**
- The VRML and Java3D repositories at Web3D Consortium
  http://www.Web3d.org/vrml/vrml.htm

3.9 INTERACTIVE WEB PAGES

This section presents a selection of the many ways of producing interactivity in Web pages.

The default process by which documents are delivered on the Web is an inherently static one:

- A client requests a document at a particular Web address (URL).
- The server at that location fetches the requested document (e.g. an HTML page, an image etc.) and transmits it back to the client.
- The document is displayed by the browser on the client machine.

There are a variety of methods available for making the Web more interactive. In order to introduce dynamic behaviour into the Web each of the stages above can be enhanced or altered.

In the browser, Dynamic HTML, JavaScript, Java and ActiveX controls can affect the display of the document. All the processing that provides the interactive behaviour is actually performed by the browser. This is often referred to as client-side processing.

In contrast, technologies such as ASP (Active Server Pages), CGI (Common Gateway Interface) and SSI (Server Side Includes) dynamically influence the page each time it is requested from the server, i.e. server-side processing. This is a tremendously powerful means of generating pages that are always up to date and adapt themselves to the user's requirements. Because the processing is taking place on the server before the page is delivered to the browser, the results will appear to be the same, regardless of the client browser type or computing platform. Such techniques are employed with great effect in the development of database-driven Web sites.

One complication of these server-side technologies is the implication for caching and indexing of documents.

Cookies assist with session and user tracking and involve both client and server in a limited way.

The topics covered in this section are:

- Dynamic content and caching;
- Dynamic HTML refers to the combination of HTML, style sheets and scripts that allows documents to be animated;

- Java applets Java byte-code pulled across the network and executed by the browser when the appropriate tag is encountered in an HTML page;
- JavaScript programs embedded inside an HTML page are executed on-the-fly by the browser;
- Common Gateway Interface a standard for fetching Web documents generated dynamically by the Web server;
- Active Server Pages a server-side technology from Microsoft used for creating dynamic Web pages;
- Server Side Includes a means of dynamically including content in a Web page. The included content may be files (e.g. header and footer files), server-generated information (e.g. current date, date of last modification of the document), or the output of a CGI script (e.g. hit counter);
- Cookies small pieces of data created by servers and stored at the browser for later use.

Distributed object technology

Software component models such as CORBA (**http://www.omg.org/ gettingstarted**) and DCOM (**http://msdn.microsoft.com/library/backgrnd/html/ msdn_dcomarch.htm**) provide a framework within which distributed software objects can communicate with each other, regardless of location or platform. The consequence of these component models for the Web is that they offer a means of easily integrating software components in order to generate new applications or to extend old ones. For example, browsers, protocols or commercial applications, with the added benefits of all the sophisticated distributed systems services and techniques that are available within the model, can be used collectively.

Existing products that use these technologies are Java Beans and ActiveX.

3.9.1 Dynamic content and caching

Caching Web pages considerably speeds up retrievals, whether it is handled by the user's browser, a local proxy server, or a regional or national caching service. However, with dynamically generated pages the benefits are not as clear cut as with static pages. If a dynamic page is retrieved from the originating server and stored in a cache, when a user retrieves it from the cache some time later, they may not see the page as it is meant to be seen, either because the information is no longer current or it is not the version of the page for the browser they are using, or some other variation determined by server-side processing. On the other hand, if pages always need to be retrieved from the originating server, users do not benefit from the speed and access improvements offered by caches, particularly where connectivity is poor.

When these issues have been weighed up, the Web protocol (HTTP) offers the content provider a means of exercising control over how long their pages are cached for. If freshness of content of dynamically generated documents is the main priority and the document should not be cached at all, this can be specified in the header by setting the 'Expires' value to zero. Alternatively, the value could be set to one day, one week, or whatever is appropriate. Conversely, where the provider (using an Apache Web server) wants to make sure that documents containing SSIs are cacheable, a tool called 'xbithack' can be used.

Dynamically generated pages also have implications for search engines. Here it is not a question of freshness of content, rather of stale indexing. Index terms collected by the search engine may no longer apply when the document is accessed some time later. One ameliorating factor is that frequently updated pages tend to attract frequent visits by search engines and, consequently, frequent updates of their index.

Finding more information

Information Resource Caching FAQ **http://www.ircache.net/Cache/FAQ**
See also Section 2.3.

3.9.2 Dynamic HTML

Definition

Dynamic HTML (DHTML) is a collective term for a set of technologies that produce Web pages that are responsive to user actions. The appearance or content of the page can change in response to actions such as mouse clicks or movements, keying in text, or other keyboard actions. Although not yet fully implemented in all browsers, DHTML represents a leap forward in the potential for client-side interaction.

DHTML is made up of three key elements:

● **Cascading Style Sheets** CSS gives authors greatly enhanced control over the presentation of Web pages by separating document display information from the actual content. With CSS it is possible to specify attributes such as text colour, margins, alignment, font size etc.

- **Scripting languages** scripts in languages such as JavaScript are embedded in the HTML page and interpreted by the browser as it loads the page. They are typically used to generate responses to user events such as mouse-clicks, form input and page navigation.
- **HTML tags** the HTML 4.0 specification provides tags to embed objects and scripts, and to support style sheets.

Other associated features of DHTML are.

- **Content positioning** allows for precise alignment and layering of blocks of HTML content such that they can be exposed, hidden, moved, expanded or contracted in response to user actions;
- **Downloadable fonts** any font required to enhance a Web page can be incorporated into the page and is downloaded on demand if required by the client browser.

DOM

The foundation for DHTML is the Document Object Model (DOM). DOM defines the anatomy of a page. Within a hierarchical framework, each element within a document can be specified. There is, for example, the document itself, the head, the body, links, images, text styles etc. Elements and styles also have their own properties. For instance, a table has height and width, a heading has a font style and font size. DOM provides the framework by which these elements and their style properties can be accessed and manipulated by client-side scripts.

The World Wide Web Consortium has issued the DOM Level 2 Specification as a W3C recommendation, thus defining a standard API (Application Programming Interface) that allows authors to write programs that work, without changes, across tools and browsers from different vendors.

Using DHTML

Because DOM allows client-side scripts to access style elements and their associated properties, it is possible to alter the appearance of objects in a Web page in response to user actions (events). For example, the style of a link could change when the mouse is moved over it.

CSS enables absolute positioning of HTML elements, using exact x, y, and z coordinates. It is therefore, possible to animate precisely positioned content, for instance moving an object to a different position on the page when it is clicked.

Unfortunately the fourth generation Netscape and Microsoft browsers inconsistently render DHTML. This is chiefly because they currently implement DOM slightly differently. Netscape Navigator 4.0 gives scripting languages less access to page elements than Internet Explorer. For example, Netscape Navigator 4.0 cannot change style properties after the page has loaded.

Another difference between Netscape and Internet Explorer is in the implementation of content positioning. Netscape uses the LAYER tag while Microsoft bases its approach on a combination of CSS (DIV and SPAN tags), Active X and its own DOM.

EXAMPLES   *Rollover*

In this example, two style classes are defined using CSS. This STYLE declaration is placed in the HEAD of the document:

```
<STYLE>

.on           {
              font-size: 16;
              font-style: italic;
              font-family: san-serif;
              text-decoration: none;
              color: red;
              }
.off          {
              font-size: 16;
              font-style: normal;
              font-family: serif;
              text-decoration: none;
              color: blue;
              }

</STYLE>
```

In the document, scripts are used to apply these class styles to objects in a dynamic way, that is, in response to user actions. Employing the JavaScript functions onMouseOver and onMouseOut the object changes style when the mouse is moved over it (in this case, the object is an empty link).

```
<A HREF = "#"
CLASS = "off"
onMouseOver = "this.className ='on';"
onMouseOut = "this.className = 'off';">
Example of a rollover
</A>
```

The result is

```
Example of a rollover
```

Due to the different implementation of DOM between browser types (see above) this example will only work correctly using Microsoft Internet Explorer. Move your mouse (without clicking) over the text `Example of a rollover`. It should change as you do so.

Finding more information

- Dynamic HTML Lab **http://www.Webreference.com/dhtml/**
- Inside Dynamic HTML **http://www.insidedhtml.com**
- Netscape DevEdge Online **http://devedge.netscape.com/**
- DHTML tutorial **http://www.dansteinman.com/dynduo/**

3.9.3 Java

Java is a programming language from Sun Microsystems designed to run in a secure manner on any platform without modification of the source code. These characteristics make it ideal for developing network applications – programs that you can download from a remote machine and execute on your own computer. The most common use of Java on the Internet is in the form of applets, which can be executed by Java-enabled Web browsers. Java's built-in security mechanisms aim to prevent inadvertent or malicious interference by the applet with any other part of the user's system.

Using

Java applets can be run by any Java-enabled browser, such as HotJava from Sun Microsystems, Netscape Navigator and Internet Explorer. The applet program is dynamically loaded across the Internet and executed inside the Web browser when the browser encounters an `<APPLET>` tag in an HTML document.

The basic components needed to write applets or stand-alone applications in Java can be freely downloaded in the form of Sun's Java Development Kit (JDK) from JavaSoft (**http://www.javasoft.com**). This includes the core class files, a compiler and an interpreter. There is a useful tutorial at **http://www.javasoft.com/docs/ books/tutorial/index.html** at JavaSoft that covers both basic and specialized aspects of using the language.

It is also possible to download and use ready-made applets from one of the many public archives on the Web.

Sun Microsystems gives examples of Java technology in action at: **http://www.javasoft. com/nav/used/index.html.**

Finding more information

The *JavaWorld* magazine is an online publication aimed mainly at programmers. It contains lots of technical information and discussion about Java.

3.9.4 JavaScript

JavaScript is a client-side scripting language used for writing small programs that are embedded inside a page of HTML. As the page loads, the JavaScript code is interpreted by the browser. JavaScript was developed at Netscape, and is recognized as standard by Microsoft's Internet Explorer as well (though Microsoft originally developed its own version of JavaScript called JScript).

By operating on the client-side, JavaScript speeds up simple interactive behaviour without needing to use the network. For example, simple verification of the data entered into a form (e.g. numbers only in telephone field) could be carried out in the browser via JavaScript inside the HTML of the form page. This reduces server load and speeds up performance at the client side. In general, the use of an embedded client-side scripting language can create a more event-driven page, reacting instantly to user input, such as mouse clicks or text entry at the browser.

Using

Scripting languages such as JavaScript are commonly used as a key component technology of DHTML. Using DHTML, properties of objects in the Web document can be accessed and manipulated, generating interactive and animated pages at the client end without recourse to interactions with the Web server.

To run a program written in any scripting language, your browser must be able to interpret the particular language that is being used. Both Netscape and Internet Explorer browsers can execute JavaScript programs.

Examples of JavaScript abound on the Web. Many examples can be found at **http:// www.developer.com/lang/jscript/** and **http://www.javascript.com**.

Finding more information

- Netscape documentation on JavaScript **http://developer.netscape.com/ docs/manuals/index.html**
- Microsoft JavaScript page **http://msdn.microsoft.com/library/ default.asp?url=/library/enus/dninvbs/html/javascript.asp**

3.9.5 Common Gateway Interface

The Common Gateway Interface (CGI) provides a standard interface between Web servers and other, external programs and applications. For example, using CGI to access a database means that non-Web information can be made available via the Web. It is a server-side technology in which the processing of information takes place at the server end and the results are sent back to the Web browser in a dynamically generated HTML page generated on-the-fly.

The typical CGI scenario is:

- the user clicks on a link in a Web page which represents the URL of a CGI script, e.g. submitting a database search request;
- the request is sent by the browser to the Web server;
- the Web server executes the CGI script, e.g. a database search for the keyword;
- the script sends HTML output back to the server and terminates;
- the dynamically generated HTML page containing the output is displayed by the browser.

A document generated using CGI will be indistinguishable, to the requesting browser, from a normal static Web document (although the content of the page and its URL may make its origins evident). Because CGI documents are created on demand they cannot be cached locally. In order to reload the same page the CGI script will need to run again on the server and regenerate the document.

The use of CGI on a Web server is usually strictly controlled by the server manager, because of the security risks inherent in effectively allowing anonymous users to execute programs on the system. To create the actual scripts or programs that do the work, any programming language can be used. Popular choices are interpreted languages such as Perl, PHP and Python, although compiled languages such as C and Visual Basic can also be used.

Collections of sample programs

- CGI Resource Index **http://www.cgi-resources.com**
- Matt's Script Archive **http://www.scriptarchive.com/**

EXAMPLES   Examples of CGI programs are widespread on the Web: counters, forms, guest books, image maps and interfaces to database collections. See a collection of CGI examples at **http://www.developer.com/lang/cgi**.

Finding more information

The W3 CGI page at **http://www.w3.org/CGI/Overview.html** contains links to more documentation and discussion about CGI.

3.9.6 Active Server Pages

ASP is a server-side technology from Microsoft for building dynamic and interactive Web pages. ASP code is embedded in the HTML page. When such a page is requested from the Web server, the server first executes the ASP instructions and then constructs the page, including any ASP-generated information, and returns it to the client. ASP is similar in concept to CGI.

Using

By default Microsoft Web servers (Internet Information Server 3 and above) can run ASPs (you may need to install/configure the server software to do this). Other server types (e.g. Apache) can be ASP-enabled using third party tools, such as from **http://developers.sun.com/prodtech/asp/**. ASP pages are browser independent.

ASP code is usually written in a language called VBScript which is embedded inside the HTML on a page within <% and %> tags. ASP pages (with extension .asp) can contain any combination of HTML and script commands.

ASP uses an in-built set of objects and components to manage specific aspects of interactivity between the Web server and browser. Objects include the Request (made to the server), the Response (returned by the server) and the Session (allows the user's visit to the Web site to be treated as a continuous action, rather than a series of disconnected page requests).

Active Server Components provide ready-made functionality. Examples include database access, determining browser capabilities, and linking to and writing into text files.

ASP scripts are text files and can be written by hand in any simple text editor. Tools are also available. Visual InterDev provides a fast way of building ASP scripts. Also some general Web authoring programs, such as Microsoft FrontPage and Macromedia HomeSite, enable you to create and edit ASP scripts.

EXAMPLES

Here is a simple example of the use of a conditional statement in responding to an order confirmation from a user:

```
<%
If varOrderConfirm = "Yes" then
Response.Write "Your goods will be despatched within two
weeks."
Else
Response.Write "Your order was not confirmed."
End If
%>
```

But the potential for interactivity goes a great deal further than this. For instance, ASP can be used to customize the Web page for the individual user providing a selection of topics that interest that user, and indicating what is new since their last visit. It could also be used to link an online store to an existing inventory database and order-processing system.

Examples of large sites using ASPs:

- Microsoft **http://www.microsoft.com/**
- Dell **http://www.dell.com**
- Gateway **http://www.gateway.com**

Finding more information

- Microsoft: Active Server Pages **http://msdn.microsoft.com/library/ default.asp?url=/nhp/default.asp?contentid=28000522** and **http://www.microsoft.com/OfficeDev/Index/ASP.htm**
- Microsoft: Active Server Pages Tips and Tricks **http://www.microsoft.com/ AccessDev/articles/ASPT&T.HTM**
- Also see useful resources at **http://www.learnasp.com**

3.9.7 PHP

PHP is a server-side scripting language and interpreter that is available on a wide range of platforms, including Apache and IIS. Originally the program was known as Personal Home Page Tools, hence the derivation of PHP. Alternatively, some users prefer the abbreviation to refer to Hypertext Pre-processor.

A PHP script can be embedded in a Web page, and then interpreted on the server, prior to being sent to the client who originally requested the page. PHP is open source, and may be downloaded from **http://www.php.net**.

PHP came about because many Web developers found that existing tools and languages were not ideal for the specific task of embedding code in markup – early developers therefore devised a server-side scripting language which they felt would be ideal for developing dynamic Web-based sites and applications.

PHP was created as an embedded script – PHP code would benefit from quicker response time, improved security, and a greater transparency for the end user. Recent estimates suggest that over 1.5 million sites are currently running PHP.

Finding for more Information

- **http://www.php.net**
- **http://www.beginnersphp.co.uk**

3.9.8 Application program interface

An API is effectively a set of functions or subroutines that a program, or application, can utilize to tell the operating system to carry out a specific task. The Windows API, for example, is composed of more than a thousand different functions that programs written in C, C++, Pascal and other languages can be called upon to create windows, open files and perform other essential tasks.

Finding more information

Diffuse Project Web site – Guide to Application Program Interfaces **http://www.diffuse.org/apiguide.html**

3.9.9 Server Side Includes

Afford a means of creating a 'template' Web page, which in turn places some standard text in a set of Web pages or applies a consistent appearance across a set of Web pages.

Using

The HTML text to be used as a template is saved in one file, and then each individual page contains a special instruction to include this file. If the Web author then wants to change the appearance of an entire site, only the template file need be changed.

When the user types a URL for a Web page, the Web server software dynamically creates a 'final' page that includes whatever is in the template (hence 'server-side'). Because this mechanism happens at the Web server end, and is invisible to the user, any Web browser may be used. SSIs are a feature of the Web server software – Apache and Microsoft IIS both support them. The syntax differs slightly depending on the Web server used.

EXAMPLES

Suppose you wished to include the following HTML in all the Web pages on your site.

```
<H2>
<IMG SRC="logo.gif">
University of London</H2>
<I>e-mail: Webmaster@lon.ac.uk<I>
```

You would save this in an ordinary text file called e.g. **header.inc**. By convention SSI template files are often saved with the .inc file extension. In order to include the above HTML in a Web page, the following syntax would be used.

```
<!--#include
file="header.inc"-->
```

SSIs can also be used to dynamically insert information such as local time, date or file information (filesize, filename, creation date etc.)

Finding more information

- Introduction to SSIs **http://www.carleton.ca/~dmcfet/html/ssi3.html**
- About Apache Server Side Includes **http://www.apacheweek.com/features/ssi**

3.9.10 Cookies

Cookies are a way of saving information from a Web server on a browser. A cookie is a small amount of data sent by a server the first time a user accesses a site and is stored, by the browser, on the user's computer. When making subsequent requests, the browser checks whether a cookie has previously been saved for that site and if so sends the cookie back to the server along with the request for the page.

The contents of a cookie can be anything the server wishes to 'remember'. It must have an expiration date and is limited in size. Cookies have often been perceived as a security risk and possibly an invasion of privacy.

Access

Cookies are not something to which you would normally require access. They are used by browser and server to help personalize your Web usage – for Web site managers, cookies are a useful way of monitoring individual usage and preferences.

However, if you should want to see what information is being collected on your behalf, the file, or files, are located on the same computer as the browser you use and possibly in the same directory, though the location can vary with different browsers.

Microsoft Internet Explorer stores cookies in a directory inside the user's local profile directory. Netscape appends new cookies to a single file called `cookies.txt`. It is possible to transfer cookies from one browser to another.

Using

A Web user may not be aware that cookies are being set by the sites being visited, although some browsers may be configured to warn the user before accepting a cookie, or even to not allow the cookie to be set. For example, Netscape 4 provides options for accepting all cookies, accepting none, or accepting only cookies that are sent back to the originating server. Similar options are available in other browsers. See Figure 3.1.

The option 'Accept only cookies that get sent back to the originating server' effectively excludes cookies to be sent to third party servers – such as those which provide banner advertising on popular sites, e.g. Doubleclick.

Since the data is stored on the client computer, a user can always delete or corrupt the relevant files if they do not wish to keep the cookies.

Scripts are written using CGI or JavaScript.

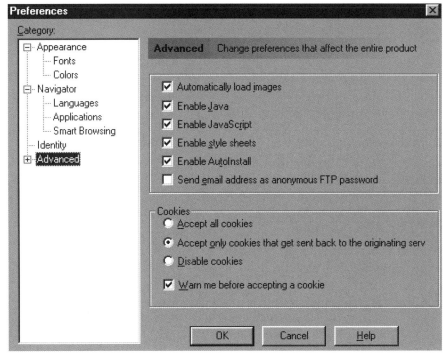

Fig. 3.1 Controlling cookies
Source: Netscape

Common uses of cookies include tracking which pages are visited by a user at a particular site over multiple visits and storing information such as name and password. Another use is with sites consisting of a sequence of ordered pages, such as a training course – the cookie remembers where the user reached on their last access. In the commercial context, cookies may be used to store information on items ordered, the usual analogy being the 'shopping trolley' to which items are added at intervals, with a final tally being made by reference to cookies.

EXAMPLES

Finding more information

- An excellent overview of cookies is at Cookie Central **http://www.cookiecentral. com/index.html**

- Another 'How to use cookies' can be found at **http://MasterCGI.com/howtoinfo/ cookies.shtml**

3.10 WEB DATABASES

As the Web becomes a mainstream technology for all sectors, and particularly commercial enterprise, there is a growing interest in Web/database integration driven from two main sources:

- the desire for a cross-platform, easily accessed interface to legacy databases;
- the requirement for up-to-date information on large, complex and constantly-changing Web sites.

Interface to legacy databases

When a database and Web site are integrated, database users do not need to have access to the database application, nor are they limited by computing platform or location. With a system of password entry, they can securely carry out traditional tasks, such as data entry and retrieval, using just their Web browser.

Dynamic Web sites

For a Web site containing rapidly changing information it is not practical to continually rewrite HTML pages to cope with the demand for up-to-date content. By using a database to store and generate Web site content, the Web server uses SQL queries to get content automatically from the (constantly maintained) database and dynamically creates the Web pages. Dynamic generation can be carried out as the page is requested. Where heavy traffic would make the load on the database too great or for pages that update less frequently, the HTML pages can be generated en masse at regular intervals and posted on the site as regular pages. The drawbacks of dynamically generated Web sites are the implications they have for indexes (such as search engines) and caches. See Section 3.9.1 for a discussion of the issues.

There are a variety of tools to choose from when setting up a Web/database system. It is only necessary to find an affordable combination of operating system, Web server, database management system and the tool that acts as the interface between the Web server and database. The interface technology could be:

- a custom application written in Perl, Java etc. accessed through CGI;
- Active Server Pages (ASP) running on the Web server;
- a specialized third-party Web database application server such as ColdFusion;
- part of an all-in-one package such as Oracle.

a web database application server interfaces with the Web server through its API. API extensions installed on the server extend the server's capabilities to use other technologies.

Database management system

Most of the database systems likely to be used in Web services will be ODBC (Open DataBase Connectivity)-compliant relational databases queried with SQL (Structured Query Language). ODBC handles the connection between the Web server and the database in addition to the translation of requests.

ODBC drivers are available for many database systems. (JDBC is the equivalent standard for use with Java-based applications.) Popular desktop database systems are Microsoft Access, FoxPro and FileMaker Pro. Examples of enterprise level systems are Oracle, Ingres, Sybase, Informix, DB2, Microsoft SQL Server and MySQL.

Enterprise level systems have the requisite power, speed and security protection to cope with multiple concurrent users and transactions. Desktop database systems are less complex and may be adequate for most uses, particularly for an intranet or a low-traffic Internet site.

3.10.1 Web database tools

Active Server Pages

http://www.microsoft.com/OfficeDev/Index/ASP.htm

See also Section 3.9.6. ASP is a server-side programming technology from Microsoft that can be used for developing a Web interface to an ODBC database. Built-in ActiveX data objects link the database to the Web server and ASP Web pages access and manipulate data from a Web browser.

ASPs may be authored using an authoring tool such as Macromedia ColdFusion MX or Microsoft Visual InterDev.

Macromedia Cold Fusion

http://www.macromedia.com/software/coldfusion

A popular cross-platform Web application tool, ColdFusion provides a fast way of building and deploying applications integrating browser, server and database technologies. It uses a tag-based scripting language (CFML), which integrates with HTML and XML and is processed by the ColdFusion Application Server. It boasts scaleable deployment and high performance, even on demanding sites, security features and extensibility with a wide range of technologies. It includes built-in support for Oracle and Sybase and also general ODBC support.

Filemaker Pro

http://www.filemaker.com/
FileMaker Pro is known as an easy-to-use organized data-sharing database for the end user. Its new ODBC import function allows querying of ODBC data sources and importing of the results. Originally Mac software, there is now a PC version.

MySQL

http://www.mysql.com/

MySQL is a very fast, multi-threaded, multi-user and robust SQL database server. For Unix and OS/2 platforms, MySQL is basically free; for Microsoft platforms you must get a MySQL license after a trial time of 30 days.

MySQL is often used as a database back-end integrated with the Web using PHP3 or CGI scripts.

Oracle

http://www.oracle.com/ip/index.html?content.html

Oracle9i is specifically designed as an Internet development and deployment platform. It combines the functions of database server, Web server, file server and application server. It includes a Java Virtual Machine and has implemented support for SQLJ, an embedded SQL language for Java.

PHP

http://www.php.net

PHP is a scripting technology/language with a syntax similar to C, Java and Perl. Originally developed for the Unix platform, there are now versions for Windows, Unix and Linux. PHP is an open source project which means that, by definition, it does not cost anything to use.

SQL server

http://www.microsoft.com/sql/

SQL server is an enterprise-level database product that is designed for large-scale use and, as a Microsoft product, it can be easily integrated with a Web site using ASPs.

Pervasive.SQL

http://www.pervasive.com/offerings/

This is an industrial strength tool for creating Web applications using back-end databases. Pervasive.SQL includes Development Studio and Application Server and will support any ODBC compliant database, as well as direct connections to Oracle, Butler SQL and FileMaker Pro, and is available for many platforms.

3.11 XML: WHAT IS IT?

XML (eXtensible Markup Language) is a new development in the evolution of (markup) languages for creating Web/Internet content. It uses 'tags' in a similar style to HTML but allows users to create their own.

However, there are important differences between XML and HTML. Whereas HTML is used to control the format or appearance of a page of text, XML is used to define the structure and processing of data. This can provide important advantages in the management and retrieval of information, and separates stylistic issues from the content. HTML contains a strictly defined number of tags that cannot be changed or extended; XML allows Web authors/information providers to create their own set of tags for individual purposes. Strictly speaking XML is a 'meta language' – that is, a language which is used to define new languages with strict rules about the structure and formatting of information written using them.

Advantages of XML are:

- additional flexibility – to create new tags;
- separation of presentation and content – better information management;
- built-in error checking and validation;
- built-in processing features – e.g to sort or search data;
- can be used to exchange data between applications;

- complex hierarchical data structures possible;
- more precise search and retrieval of data possible.

EXAMPLES

Example of XML document

Suppose you wish to structure the play 'Macbeth' as XML. It might look something like this.

```
<?xml version="1.0"?>
<play>
<playtitle>Macbeth</playtitle>
<act number="1"><br /> <scene number="1" location="a desert
heath">
<directions>Thunder and lightning. Enter three witches.
</directions>
<line person="first witch">
Where shall we three meet again. In thunder, lightning, or
in rain?
</line>
</scene>
</act>
</play>
</code>
```

Note that the rules of XML are stricter than HTML. For example, HTML allows single tags without a closing tag (e.g. <HR>), but XML insists on every element being properly closed. Also, XML is case sensitive. Notice an important difference between HTML and XML – there are no formatting instructions in XML as there would be in HTML.

3.11.1 eXtensible Style Language

The details of how the individual elements are to be formatted are stored elsewhere – either using CSS (Cascading Style Sheets), or another type of language called the eXtensible Style Language (XSL). This is similar in concept to CSS, but is more complex (XSL contains programming constructs which can be used for processing/sorting data).

Without the style sheet instructions, browsers would not know how to display the content. Keeping the formatting instructions separate from the structure and content of the XML document gives two main benefits:

- content and style can be altered without affecting either each other or the structure of the document;
- alternative styles can be presented for different environments, e.g. a style for printing rather than screen display, or a style for display on a mobile phone rather than a Web browser.

Document Type Definitions

It is possible to define the exact rules for an XML structure in what is called a Document Type Definition. A DTD specifies which tags are nested within other tags, what order they can be used in, which parts are optional or compulsory etc.

A DTD can then be used to validate XML documents using this DTD to check that it is correct.

Implications of XML

If one considers ordinary pages of textual information, XML can be used as a more efficient way of managing and structuring information. This can lead to important advantages in terms of information management (less duplication/redundancy, greater accuracy, more control over revisions, error checking and providing different formats/versions of information for different circumstances).

However, XML has the advantage that it can be used to create and structure other forms of information – for example, abstract languages such as music, mathematics or chemistry. Such information can then be displayed, processed in other ways (e.g. playing music, displaying 3-D molecules), or used as a format for exchanging data with other applications. None of this is possible using an HTML type of approach.

On the other hand, in the early stages it is much harder to define and construct an XML page or DTD, and specialist/abstract applications as described above require substantial technical/programming skills.

3.11.2 XML browser compatibility

The following summarizes the compatibility of commonly used browsers with XML.

- **IE4** partial support for XML, reasonable CSS;
- **IE5** good support for XML and CSS;

- **Netscape 4** no XML, moderate CSS support;
- **Netscape 5** good support for both XML and CSS.

Finding more information

- What is... XML? Ariadne Web article by Brian Kelly **http://www.ariadne.ac.uk/issue15/what-is/intro.html**
- W3Cs XML Home page **http://www.w3.org/XML**
- O'Reilly Network XML Homepage **http://www.xml.com**

Examples of XML applications

- MathML (Mathematics Markup Language) **http://www.w3.org/TR/REC-MathML**
- CML (Chemical Markup Language) **http://www.xml-cml.org**
- SMIL (Synchronized Multimedia Integration Language) **http://www.w3.org/TR/1998/PR-smil-19980409**

3.12 METADATA

Organizing the Web

The use of metadata to add cataloguing information to Web resources offers potential to improve the organization of Web resources and allows the development of more sophisticated search tools.

Metadata

Metadata is simply 'information about information'. A library catalogue record or the publishing details at the front of a book are examples of metadata. The lack of metadata on the Web is seen as a considerable barrier to effective searching. Imagine trying to search a library catalogue that gave no information about the authors or titles of the books in the library. Yet it is almost impossible to search for the author of a Web page, and many Web pages are untitled. Restricting searches by date is also problematic – what exactly is the 'date' of a Web page? When it was first written or last updated? Even if date information is added to a Web page, there are no rules to govern the format of a date – for example, is 03/04/02 the 3rd of April or the 4th of March?

Incorporating metadata in a Web page is rather like giving the page its own catalogue record. Metadata is written into the code of a Web page, so that it is not displayed on the page but it can be indexed by search tools. As well as assisting with resource discovery, metadata can also be used for administrative purposes, such as intellectual property rights management and content rating.

Web pages are written in HTML, which uses 'tags' to define parts of a Web page. 'Meta-tags' are placed in an unseen part of the Web page called the HEAD (the visible section which appears in the browser window is written in the BODY of a page), and can include subject, creator and description tags. Metadata can either be written manually in HTML, or via built-in tools using Web authoring packages. Some metadata schemes, such as Dublin Core, have produced automatic metadata generation tools, which can create metadata for a Web page at the click of a mouse.

Metadata schemes

Just as library cataloguers have to adhere to recognized cataloguing standards, various metadata schemes have been developed to enable standardization of metadata. One of the most widely used schemes is called Dublin Core. This defines 15 different metadata 'elements' (equivalent to 'fields' in cataloguing), including title, creator, publisher and resource type. As there are many different schemes in existence, the Resource Description Framework (RDF) is an initiative from the World Wide Web Consortium to provide a foundation for exchange and interoperability between different metadata schemes.

Problems with metadata

Not everyone thinks metadata is a good thing. It requires time and effort from Web page creators, yet the benefits of incorporating it may not be immediately apparent. Even a British Library director has recently suggested that investing time and money in metadata creation is ill-advised, since most people are interested in full-text Web searching, rather than field searches; selecting Web sites from a list of results, rather than looking for one specific site [Dropping the Metadata Mindset, Library and Information Update, May 2003, 2(5), 12]. Furthermore, the use of metadata is open to abuse by Web authors who want to get their sites listed higher in search engines. For example, they can repeat keywords over and over again, known as 'keyword spamming'. Partly as a result of this, no major search engines use the 'meta keyword' tag any longer. However, it does still have potentially useful applications in specific projects and sectors (for example, government Web sites).

EXAMPLES This is an example of metadata (Dublin Core Scheme, DCS).

```
<meta name="DC.Publisher" content="Netskills, University
of Newcastle, UK">
<meta name="DC.Date" content="2003-07-10">
<meta name="DC.Identifier"
content="http://www.netskills.ac.uk/">
<meta name="DC.Format" content="text/html - 6,975 bytes">
<meta name="DC.Type" content="Text">
```

Finding more information

- Dublin core metadata initiative **http://dublincore.org**
- W3C Metadata and Resource Description **http://www.w3.org/Metadata/**
- DESIRE Project: Information toolkits **http://www.desire.org/toolkit/**
- UKOLN Metadata resources **http://www.ukoln.ac.uk/metadata**
- Resource Description Framework **http://www.w3.org/RDF/**
- An 'anti-metadata' article **http://www.well.com/~doctorow/metacrap.htm**

3.13 ROBOTS

Robots are automatic software programmes or agents designed to carry out highly repetitive work, or work beyond the scope of human intervention due to scale. Web robots are also known as Web wanderers, Web crawlers, or spiders – their main function is to 'wander' the Web, navigating through hyperlinks and performing tasks, such as recognizing and indexing resources.

The current generation of Web robots is large. Current estimates suggest that there are over 160 well-known robots, written in a variety of different languages. Some use libraries that are written to aid Web agent design – two popular libraries used for this purpose are *libwww* for the C language and *LWP* for Perl.

Most robots navigating the Web are used by search engines to index keywords and other metadata to build indices for resource retrieval. Other robots are used to maintain hypertext structures or to summarize resources in different ways.

Generally, Web robots can be categorized as:

- exploratory Web crawling (e.g. resource discovery or broken link discovery);
- directed Web crawling (e.g. of URLs submitted to a search engine);
- restricted Web crawling (e.g. all URLs within a DNS domain).

There are two methods by which Web authors and administrators can attempt to influence which areas of their Web site are visited by robots – the Robot Exclusion Protocol, and the Robots META tag. It is important to note that both require the robot to cooperate with these directions or preferences, and cannot force the robot to behave as specified.

Robot Exclusion Protocol

A file called `robots.txt` can be placed in the root directory of the Web server. In this file is a set of disallow statements defining parts of the Web site that the robot should not index. A sample `robots.txt` file is as follows.

```
User-agent: *
Disallow: /cgi-bin/
Disallow: /tmp/
```

The Robots meta tag

The Robots meta tag enables HTML authors and content providers to indicate to visiting robots whether or not a document may be indexed or used to traverse additional links. It differs from the `robots.txt` file in that one doesn't require access to a Web server's root directory.

Meta tag placement

Like any meta tag, the Robots meta tag should be placed in the HEAD section of an HTML document.

```
<html>
<head>
<meta name="robots" content="noindex,nofollow">
<meta name="description" content="This Web page...">
<title>Welcome</title>
</head>
<body>
.  </body>
</html>
```

Meta tag structure

The content of the Robots meta tag includes directives separated by commas. The currently defined directives are `[NO]INDEX` and `[NO]FOLLOW`. The `INDEX` directive specifies if a robot should index the page and the `FOLLOW` directive specifies if a robot should follow links on the page. The defaults are `INDEX` and `FOLLOW`.

```
<meta name="robots" content="index,follow">
<meta name="robots" content="noindex,follow">
<meta name="robots" content="index,nofollow">
<meta name="robots" content="noindex,nofollow">
```

Finding more information

The Web Robots pages **http://www.robotstxt.org/wc/robots.html**

3.14 ACCESSIBILITY

Recent legislation in both the UK and the USA has now made educational institutions legally responsible for ensuring that opportunities for learning are accessible to all students, irrespective of disability or impairment. This supplements other legislation that already existed in non-educational organizations. Most European countries have adopted similar legislation – further details can be found at: **http://www.w3.org/WAI/Policy**.

In the UK, the TechDis initiative (a JISC funded advisory service) has created a number of resources to enable Web designers to design fully accessible pages. These include some of the following:

- Navigation and page layout;
  website navigation design and page layout.
- Visual presentation and customization;
  design, colour and presentation issues including the requirements for user control.
- Text descriptions for images;
  implementation and appropriate use of various tags or attributes for images.
- Accessible markup – forms, lists, scripts and tables;
  use of an appropriate markup language to achieve accessible elements.

- Use and presentation of written language;
  use of clear and concise, recognizable language conventions and configuration of letters, words, sentences and paragraphs.

- Accessible issues for other media types;
  providing accessible media (e.g. video and audio files), accessible document formats (e.g. PowerPoint and PDF files).

- Help, searches, errors and documentation;
  contextual help, dealing with errors and other useful documentation.

These are more fully explored at **http://www.techdis.ac.uk/**

In addition, there are a number of resources that enable users to evaluate their pages against these precepts, including an online Web accessibility tool that will check supplied URLs and respond with an e-mail evaluation report. These resources can be found at:

- TechDis User Style Sheet Wizard
  http://www.techdis.ac.uk/indexphp?p=3_6_20051205110543

- TechDis User Preferences Toolbar
  http://www.techdis.ac.uk/indexphp?p=1_20051905100544

- TechDis Web Accessibility Evaluation Tool
  http://www.techdis.ac.uk/indexphp?p=3_6_20051905120529

Finding more information

- W3C Web Accessibility Initiative **http://www.w3.org/WAI/**
- Nielson useit.com documents or papers **http://www.useit.com/papers/ heuristic/heuristic_evaluation.html**
- Cast's Bobby Web accessibility evaluation tool **http://bobby.watchfire.com/ bobby/html/en/index.jsp**
- TechDis resources page **http://www.techdis.ac.uk/indexphp?p=3**

See also the graphics (3.5 and 3.6) and multimedia (3.7 and 3.8) sections for specific accessibility issues.

4

PROTECTING USERS AND INFORMATION

If on one hand the Internet is the widest means of exchanging and publishing information, on the other there is a big effort being made to increase the level for security for protecting information and personal data. For some kinds of applications such as the transmission of sensitive data, e-commerce and home banking, security is a must.

This chapter describes how users can access applications in a secure way and how they can protect their data. Topics discussed in this chapter are:

- Digital signatures
- Encryption
- PKI
- Firewall
- Viruses
- Spam.

4.1 SECURITY RISKS

Before the network age, managing computer security was simple. There was just one point to defend from enemies and intruders – the mainframe computer that took care of all the work. Users communicated with it using two simple input/output devices, a keyboard and a monitor. In the mainframe age that big computer was locked in its room and only authorized personnel could get close to it. In those days the computational model was a centralized one. Today in the network age, better known as the Internet age, the computational model has changed and the security problems have increased. In today's distributed environment every computer connected to the network is a potential threat and, of course, a potential victim. Computers, network resources, storage network devices and communication channels all have to be protected from every other computer and network. Every computer on the Internet could be a potential threat from which others have to be protected.

Tomorrow the computational model will change again – the revolution has already started. Networks are, in fact, starting to fragment themselves. Wireless networks, the GRID and the Peer-to-Peer (P2P) networks are growing. Nevertheless that is tomorrow's problem. This guide describes today's security problems and solutions.

The most common areas of Internet security risks are:

- the increase in the speed and ease of access to every type of resource;
- the rapid and widespread transmission of viruses as a result of worms (a special kind of virus that spreads from computer to computer using the network without human intervention);
- easy transmission of data worldwide, either accidental or deliberate;
- easy technical aids to 'e-stealing';
- poorly configured Internet systems leaving loopholes.

What is a hacker? A hacker, according to some people, is just a romantic hero or heroine struggling for freedom of opinion and knowledge. The hacker is always looking for an intellectual challenge. The hacker does not do things for money, for vengeance or to cause damage, but is only looking for a personal challenge to gain knowledge on how things work. The cracker, on the other hand, is a person doing damage for money or for vengeance. There are in fact a variety of sources of attack for networked computer systems, categorized by the motives of the attacker:

- joy riders who do it for fun;
- vandals acting maliciously to cause damage;
- score keepers who compete with their peers in the challenge of hacking;
- spies (industrial or otherwise) who set out to steal valuable information.

4.1.1 Maintaining a secure environment

If we begin by noting that the strength of a chain is the strength of its weakest link – hence, the overall security of a system can be no stronger than the security of its weakest component. There are some general guidelines for maintaining the security of logins and passwords on an Internet host, and associated access to file space, electronic mailboxes and Web space. Users largely rely on system managers to take care of the overall security and integrity of a system. However, if someone is intent on breaking in, any weakness in the system can provide an initial entry point. This can be a single user who is slack about user-id or password security. Standard computer security is important for network security. If a password is broken, network login details may be obtained from a computer if it falls into the wrong hands.

In summary:

- Keep passwords secret. Do not give them to anyone else and, especially, do not include login and password details in e-mail messages.
- Use a password that cannot be guessed and avoid words that can be found in a dictionary. 'The dictionary attack' is an automated attempt in which software tries to guess a password using all the words that can be found in a dictionary. The recommended practice is, therefore, to create a password that contains a random mixture of letters using upper and lower case, and include some numbers too.
- Change passwords frequently.
- Keep computers secure. Do not leave yourself logged on to an unattended machine.

4.1.2 Security requirements

There are a number of basic security requirements which will allow the secure exchange of data in an open and distributed environment such as a network:

- **confidentiality** the data cannot be read by any unauthorized person;
- **integrity** the data has not been tampered with during transmission so the data sent is the data received;
- **authentication** the identity of the system or person with whom data is exchanged;
- **non-repudiation** the source of data cannot be denied in the future.

Encryption is one way of meeting these requirements and forms the basis of many of the tools (protocols and secure data formats) for security and privacy, for example Secure Sockets Layer (SSL), Secure/Multipurpose Internet Mail Extensions (S/MIME), Pretty Good Privacy (PGP) and Secure Shell (SSH).

Section 4.3, encryption, explores some of these tools, in particular those related to user requirements rather than those specific to the security concerns of Web site administrators or system managers.

There are security requirements that can be met without reliance on encryption that are of lesser interest for end users:

- **availability** ensuring that a service is provided continuously;
- **consistency** maintaining the same service without alteration;
- **disaster recovery** backing up of data and recovery of services after some disaster, natural (e.g. fire, flood, earthquake) or otherwise;
- **auditability** being able to track back to a previous known stable state of the data;
- **authorization** restricting access to information.

Organizations attach different importance to different types of security. An online shop or bank would attach great importance to both availablity and disaster recovery.

4.2 SECURITY FOR APPLICATIONS

The number of security applications grows daily, of which the most common are remote system management, Web and e-mail. Every time a user wants to connect to their bank to see their account online or every time they buy something online they are probably using the SSL protocol, better known as HyperText Transmission Protocol, Secure (HTTPS).

Every time they sign or encrypt an e-mail they are probably using S/MIME, the application most frequently used to secure e-mails. There are some alternatives – like Secure Electronic Transaction (SET™) to execute business transactions, or PGP to secure mail – but the majority of the applications use SSL and S/MIME.

4.2.1 The SSL protocol

When a user connects to a Web server, how can they be sure that they are really connecting to the server to which they think they are connecting? How can the end user be sure they are not connecting to a malicious server masquerading? When users are shopping online how can they trust sending their credit card number over the Internet without fearing that it could be stolen on the way to the remote server? Finally, how can they buy something from an online shop without fearing that someone will change their order and consequently the bill they will receive? For example, one for 10 books could be inadvertently or maliciously changed in transit to one for 100 books, or even 1000 books, just by adding zeroes. These problems – authentication of the server, encryption of data in transit, and integrity of the data – can be solved by the Secure Sockets Layer/Transport Layer Security (SSL/TLS) protocol.

The sequence of events that takes place when a user connects using SSL (or HTTPS), is as follows:

- The first thing an SSL-enhanced client like Netscape, Mozilla™ or Internet Explorer does when connecting to a SSL Web server is say HELLO. (Mozilla is a trademark of the Mozilla foundation.)
- The server in turn responds to the HELLO by sending its public key certificate (PKC) that binds to the client, binding the DNS name of the server to the server public key.
- The client generates a random number that will be the shared secret used by the client and the server to encrypt data.
- The client now encrypts this newly generated random number with the public key found in the certificate received from the server in the HELLO phase.

Only the server can decrypt that message because no one else has the private key related to the public key set by the client in the server certificate. No one but the client and the server stated in the PKC can know the random number. With this shared secret, the client and server can now enjoy secure encrypted communication. As well as having a shared secret to carry out encryption, thanks to the certificate, the client has also authenticated the server.

In the SSL protocol the server is always authenticated. Sometimes the client also needs to be authenticated by the server and in this case the client sends its PKC to the server and responds to a cryptographic challenge.

All the major browsers have an icon looking like a padlock. When this icon shows as a closed padlock, communication is secured and encrypted. Mozilla and Internet Explorer use the icons shown in Figure 4.1.

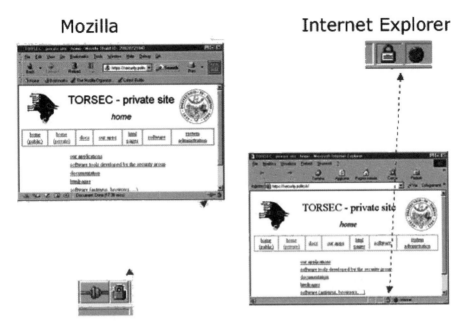

Fig. 4.1 Communication is secure and data is encrypted
Source: TORSEC private site

The architecture more commonly used for e-commerce and buying online is depicted in Figure 4.2.

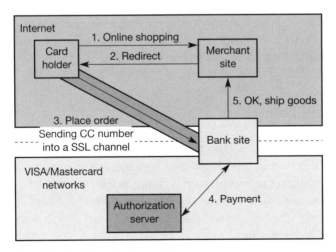

Fig. 4.2 Security architecture for online transactions

As Figure 4.2 shows:

1. The buyer goes to the merchant's site and can go through the merchant's products and special offers and put some goods into a virtual basket. Then comes the moment to place the order and pay the bill. The merchant's site usually offers a page with the list of goods just bought and the total amount to pay.

2. When the user clicks and proceeds, the client browser is redirected to a bank site that establishes an SSL connection. The page has the same look and feel of the merchant's site, but it is on the bank's computer.

3. At this point the user can fill in a form with a credit card number, which is protected by the encryption afforded by SSL.

4. This is securely transmitted to the bank server.

5. The bank server at this point can send a notification to the merchant that the bill has been paid and the merchant will send the goods to the buyer.

Banks are routinely offerring this service commercially. The Italian bank, Banca Sella (**http://www.sellanet.it**), was one of the first to propose this type of service.

An alternative way of doing e-commerce is through SET. This was a protocol developed in 1997 by Visa International and MasterCard International. The intention was to propose a way of securing online payment that maintained the privacy of the buyer. The information about goods bought did not go to the bank and the information on the buyer's bank account did not go to the merchant. The protocol was based on a double digital signature with the use of digital certificates, but it suffered from two major problems – it was very expensive to deploy and it relied on the user's ability to install a personal wallet on their own computer. Because of this SET was never adopted as a standard.

4.2.2 E-mail

What security services are needed from an e-mail system? Even non-technical users would hope that nobody would read their messages and nobody would modify the contents of messages or masquerade as someone else. Users need authentication of the sender, integrity of the message, non-repudiation and confidentiality from an e-mail service. The first three of these can be achieved using a digitally signed e-mail, the last with encryption.

There are two main ways of obtaining these security services:

- PGP – or the open source version GNU's **Not Unix Privacy Guard** (GnuPG)
  http://www.gnupg.org
- **S/MIME http://www.imc.org/ietf-smime**

PGP

There are two versions of PGP. One is commercial and is maintained and developed by the PGP corporation established in August 2002 and run by the PGP inventor himself. The other is an open source version called GnuPG, which is maintained by the Free Software Foundation. PGP uses public key cryptography with a ring of trust. The trust of public keys is exchanged on a meeting basis and works like this.

- I know you and I sign your key.
- I can trust your key because you give me it personally.
- I can partially trust someone else's key because you fully trust him or her.
- The more friends you have, the more your key is trusted.

What is lacking in PGP is someone 'super parties', a trusted third party like a certification authority (CA) that ensures trust in the binding of keys to holders. Because of this lack, the history of PGP has been troubled.

S/MIME

S/MIME is an evolution of MIME, the technology that permits, for example, the sending of e-mails written in HTML with different fonts or with pictures inside and files attached. It allows e-mails to be boxed with different contents in different formats. S/MIME is a protocol developed by the RSA Laboratories to add security to MIME. It was developed in 1995 with two main aims: security and interoperability. The purpose of S/MIME is to permit the exchange of encrypted and signed content between two applications developed by different vendors.

S/MIME adds security to MIME by including the option to sign and encrypt e-mails. To work S/MIME needs PKCs – one from the sender for signing e-mails and one from the recipient for encrypting e-mails. Almost every mailer except Eudora supports S/MIME.

Secure downloading of e-mails

In dealing with the security of the e-mail system one more big problem arises – the downloading of e-mails. This is done by sending a username and a password over the network in the clear. Someone 'sniffing' (looking at what is crossing the network) could get the username and the password, and even the content of the e-mail if it is not encrypted. If someone who was sniffing stole the username and password, they could then easily download all the mail, instead of the real owner, causing what is called a denial of service. The user is unaware of this attack and simply thinks that no one is writing to him or her. The way to solve this problem is to encrypt the username and password. There are two ways of doing this. One is to use Authenticated Post Office Protocol (APOP), an extension of the POP protocol used to download e-mails. This is a solution used mainly by Qualcomm with its WorldMail server **http://www.eudora.com/worldmail/features.html**.

The other solution is to download e-mail on a secure SSL channel. In this way the user authenticates the server, and the username and the password cross the network encrypted.

4.2.3 Remote system connection

When making a terminal connecting to a remote system, it is preferable to authenticate the remote computer, exchanging encrypted data using SSH or Telnet over SSL.

SSH is a protocol that can be used to secure terminal access connections. SSH connections use only public keys, unlike SSL that uses a PKC. The great drawback of the original version of SSH is that the public key has to be exchanged manually between the client and the server. In a recent version this problem was corrected and now it is possible use SSH with PKCs. This complicates the system because it relies on a public key infrastructure (PKI).

The other solution is to connect using Telnet over SSL. This uses the standard SSL protocol authenticating the server and eventually the client with PKCs. The drawback of this solution is, again, that it relies on the services of a PKI.

Finding more information

- Phil Zimmermann home page **http://www.philzimmermann.com**
- PGP Corporation home page **http://www.pgp.com**
- The GNU Privacy Guard home page **http://www.gnupg.org**
- Using PGP: two case studies **http://www.ja.net/documents/gn_pgp.pdf**
- Secure Electronic Transaction (SET) **http://www.setco.org**
- SSH: The commercial version **http://www.ssh.com** and the free version **http://www.openssh.com**

4.3 ENCRYPTION

Encryption – cryptography followed by decryption – allows text to be coded and decoded into and out of a form that is indecipherable by unauthorized readers. It is the process of using a code or cipher to scramble readable text into ciphertext that can be read only by someone with the cipher for decrypting it.

Encryption on the Internet has many uses, from the secure transmission of credit card numbers via the Web to protecting the privacy of personal e-mail messages. Some of the security requirements seen earlier in this section are achieved by using encryption. Confidentiality, integrity, authentication and non-repudiation are most important from the user point of view.

4.3.1 Methods of encryption

Single key encryption

Single key, or symmetric, encryption is a form of cryptography in which the sender and receiver have the same key. This single key is used by the sender to encrypt the data and by the receiver to decrypt the data.

Before the secure exchange of encrypted data can take place, the sender and receiver need to have access to the same single key. It is not advisable to transfer copies of this key over an insecure network, such as the Internet, as it might be possible for a third party to intercept the message and obtain a copy of the key. This would allow the third party to decrypt any encrypted messages. An alternative is to write the key onto a floppy disk, or other removable media, and send it through the normal postal system. Figure 4.3 shows how single key encryption works.

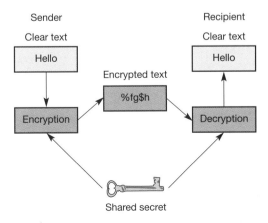

Fig. 4.3 Single key encryption

Examples of single key encryption include International Data Encryption Algorithm (IDEA), Data Encryption Standard (DES), Triple Data Encryption Standard (3DES), Rivest's Cipher 2 [alternatively known as Ron's Code 2 (RC2)] and RC4.

Public key encryption

Public key, or asymmetric, encryption uses two types of key – a public key, which may be freely given out to others, and a private one, which is known only to its owner. The true value of public key encryption is that everything is encrypted by one key, the public one, and can be decrypted only by the complementary key, the private one. The heart of public key encryption is that the public and private keys are complementary and are generated together. A data stream encrypted by one key can be decrypted only by its complementary key. Figure 4.4 outlines how public key encryption works.

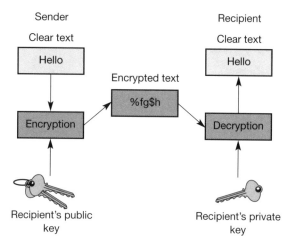

Fig. 4.4 Public key encryption

Using public key encryption to exchange data is a three-step process:

● The sender and receiver exchange their public keys (their private keys are never given out).
● The sender uses the recipient's public key in encrypting a message then sends it.
● The recipient's complementary private key is used to decrypt the received message.

Note that once the message has been encrypted using the recipient's public key, even the sender will no longer be able to decrypt the resultant message. So every time the sender encrypts a message for someone, the message is also encrypted with the private key to make it readable in future.

Another important property of public key cryptography is that its practically impossible to compute the private key from the public key, and is certainly beyond the computational capabilities of most users. This property is called irreversibility.

An example of public key encryption is RSA, the original public key encryption system invented by Rivest, Shamir and Adleman. To understand the mathematical principles that form the basis of RSA with a simple example look at 'finding more information, below.

Another algorithm is the Digital Signature Standard (DSS), sometimes called the Digital Signature Algorithm (DSA), published in 1994 by the Federal Information Processing Standard (FIPS). This was designed only to sign messages and so can not be used to encrypt messages.

4.3.2 Keys and computational power

Cipher keys come in various sizes and are measured in numbers of bits. Generally, the more bits used for the key the stronger its resistance to being compromised by unauthorized entities.

Owing to the nature of cipher algorithms, public key ciphers need to have keys longer than single key ciphers to achieve the same level of security. Single key 128-bit encryption provides an acceptable level of security, but encryption with a 40-bit key may not necessarily withstand a concerted effort to break the code.

For public algorithms a 1024-bit key is reasonable. A disadvantage of the public key algorithms compared to the single key approach is the computational power needed to undertake the encryption and decryption. The time needed to encrypt a data stream with a public key cipher algorithm is at least ten times longer than with a single key cipher algorithm.

While single key encryption systems certainly provide an efficient approach to encryption and decryption, there remains the difficulty of securely exchanging keys between the users over an essentially insecure Internet. For this reason the public key approach, as outlined in Figure 4.5 is usually preferred.

Finding more information

- Daniel D. Houser Digital Encryption Standard: A New Look at the DES Lifecycle (April 5 2001) (an interesting paper on DES also dealing with the cost of breaking the scheme) **http://rr.sans.org/encryption/DES.php**

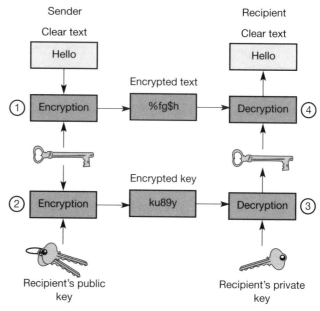

Fig. 4.5 Public key (asymmetric) encryption uses two types of key

- RSA Laboratories Frequently Asked Questions About Today's Cryptography, *Version* 4.1 **http://www.rsasecurity.com/rsalabs/faq/**
- RSA Laboratories, What is RC2? **http://www.rsasecurity.com/rsalabs/faq/3-6-2.html**
- To understand the mathematical principles at the heart of RSA through a simple example try RSA Algorithm JavaScript Page, University Honors College, Oregon State University Peer Mentoring **http://www.orst.edu/dept/honors/makmur**
- Federal Information Processing Standards Publication 186 (May 1994), Announcing the Standard for Digital Signature Standard **http://www.itl.nist.gov/fipspubs/fip186.htm**

4.4 AUTHENTICATION, AUTHORIZATION AND ACCOUNTING

Authentication, authorization and accounting, usually collectively referred to by the acronym AAA (triple-A), are three security functions used together by computer systems, for example networks or services, to control which users are allowed access, what functions they are allowed to use and how much resource they have used.

4.4.1 Authentication

Authentication is the way users show that they are who they claim to be. It is used every time a user's identity must proved – for example, it is the way a user is identified to:

- a network to gain connectivity (e.g. when dialling up to ISP with a modem, or when accessing a network by a wireless link);
- a service (e.g. accessing a computer and using machine computing cycles, for instance in GRID services);
- an application (e.g. Web connecting to a Web server or when connecting to a database to fetch some data).

Authentication can be accomplished by matching something a user knows, like a password, with something a user has, like a smart card with a stored private key, or by something specific to an individual user, for example biometrics identification. Biometrics (for instance, the recognition of a fingerprint, hand geometry, iris or voice) is a very good way of identifying users, but it has some drawbacks. We have only ten digits so in your whole life you can only change your 'fingerprint password' ten times. Biometric data are stored in databases in digital form and, if the databases are not well secured, can be stolen and injected into the system doing the authentication. Consider someone who stole biometric data and entered it into a bank online system when asked for it.

A better method of authentication is to use a combination, a good example being the need of a fingerprint plus a password. In some instances, reliance on just one authentication approach may not provide sufficent security.

4.4.2 Authorization

Authorization is the process of giving the user access to system resources. To use a system resource like a printing service, the user needs authorization from the system administrator. This authorization can be provided on a user-by-user basis or on a group basis. For reasons of manageability, users are usually grouped. For example, in a team of related workers all members of the group might be granted read and print access to a data file (perhaps the group budget information). Maybe only the manager of the group may be granted read, print and write access, however.

4.4.3 Accounting

Accounting enables the system to track which services are being used and by whom. In this way the system owner can record how many resources were used and for how long a user stayed connected to the system. All those logs can be used for billing purposes, or simply for the purpose of providing statistics.

Finding more information

- For biometrics information **http://www.biometrics.org/html/ introduction.html**
- TERENA Task Force for Authentication and Authorization **http://www.terena.nl/ tech/task-forces/tf-aace**

4.5 DIGITAL SIGNATURES

A signature, as defined in the Longman Dictionary, is 'a person's name written by himself/herself, e.g. at the end of a letter, or on a cheque or official paper'. A signature is a way of authenticating the signer, and of avoiding the signer later repudiating the signed document.

What about the digital world?

According to the ITU [Telecommunications Union Standardization Sector (ITU-T) Recommendation X.200] a digital signature is 'data appended to, or a cryptographic transformation of, a data unit that allows a recipient of the data unit to prove the source and integrity of the data unit and protect against forgery, e.g. by the recipient.'

4.5.1 Creating a digital signature

In the simplest terms a digital signature is a stream of bits appended to a document. The purpose of a digital signature is to provide assurance about the origin of the message and the integrity of its content. When a message with a digital signature is transmitted and received, the following parties are involved:

- the signer who signs the document;
- the verifier who receives the signed document and verifies the signature;
- the arbitrator who rules on any disputes between the signer and the verifier, if there is a disagreement on the validity of the digital signature.

Digitally signing a document begins with producing a summary of the document using mathematical functions known as hash functions. Some examples are Message Digest-5 (MD5), Secure Hash Algorithm-1 (SHA-1) and Réseaux IP Européens (RIPE) Message Digest-160 (RIPMED-160). The output of a hash function, a document summary called the hash, always has the same number of bits (e.g. 128 for MD5 and 160 for SHA-1) regardless of the length of the input document. It is obvious that different documents will produce different hashes. It is considered virtually impossible to have an identical hash, even from two similar documents.

The hash function is encrypted by the signer using his/her private key and forms the digital signature of the encrypted document.

The verifier receives both the document and the signature, calculates the summary of the document using the same hash function used by the signer. The signature is decrypted using the signer's public key. The last step is to compare the decrypted summary with the one previously computed by the verifier from the document. If the two summaries are identical then the signature has been verified. The verifier is now sure of the identity of the signer and that the data has not been modified.

Figure 4.6 shows the signing process in steps.

Let us suppose that Alice is the signer and Bob the verifier:

- Alice calculates the summary of the document, the hash;
- Alice encrypts the summary with her own private key to create the digital signature;
- Alice sends the digital signature and the document to Bob, the verifier;
- Bob calculates the summary of the document, the hash;
- Bob decrypts the digital signature with Alice's public key and obtains a summary;
- Bob compares the two summaries he has made;
- if they are equal Bob is sure that the document was not modified and that Alice really did sign the document herself.

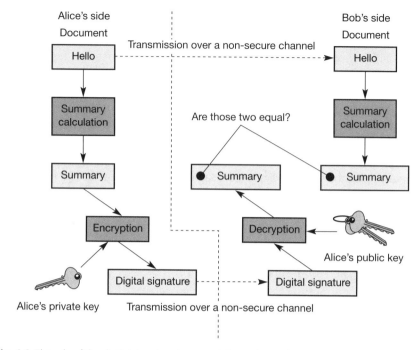

Fig. 4.6 The role of the digital signature in secure information exchange

4.5.2 Certificate authorities

How can verifiers be sure of the owner of a public key? Let us suppose that the sender, Alice (see Figure 4.6), sends a signed document to Bob. Bob needs Alice's public key to verify the signature. But, how can he obtain it? He cannot just simply go to Alice's Internet home page and download it. He cannot be sure that the home page he is using to download Alice's public key really belongs to Alice. He cannot trust her home page, since on the Internet everything is possible – he cannot even trust someone else who claims to have Alice's public key. There is a need for someone or something that can be trusted to guarantee the link between Alice and her public key. The trusted party is a certification authority (CA) and the tool to bind the key to an identity is a public key digital certificate. The mechanism for obtaining, updating and revoking a certificate is outlined in Sections 4.6.1 and 4.6.2.

A public key infrastructure (PKI) is a set of software, hardware, people and procedures, including CAs and registration authorities (RAs), that deal with the whole PKC life cycle, from its issue to its expiration or revocation.

Examples of PKI

- VeriSign **http://www.verisign.com/products/pki**
- EuroPKI **http://www.europki.org**

4.5.3 Digital certificates

A public key digital certificate (see Figure 4.7) is a way of binding a public key to an identity. Digital certificates used today adhere to the X.509 standard and always contain the following data elements:

- the serial number of the certificate;
- the subject (the public key owner);
- the certification authority (CA) that has issued the certificate;
- the subject's public key;
- the private key (the seal or signature of the CA) guaranteeing that the link between the subject and his or her public key cannot be forged;
- the certificate revocation list (CRL) publication point;
- an expiration date, because certificates have a restricted lifetime.

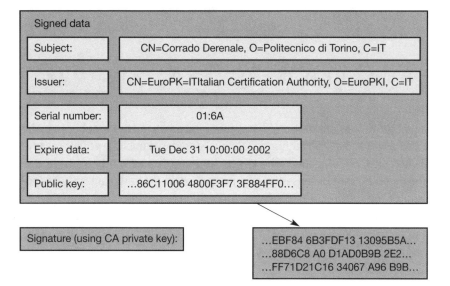

Fig. 4.7 Public key digital certificate

Optionally they can contain the organization and department for which the subject works, as well as other attributes.

See the RFC 3280 Internet X.509 Public Key Infrastructure Certificate and Certificate Revocation List Profile for a complete list, available at: **http://www.ietf.org/rfc/rfc3280.txt**.

Finding more information

- [RFC 3280] Internet X.509 Public Key Infrastructure Certificate and Certificate Revocation List (CRL) *Profile* (April 2002) **http://www.ietf.org/rfc/rfc3280.txt**
- There is a well-produced digital signature resource centre at **http://www.digitalsignature.be**
- Digital Signature Pictorial Tutorial is easy to understand **http://www.digitalsignature.be/pki_guide.cfm**
- An Introduction to Digital Signatures: the technology **http://www.ja.net/documents/gn_pgp.pdf**
- There is a directory of ITU-T recommendations at:
  - The Directory: Public key and attribute certificate frameworks X.509 (March 2000) **http://www.itu.int/rec/recommendation.asp?type=folders&lang=e&parent=T-REC-X.509**
  - IETF pkix working group public key infrastructure (X.509) (pkix) **http://www.ietf.org/html.charters/pkix-charter.html**

4.6 PUBLIC KEY INFRASTRUCTURE

Digital certificates are data structures that bind an identity to a public key. They are issued by a certification authority (CA) and stored in a public repository ready to be downloaded when needed. The key and the certificated attributes have a limited lifetime and expire because the information inside the certificate may change, for example the subject may go to work for a different organization. From time to time a key has to be renewed for security reasons – it may be lost or stolen. In a word, keys can be compromised before they expire and in such event the public key certificate (PKC) has to be revoked.

4.6.1 Public key infrastructure

A public key infrastructure (PKI) is the set of hardware, software, people, policies and procedures needed to issue, manage, store, distribute, set expiry dates for and revoke PKCs. The major areas of concern of PKIs are initialization, registration, certification, key update and key compromise.

- **Initialization** is the first contact between the PKI and the subject requesting a PKC. This is when trust is established between the user and the CA.
- **Registration** is when a subject makes him or herself known to a CA directly or through a registration authority (RA). It involves the subject providing the PKI with the attributes that the subject wants to certificate with the public key.
- **Certification** is the process in which a CA belonging to the PKI issues the PKC for the subject and posts it into a public repository.
- **Key updating** is the process of renewing the certificate with a new key pair.
- **Key compromise** leads to certificate revocation. When a key becomes compromised, for example because it is stolen or lost, the PKI has to react very quickly to revoke the compromised PKC and to publish the information of this revocation in a new certificate revokation list (CRL). The first thing a certificate owner has to do on becoming aware of a key being compromised is to tell the CA. which then revokes the certificate, putting it on a CRL. The CRL is published for public downloading.

4.6.2 Obtaining a public key certificate

The procedures for obtaining a PKC for signing e-mail or connecting to a secure Web server (in most cases) follow those mentioned in the previous sections.

Netscape Navigator

Let us suppose that the client Netscape Navigator version 4.76 or higher is being used. The first thing the applicant has to do is to initialize the process by, for example, connecting to a CA site and downloading its PKC. After that the applicant has to register. Usually this is accomplished by filling in an online form with personal data. When the form is sent to the CA server, Netscape automatically generates the key pair. The private key is saved inside the Netscape Personal Security Environment (PSE) and the user is asked for a password to protect access to the private key. In the case of more secure PKI systems, where the precise indentity of a user needs to be established, the individual may be required to present themselves to the CA operator in person, together with some proof of identity (a passport for example). This is called personal authentication and gives more value to the PKC because someone who trusts the PKC knows that the authentication of the owner was proven. The CA receives the certificate application and, after a variable time that depends on the CA's internal procedures, issues the certificate, stores it in a public repository and sends a notification to the applicant (certification). The applicant goes to the repository using the same computer as that used to make the request and downloads the certificate.

Internet Explorer

The same procedures have to be followed with Microsoft Internet Explorer. The only difference is that in the Microsoft Windows environment the PSE is called the Certificate Store (CS). The operating system uses the CS to store personal certificates, CA certificates and CRLs. Finding the contents of the CS is quite easy. Select the button 'Tools' from the Menu in the Explorer window and then select 'Internet Options'. From the 'Internet Options' select the 'Content' tab and from there the button 'Certificates'.

4.6.3 Signature verification

If a relaying party (RP) has to verify a signature, there are at least five steps that have to be taken. The first four involve the certificate validation process, and the last is the signature verification – a 'simple' cryptographic control. Verifying the validity of a certificate means verifying that the certificate has neither expired nor been revoked or maliciously forged.

1. Fetch the certificate of the signer from the PKI repository. It may be that the certificate is appended to the signed document, as happens with S/MIME.
2. Check the validity period and the signature of the CA on the certificate. This is a cryptographic verification.
3. Fetch the latest CRL from the PKI repository.
4. Check that the certificate is not in the CRL. If steps 1 and 4 succeed, then the certificate is a valid one.
5. Check the signature using the valid certificate.

Finding more information

- A. Arsenault & S. Turner, Internet X.509 Public Key Infrastructure: Roadmap (July 2002) **http://www.ietf.org/internet-drafts/draft-ietf-pkix-roadmap-09.txt**

- If you are interested in the history of key management from its origin read C. Ellison et al. SPKI Certificate Theory (September 1999) **http://www.ietf.org/rfc/rfc2693.txt**

- Another reference worth the effort, even if it is a little more technical, is Peter Gutman, PKI: It's Not Dead, Just Resting, IEEE Computer, Vol. 35, No. 8 pp 41–49 (August 2002).

4.7 SMART CARDS AND TOKENS

A smart card is a credit-card sized plastic card with an embedded computer chip with computational and/or memory capacity and is able to communicate externally. There is a broad field of applications for smart cards, from prepaid phone cards and credit cards to mobile phone subscriber identity module (SIM) cards. Thanks to their computational power, some smart cards can be used to generate the public keys necessary for public key cryptography and can also compute digital signatures. They can store confidential data, like private keys, in a secure way and are also practical because they can fit inside a wallet. Lastly, smart cards can be printed with, for example, a photo of the owner or the logo of the company that issued them providing an additional level of security.

4.7.1 Smart card types

There are two categories of smart cards – contact and contactless. In a contact smart card the micromodule containing the chip is directly visible on the surface of the card – see Figure 4.8. This kind of smart card requires insertion into a smart card reader.

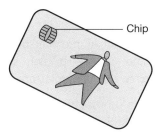

Fig. 4.8 A contact smart card

A contactless card has the micromodule hidden between the two plastic faces and requires only close proximity to the reader, from 20 to 30 centimetres. Both the reader and the card have an antenna and it is via this electromagnetic link that the two communicate. See Figure 4.9.

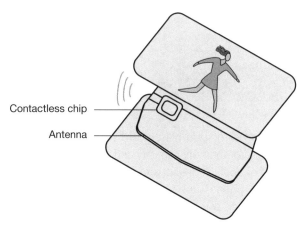

Contactless chip

Antenna

Fig. 4.9 A contactless smart card

The smart card chip can be memory-only, or a microprocessor and some memory. Memory-only chips are inexpensive and can be used for mass production prepaid cards, like prepaid phone cards. Microprocessor cards with memory are expensive but can manipulate information and execute code from their memory. They are, in fact, miniature computers, with a central processing unit, memory, operating system and input/output ports and storage. Today there are three operating systems on the market:

● Sun **http://java.sun.com/products/javacard/**

● MULTOS from Maosco Ltd **http://www.multos.com/**

● customized operating systems for specific applications.

There is a consortium trying to build an interoperable management infrastructure, but standardization is still some way off. For more information go to the Global Platform consortium site **http://www.globalplatform.org/default.asp**.

Microprocessor smart cards can be used for a range of applications, from credit cards to Global System for Mobiles (GSM) cards. The two most relevant applications in the security field are carrying electronic authentication and/or digital signatures.

Instead of going into the office, turning on the PC and typing a login name and password for authentication, a user could simply insert a smart card into the reader and type a code to unlock the card. Without a card no one can enter the system. This is the simplest authentication application. It works by simply authenticating the user via one RSA private key stored in the smart card.

After having authenticated themselves to the system, later in the morning the user might have to send a signed e-mail. All that has to be done is to write the e-mail and again unlock the smart card. The signature is done with the private key that it stores, the same key used to authenticate the user to the system earlier in the morning.

The microprocessor power of the smart card can be used to encrypt and decrypt data and the memory can be used to store a private key. A smart card is a very good place in which to keep sensitive and confidential information, like a private key, because smart cards are designed and manufactured with security in mind. They are more secure than magnetic strip cards that can be used only to store data. Smart cards are active and can react if someone wants to read the contents by probing the chip with electrical signals. They are also tamperproof as they prevent unauthorized access to the data they contain.

A private key is generated directly on the smart card using the computing power of a microcontroller. For example, when someone wants to sign a document the hash of the document is sent to the smart card microcontroller. The hash inside this is encrypted using the private key stored in the card memory and the result is sent to the application that requested the signature, for example the mailer. The steps involved in signing an e-mail using a smart card are:

- the user writes an e-mail;
- the mailer computes the summary (hash) of the e-mail and sends it to the smart card microcontroller;
- the smart card microcontroller encrypts the hash with the private key stored into the smart card;
- the smart card sends the encrypted hash to the mailer;
- the mailer attaches the encrypted hash to the e-mail in a format called PKCS#7 and sends it to the mail recipient.

4.7.2 Certificates on USB tokens

The private key and its corresponding certificate are usually stored on the smart card. The great drawback is that cards need specialized readers. Universal serial bus (USB) tokens, however, do not. A USB token can contain a similar security chip to a smart card but, as it is embedded into a plastic case with a USB controller, the device can be plugged into the commonly available USB port.

Finding more information

● Andrew Phillips, Planning for Smart Cards, January 29 (2002)

● The major world smart card vendor GemPlus **http://www.gemplus.com**

● Some token vendors: Rainbow technologies with the iKey 2000 **http://www.rainbow.com/products/ikey/ikey2000.asp** and EToken from Aladdin **http://www.ealaddin.com/etoken/default.asp?cf=tl**

4.8 FIREWALLS

In building construction terminology, a firewall is a wall designed to prevent flames spreading from one room to another or from one building to another. In information technology terminology, a firewall is a security system put between two networks at different security levels. The firewall system prevents intruders, thieves or vandals coming from a network with a lower security level and damaging the safer and more protected network.

Attacks can be grouped into three main categories:

● intrusion

● denial of service

● information theft.

Firewalls are tools for preventing those attacks on networks.

4.8.1 How firewalls work

Usually a firewall is put between the local area network (LAN) of the organization and the Internet – and it is called the Internet firewall – see Figure 4.10. The firewall can either be a dedicated PC running firewall software, or a purpose built hardware firewall placed on a single link between the LAN and the global Internet. It is essential that there are no other links between the LAN and the Internet, otherwise malicious traffic may be able to avoid being stopped in the firewall. A single firewall is capable of protecting all the hosts or PCs that are connected to the LAN.

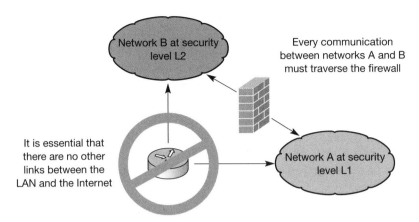

Fig. 4.10 Generic firewall construction

Firewalls can be designed to filter at different levels depending on which layer in the protocol stack it inspects. It can inspect just the IP layer and so react to the IP address, or it can work at the application layer of the Transmission Control Protocol/Internet Protocol (TCP/IP) stack and screen the content of the Web pages or File Transfer Protocol (FTP) file.

A firewall can analyze all aspects of the data that flows to and from the LAN and may selectively filter on addresses or information content. It has a set of rules that permit or deny a certain type of traffic from flowing from the Internet to the LAN and from the LAN to the Internet. A firewall can stop IP addresses belonging to the information coming from outside the LAN from reaching a computer inside. Only the authorized information can traverse the firewall.

A firewall can also examine the content of the information and prevent it from passing through. For example, the filter rules may have been designed to detect content such as images with a given type (for instance `xxxxsex.jpg`) and prevent such images being transmitted to the LAN.

4.8.2 Personal firewalls

Nowadays personal firewalls are popular. This kind of firewall does not protect a network, but just a single computer.

Why should a user install a personal firewall? The answer is that because threats come not only from outside the network but also from inside, it may be necessary to protect your personal computer from other users on the LAN.

A personal firewall is software that alerts the user if someone tries to access computer resources, like files or services. Sometimes the computer runs services that are unknown to the user, for instance as part of a standard operating system installation. Others may be instituted when application software is installed. Bearshare filesharing software is an example of an application that installs and runs a personal Web server on the host that runs the application. The consequence of running such a service on your machine is that it may be possible for attackers to gain access to any files or resources on your machine – not just those resources being shared in file sharing activity. A personal firewall blocks any efforts to connect to the unwanted services open on the computer and alerts the user if someone is trying to connect and use that service.

A personal firewall should not be seen as a subsitute for a network firewall protecting a LAN. Personal firewalls are a complement providing another layer of protection. This can be worthwhile for organizations or individuals where the value of the data is either high or sensitive in nature.

The most important role for a personal firewall is on computers that are offering public services. Such computers are common targets for hackers.

Does your home computer contain data that can be of any value to someone else? If so, then it is a good idea to install a personal firewall that will help to keep intruders from scanning and stealing information from the hard disk. If, however, the data are not particularly valuable to anyone else and the software is frequently updated, think twice before incurring the expense of a firewall. A personal firewall can be useful, but don't become paranoid. Frequently updated applications and antivirus applications against worms and Trojan horses (see Section 4.9) make it difficult for someone to use the Internet to get into a dial-up home computer.

Finding more information

- Wolfgang Weber, Firewall Basics (October 1999).
- 4th International Conference on Telecommunications in Modern Satellite, Cable and Broadcasting Services, TELSIKS'99, Proceedings of Papers, Vol. 1, Nis 1999.
- Elizabeth D. Zwicky, Simon Cooper and D. Brent Chapman, Building Internet Firewalls, O'Reilly UK 2000.

Personal firewalls:

- MacAfee.com Personal Firewall **http://www.mcafee.com/myapps/firewall/ default.asp**
- Sygate Personal Firewall PRO 5.0 **http://soho.sygate.com/products/pspf_ov.htm**

- JANET technical guides: The Use of Firewalls in an Academic Environment GD/JANET/TECH/002. A reprint of the original JTAP report is available on paper from JANET Customer Service. An electronic version can be found on the JISC Web site at **http://www.jisc.ac.uk/index.cfm?name=project_firewalls**

4.9 HOSTILE CODE

Hostile code is one of the greater menaces to networks and computer systems. From a survey by the Computer Security Institute and the Federal Bureau of Investigation published in 2002 on computer crime and security, the most widely used type of attack on computer systems is the use of hostile code. Of the surveyed sample, 85 per cent had had some problem as a result of hostile code. It exploits the flaws of software code or of a system's configuration to damage it. It is divided into four categories:

- viruses
- macro and e-mail viruses
- Trojan horses
- worms.

4.9.1 Viruses

A virus is a program, a piece of hostile executable code, sometimes called *malware*, that inserts itself into another executable program. In this way the virus propagates itself when the infected program is executed. A virus is passive, because it requires someone, such as the unlucky user, or something, such as another computer program, to launch and execute the infected program. Before being launched, the virus remains dormantly on the hard disk. When activated by inadvertent execution, the code is put in the central memory of the computer and begins to run like any other program, but with bad intent. When activated, a virus usually inserts a copy of itself into the most common executables it can find on the victim's hard disk, a process known as auto-replicatation.

An infected program usually spreads from one computer to another by being copied from a floppy disk or downloaded from the Internet and then launched, so it is a good thing to scan executable files for viruses before running a program borrowed from a friend or downloaded from the Internet.

Another way a virus can replicate itself is by writing itself to a special part of the floppy disk that is invisible to the common user. This is the master boot sector, and is the part where the computer looks for the operating system when being booted. If the disk is infected, the computer finds the virus and runs it. When active, this sort of virus writes itself onto every floppy disk inserted in the drive of the infected computer until it is detected and removed.

Other than replicating themselves, what damage can viruses cause? Potentially, viruses can affect everything a user can do. Two examples are the Chernobyl and Michelangelo viruses. Chernobyl was activated on 26 April 1999, the anniversary of the Chernobyl nuclear accident. It deletes all the files on a hard disk and tries to rewrite the system BIOS. This is a vital part of a computer system and it is required when booting. If it is missing, or corrupt, the computer will not load the operating system. If a computer has been damaged by the Chernobyl virus, the Computer Emergency Response Team (CERT®), a special organization for Internet security, recommends you to contact your computer vendor or motherboard vendor to find out how to recover the system BIOS. Michelangelo is a computer virus that affects PCs running MS-DOS, PC-DOS, DR-DOS etc. This virus was detected for the first time in 1991 and infects the floppy disk boot sector and the hard disk master boot record. This virus is triggered on 6 March (Michaelangelo's birthday) and overwrites some critical system data rendering the hard disk unusable.

Finding more information

- Chernobyl virus **http://www.cert.org/incident_notes/IN-99-03.html**
- Michelangelo virus **http://www.cert.org/advisories/CA-1992-02.html**

4.9.2 Macro and e-mail viruses

Computer users exchange documents more frequently than programs, so what about documents infecting computers?

Macros (essentially simple programs) that can be run by applications such as Microsoft Word, Excel or Outlook can also be infected by viruses. When the unlucky user reads an infected document, the virus will run in the background unnoticed. Similarly, there are viruses that can be attached to e-mails. As soon as the recipient opens the content of such an infected message the virus will be executed. Often these viruses, written in Visual Basic Script, start to send e-mails containing copies of themselves to every contact found in the victim's address book.

It is important to remember that the virus is only activated when the recipient opens the message, but this action is often encouraged by the use of spurious subject titles such as 'I LOVE YOU' or 'Anna Kournikova'. These two viruses caused a lot of damage in 2000 and 2001 respectively.

The 'love letter' worm was a macro attached to an e-mail with an enticing subject to lure the receiver to open it. In addition, because it probably came from the infected mailer of an aquaintance, it appeared to come from a trusted sender. The name of the attachment, the actual macro virus, was `LOVE-LETTER-FOR-YOU.TXT.VBS` and it carried a Visual Basic script that, when opened, replaced some of the user's file with a copy of the virus. The strength of that virus was in the false subject exploiting the human urge to be loved. For more details see: **http://www.cert.org/advisories/CA-2000-04.html**.

The 'Anna Kournikova' macro virus relies on the user's curiosity to spread itself. It suggests to the receiver that the e-mail carries a picture of a beautiful girl, but instead the user contracts a virus. For more information see **http://www.cert.org/advisories/CA-2001-03.html**.

Another example of this class of infection is the well-known 'Melissa' macro virus. Melissa was the first major mass e-mail virus that spread itself in a Microsoft Word document attached to an e-mail with the subject: 'Important Message From [UserName]' where 'UserName' was the name of the user whose computer was infected. The effect of this virus is that the user's documents (including confidential ones) can be sent out on the Internet. For more information see **http://www.cert.org/advisories/CA-2001-03.html**.

E-mail viruses can also cause a lot of damage to the mail infrastructure of the Internet through the enormous amount of traffic that viruses generate as a result of repeated replication. In some cases they have crashed e-mail servers that were unable to cope with the sheer volume of traffic.

4.9.3 Trojan horses

Trojan horses are a special kind of *malware* that open doors of systems to intruders. The name is taken from the ancient wooden horse used by the Athenians to defeat the city of Troy, as described in the Homeric poem 'The Iliad'.

The term 'Trojan horse' is used to describe software that permits remote hackers to take control of a computer, download files, install applications, modify files and even turn off the system. They are relentable programs and are installed inadvertently by the user after an infection of a downloaded file or application.

One of most famous Windows Trojan horses, the 'Back Orifice', is so powerful and disruptive that it is now considered as a program for remote managing! Details of Back Orifice are available at **http://www.cert.org/vul_notes/VN-98.07.backorifice.html**.

4.9.4 Worms

Worms are far more powerful than the other kind of malicious code. Worms come from the Internet and they can replicate themselves without any human intervention. While viruses are passive and need human intervention to run, worms are active. Worms do not need human intervention, they can replicate and activate by themselves and are therefore very dangerous.

Worms are programs that replicate themselves using program errors (bugs) in network resources. They can inoculate themselves into computers utilizing an error in the server, from where they begin to scan the network looking for other computers to infect. The rate of spreading of a worm is amazing – 'Code Red' took 15 minutes to infect thousands of computers and even attacked the official US Whitehouse site. Details of Code Red can be found at **http://www.cert.org/advisories/CA-2001-19.html**.

Other than looking for other computers to infect, worms can also cause damage by attacking the network and its components.

Note that a worm is a piece of code and a code is a program. What a program can do in the context of information technology is limited only by the imagination.

4.9.5 Defences

Up to now only threats and menaces have been considered. This section explores how computers can be protected from these types of malicious code.

Protecting a system from viruses

The best thing to do is install good antivirus (AV) software. Try **http://www.mcafee.com** or **http://www.norton.com**.

An AV program works in two ways: it both scans and is event driven. In scanning mode the AV software scans the master boot sector and all the files of the hard disk looking for a virus. A virus is a piece of code and a piece of code is simply a pattern of bits. An AV program scans the master boot sector and all the files looking for patterns of bits that are known to represent viruses. This is the reason why an antivirus has to be updated very frequently – every day there are new viruses out there! It is good practice to scan a system once a day looking for a possible infection. Every AV program has the capability to schedule scanning and start it automatically, maybe during a lunch break or overnight.

The second way an AV package works is by being event driven. AV software should always be active, so whenever an event happens, for example when a new file is downloaded from the Internet or when a floppy disk is inserted into the drive, it is scanned automatically without any user intervention.

In summary, to protect from viruses:

- install a good antivirus package;
- scan the system frequently;
- update the software and virus definitions frequently;
- set the program to react to events.

Protecting a system from macro viruses and e-mail viruses

Some AV packages, McAfee and Norton for example, also react to e-mail downloads. They scan the arriving e-mail and show an alert if malicious code is found. These packages also react to the loading of a file like a .doc file containing a macro, and before the macro can run they scan it. Many organizations with their own mail servers scan all e-mail before it is delivered to the user, thus preventing infected e-mails being downloaded to the user's computer.

Another thing to do is to stay alert. If some strange and unexpected e-mails are received, simply do not open them – delete them as they are.

Protecting a system from Trojan horses

Although Trojan horses are not strictly viruses, because they do not directly damage the system but open back doors (unwanted services) to intruders, they are recognized by AV applications. In order to protect a system from Trojan horses, take the same actions as used to protect from viruses.

Because Trojan horses open back doors in a system those backdoors can be locked by using a personal firewall. This puts itself between the network and the unwanted open services of a system and alerts a user if someone knocks on those doors trying to use the unwanted services.

Protecting a system from worms

This is very difficult indeed. The only way to prevent a worm is by fixing the software bugs that permit worms to exist, spread and infect. The only thing a user can do is to update software, applications and operating system as soon as a new patch is released.

Remember one more thing – do not run applications that are not used. Why run a Web server on a computer if it is not actually needed? This prevents the bugs in the unused applications causing damage. Unluckily, as previously stated, some software installs and runs services like Web servers without the system owner noticing. To prevent worms attacking and infecting such an application you should deploy a personal firewall that warns the user when someone is trying to use the unwanted application by sending a worm.

A more complete defence could be achieved by closing all the security holes that a piece of software could have, which is just not possible.

Conclusions

The enormous spread of malware and the difficult problem of frequently updating AV packages and all the other software designed to minimise the problem of being infected causes a great deal of work for system administrators. Every day many security companies, like CERT or the mailing list BugTraq at Security Focus OnLine, publish security alerts. The trend is to outsource security administration. Some companies offer to keep the operating system, firewall, intrusion detection system, antivirus and other applications updated and running.

Finding more information

- CSI/FBI Computer Crime & Security Survey, Computer Security Issues & Trends 8, no.1 (Spring 2002)
- CERT coordination centre **http://www.cert.org**
- Security Focus Online and BugTraq **http://online.securityfocus.com**
- H. Carvey, Detecting and Removing Trojan Horses and Malicious Code from Win2K **http://online.securityfocus.com/infocus/1627**
- The McAfee antivirus site **http://www.mcafee.com/**
- Symantec home page **http://www.norton.com/**

4.10 SPAM

Spam arises due to unsolicited e-mail, including advertisements. Everyone who deals with e-mails has been spammed at least once.

Spamming is the flooding of the Internet with many copies of the same message with the intention of reaching the largest possible number of Internet users.

4.10.1 Spam from different points of view

Let us try to analyze what spam is from different points of view – that of the user, the company, the spammer, the ISP and the mail server administrator.

From the user's point of view, spam is finding an e-mailbox full of useless messages about how to see sexy girls dancing in front of Webcams or similar unrequested items. The spam messages, as well as being useless, can generate confusion and the loss of genuine messages. Finding one important message among a mass of trash can be very difficult. From the user's point of view, spam can be costly because it consumes resources. A user dialling up to the Internet spends money on telephone calls, and some money is lost because the bandwidth is used to download unwanted messages.

From the company's point of view, spam causes a loss of productivity and reduces the availability of resources, disk, bandwidth and so on.

From the spammer's point of view, spam is a very good way of reaching many users with, for example, advertisements. It is also a very good way of using someone else's resources for the spammers's own purpose. In fact, spammers do not use their own mail server to deliver mail, but someone else's. Spammers use targeted third-party mail servers to flood the Internet so they do not have to pay for Internet resources nor for computers and they can also maintain anonymity. This is another good reason for the spammer to spam – using someone else's server is a way of laying the blame on the mail server's owner.

From the ISP and mail server administrator's point of view, spam is theft because it is they and not the spammer who carry the cost of the spam.

4.10.2 How to stop spam

From the considerations above everyone, spammers apart, would like to stop spamming. However, users can do very little about it – they can try using spam filtering, but often with poor results. A list of hints on stopping spam follows this section.

Some people think that spam cannot be stopped by technical means alone, but that strong legislation against unsolicited e-mails containing commercial advertisements is also needed. To this purpose the Coalition Against Unsolicited Commercial e-mail (CAUCE) exists. In the European Union, the e-Privacy Directive Proposal COM(2000) 385 states, 'The use of automated calling systems without human intervention (automatic calling machines), facsimile machines (fax) or electronic mail for the purposes of direct marketing may only be allowed in respect of subscribers who have given their prior consent.' It seems that spam should stop according to the law, but only the mail system administrators really have the power to act against spamming by correctly configuring their mail systems.

The first thing for administrators to do is to deny the relay of e-mail messages from mailers outside the served domain. The mail server of the goodguy.com (for example) domain has to refuse to relay any mail not coming from a client belonging to this domain. Only mail sent from a mailer inside the goodguy.com domain should be able to pass through the goodguy.domain mail server.

Mail servers should not accept mail from the domains appearing in a blacklist. If a mail server allows spam because of some misconfiguration then it could risk being put into a blacklist. In this case it will be banned from the community and not be able to send or receive mail anymore. So all mail servers should be configured not to accept mails from the servers listed in a blacklist such as the Realtime Blackhole List (RBL).

Finding more information

- To fight spam on the Internet some definitions and hints are available at **http://spam.abuse.net**.
- The Mail Abuse Prevention System LLC (MAPSM) is an organization based in Redwood City, California that provides spam prevention resources to Internet-connected organizations, as well as services to end users **http://mail-abuse.org**
- Realtime Blackhole List **http://spam.abuse.net/userhelp/#filter**
- List of user filters **http://spam.abuse.net/userhelp**
- Coalition Against Unsolicited Commercial e-mail **http://www.cauce.org**
- European Coalition Against Unsolicited Commercial E-mail **http://www.euro.cauce.org/en/index.html**
- Legislative proposals for a new regulatory framework for electronic communications (12 July 2000) **http://europa.eu.int/comm/ information_society/policy/framework/index_en.htm**
- JANET guidance notes: Investigating a denial-of-service attackGD/NOTE/001 (01/01) JANET and Internet Filtering GD/NOTE/006 (01/06).

5

REAL-TIME COMMUNICATION

This section describes the various tools and technologies that can be used to communicate between people in real time on the Internet.

Tools involving real-time communication between parties require them to be connected at the same time, for example during Internet video or audio conferencing. This type of communication is known as synchronous communication. Synchronous communication tools support a variety of media types, ranging from plain text to full multimedia.

5.1 INSTANT MESSAGING AND CHAT

The terms instant messaging (IM) and chat both refer to technologies that offer text-based synchronous communication between people. Instant messaging usually refers to communication between two people, whereas chat usually refers to communication between more than two people. In this book, instant messaging will be used to cover standards or technologies that are primarily one-to-one, and chat will be used to cover standards or technologies that are primarily many-to-many. Synchronous text-based communication, such as instant messaging and chat, differs from asynchronous text-based communication, such as e-mail and network news, in that the former usually consists of exchange of short messages (typically a single sentence), whereas the latter usually consists of longer messages. Instant messaging can thus be considered as a synchronous version of e-mail. Because of the real-time nature of instant messaging and chat, abbreviations are used extensively, sometimes making it unintelligible to the uninitiated.

There are no universally accepted standards for instant messaging and chat, so in the following sections they will be described in terms that do not refer to a single specific technology, but as being generic and focussing on the commonality between different technologies. There is not always a clear distinction between instant messaging (one-to-one) and chat (many-to-many), since most technologies support both modes of operation, but often a technology will have an emphasis on either one or the other.

5.1.1 Instant messaging

A prerequisite for establishing any kind of communication is that the sender knows the identity or address of the receiver. For e-mail, the identity or address is the e-mail address, while for instant messaging and chat this can be a number, a nickname or an e-mail-like address. In the case of asynchronous communication there is no need to know whether the intended recipient is present or not, but in the case of instant messaging the notion of presence and a mechanism for advertising and detecting presence is usually available. This means that a user of an instant messaging system can advertise his or her presence to other users and is, conversely, able to detect the presence of other users. This is often used to display the status of other known users in a so-called 'buddy list'.

Associated with presence is the notion of status, which is an indication of presence, availability and activity. For example, a user might be present but temporarily unavailable, doesn't want to be disturbed or is idle for some time. A typical example of a buddy list is shown in Figure 5.1.

In some systems it is possible to be anonymous or invisible and it is generally possible to control the amount of personal information that other users can see. Once users have exchanged identities (and possibly allowed each other to detect their presence) they can begin to exchange instant messages. Identities can be exchanged, e.g. via e-mail, but it is also possible to locate other users by searching in a directory.

Instant messaging is usually built on a client–server architecture. Some IM technologies use the server only for presence – letting clients exchange messages directly – while others route the messages through the server. In addition to exchanging messages, some technologies also provide client-to-client file transfer and multi-user chat.

Fig. 5.1 Typical instant messaging buddy lists

Source: AOL Instant Messenger screenshot

5.1.2 Chat

In describing chat, the metaphor of 'room' is often used to define a virtual venue where a number of people can meet to talk. This is also referred to as a channel. Presence and status in chat is usually signalled when a user enters or leaves a chat room or channel, and there are usually commands available to list the users present in a room at any given time, and to obtain information about individual users. Some chat technologies provide a means for users to initiate private conversations – essentially an instant messaging session. It may be possible to be in several rooms at once and to follow another user as that user leaves one room and enters another. Badly behaving users can be very disruptive in a channel open to everyone and there are usually ways of dealing with annoying users, either by banning them temporarily or by configuring the client to ignore messages from specific users.

Chat – like instant messaging – is usually built on a client–server architecture. The rooms or channels exist on a server, or a network of servers, and clients connect to a server and join a room. The client may be a stand-alone application or it may be Web based (e.g. a Java applet). In instant messaging, users often know each other's real-life identities, whereas in chat sessions users often hide their real identities and engage in anonymous conversations.

Instant messaging and chat are, at the same time, some of the most popular and some of the least standardized applications of the Internet. This is in contrast to most other popular uses of the net, such as the World Wide Web, e-mail, network news and ftp. Whatever the reason for this situation, it is clear that users will benefit from a standardized approach to instant messaging. As instant messaging begins to make inroads into corporate culture there will also be a larger demand for a single standard or for interoperation between standards.

The only well-established standards in the area of instant messaging and chat are Internet Relay Chat (IRC) and T.120 ('Data protocols for multimedia conferencing'). IRC is very popular for chat, while T.120 is used mostly in conjunction with H.323-based audio and videoconferencing, but neither of these has any major influence on mainstream instant messaging, which is dominated by proprietary technologies.

There are several ongoing activities in the Internet Engineering Task Force (IETF) working towards a set of standards for instant messaging. These activities are organized in the following working groups:

● Instant Messaging and Presence Protocol (IMPP);

● Presence and Instant Messaging Protocol (PRIM);

● Application Exchange (APEX);

● SIP for Instant Messaging and Presence Leveraging Extensions (SIMPLE);

● Extensible Messaging and Presence Protocol (XMPP).

As already mentioned, there are established standards for chat (IRC and T.120), and while instant messaging and presence is available in many non-standard implementations, these do not interwork and standardization is progressing mainly though the work of the IETF working groups. SIP (the focus of the SIMPLE working group) and Jabber (the focus of the XMPP working group) are already mature technologies in widespread use and they will be covered along with the established standards, even though the standardization process is still in progress. T.120 is described in Section 5.3.3.

5.1.3 Internet Relay Chat

IRC was developed by Jarkko Oikarinen in 1988, where it was initially deployed on a single server at the University of Oulu in Finland. Subsequently servers were set up at MIT and IRC then spread to the rest of the world.

IRC is based on a client–server architecture, where the servers are connected in a network. There is not one single IRC network, but a number of both larger and smaller networks. A client connects, through one of the servers in the network. Once connected, the client can access a number of channels. A channel is a virtual venue where all those who have joined can exchange text messages, i.e. chat. Channel is the term used in IRC, but in other technologies the term 'room' is often used. Some of the larger IRC networks have tens of thousands of channels, each of which is usually devoted to discussion of a particular topic. There are IRC clients for most operating systems and there are usually several to choose from for each platform.

Identity is very loosely defined in IRC, where it is essentially based on a nickname that the user can choose freely and even change during a session (although on some networks nicknames are password protected). It is possible both to advertise one's real name or to remain anonymous. IRC does not support any form of presence or user location mechanism, but once a channel is joined it is possible to list users in that channel. IRC is centered around group chat, but also supports other modes of communication, such as private conversations among a subset of people in the channel and client-to-client communication which uses a direct client-to-client connection. It is also possible to exchange files using this direct connection. Client-to-client messaging can be considered to be an instant messaging session initiated from a channel.

Useful sources of information are:

- IRC.org **http://irc.org/**
- Internet Relay Chat help archive **http://www.irchelp.org/**

5.1.4 Jabber

Jabber was started by Jeremie Miller in early 1998 in the form of the first Jabber daemon (jabberd), which evolved along with the the Jabber protocol. From the outset an open source project, the Jabber protocol is now managed by the Jabber Software Foundation and an effort to make it an IETF standard is being made by the XMPP working group. Alongside these not-for-profit activities, the company Jabber Inc. was formed, which sponsors development of the Jabber protocol, server and clients. There are servers other than the original jabberd and a choice of clients exist for Linux, Unix, Mac OS and Windows.

Like most instant messaging and presence technologies, Jabber is based on the client–server model, but unlike most other IM systems anyone can operate a server, be it either private (within an organization) or public. A user's identity is related to the server on which the user has an account. A Jabber ID (JID) has the form `<user>@<server><server>[/<resource>]`. Where `<user>` is the username which must be unique on a given server, and `<server></server>` is the fully qualified domain name of the server. The optional `<resource>` specifies a specific resource belonging to the user. This allows a user to run several clients at once so, for example, a user can have a resource called 'work' and a resource called 'home', both belonging to the same account.

In order to send someone instant messages using Jabber it is sufficient to know that person's Jabber ID. Jabber IDs can be exchanged through other channels, such as e-mail, but it is also possible to search a user database with the user's name or e-mail address. Messages in Jabber are not exchanged directly between the clients but pass through one or more Jabber servers.

Unlike most other IM systems, Jabber allows a user to control who may subscribe to (i.e. detect) the user's presence. In Jabber this is handled through the subscription handshake, which works like this.

- First user A sends a subscription request to user B, using B's Jabber ID.
- User B then receives user A's request and can accept or reject it.
- Assuming that B accepts A's request, B's client then sends a subscription request to A.
- Once A accepts B's request the handshake is complete and A and B can detect each other's presence.

In most clients this will result in users appearing on each other's buddy lists. Note that being able to subscribe to another user's presence information is not a prerequisite for being able to send that user messages – it only means that it is possible to see when the other user is online and available.

In addition to the instant messaging and presence functionalities offered by Jabber, it also supports file transfers between clients and group chat. Using group chat is similar to using IRC, and a group is specified by a server and a room in Jabber. A room is similar to a channel in IRC. Jabber users can exchange instant messages with users of other IM services, provided that they have an account on that other IM service, but using their Jabber client. This is made possible by using a so-called 'gateway', which is a server component that interfaces with other IM services.

Useful sources of information can be found at:

- Jabber Software Foundation **http://www.jabber.org/**
- IETF XMPP Working Group **http://www.ietf.org/html.charters/OLD/ xmpp-charter.html**
- Jabber Studio **http://www.jabberstudio.org/**
- Jabber, Inc **http://www.jabber.com/**

5.1.5 Resources

Instant messaging clients/systems:

- AOL Instant Messenger (AIM) **http://www.aim.com/**
- Gaim – a multiprotocol instant messaging client **http://gaim.sourceforge.net/**
- iChat – AIM compatible client for the Mac **http://www.apple.com/macosx/ features/ichat/**
- ICQ instant messenger **http://www.icq.com/**
- Jabber clients – for Windows, Linux, MacOS, and others **http://www.jabber.org/ software/clients.shtml**
- Trillian – a multiprotocol instant messenger for Windows **http://www.trillian.cc/ index.php**
- Yahoo! Messenger **http://messenger.yahoo.com/**

5.2 CODECS

The term 'codec' means COmpresser/DECompresser or COder/DECoder – and both terms are good descriptions of what a codec does. A codec can either take uncompressed input and code the data into a compressed coded version for transmission or storage, or it can perform the reverse role turning compressed data into an uncompressed signal.

A codec can be either lossless or lossy. A lossless CODEC recreates the original input exactly bit by bit, while with lossy codecs some information is discarded. Lossless codecs are not able to achieve the large compression ratios necessary to compress audio and video to a level where it can be transmitted over common data networks, so lossy codecs are commonly used.

When dealing with lossy codecs it is important to notice that what is standardized is almost always the format of the bit stream and the action of the decoder, whereas the implementation approach of the coder is left unspecified, except for the fact that it must produce a bit stream conforming to the standards. The big advantage of this is that it is possible to improve on the design of the coder, and let manufacturers compete on performance and features while maintaining compatibility with all existing decoders. Since the quality is almost entirely determined by the abilities of the encoder, this also has the implication that quality is not standardized. This point is worth considering when deciding what equipment to buy. Simply because both vendors A and B support codec X, it doesn't mean that both products produce output of the same quality. It is also worth noticing that the result of good encoding should result in a good signal emerging at the remote end of the connection. Conversely, a poor codec at the local end will result in a poor signal being received by the recipients. This is important to consider when evaluating equipment for videoconferencing.

5.2.1 Audio codecs

To choose an appropriate audio codec for given circumstances, it is useful to consider some of the important characteristics of audio codecs. One is most often interested in achieving the best possible quality within the constraints of the available bandwidth. In videoconferencing and streaming, the available bit rate is always shared between the audio, the video and other traffic. By lowering the bit rate used by the video one can free more of the bit rate for the audio and vice versa. Good quality audio is usually preferred when there is a trade-off between audio and video quality, since bad audio puts a much bigger strain on the listener than bad video does on the viewer. If the audio becomes unintelligible almost all information is lost, whereas video, even at very low frame rates, can be acceptable (depending on the application).

The main characteristics of an audio codec are audio bandwidth, bit rate and delay. Audio bandwidth is expressed in hertz (Hz) and is a measure of the frequencies that can be represented. Sometimes the sampling rate is specified instead. To obtain a satisfactory reconstruction of the original signal, the sampling rate must be at least twice the audio bandwidth – so to represent a 3 kHz signal, a sample rate of at least 6 kHz must be used. The bit rate is simply the number of bits per second required to transmit the coded signal. Unfortunately this is also often referred to as the bandwidth. The bit rate is measured in bit/s. The delay of a CODEC depends on the algorithmic complexity and the frame size. It is measured in milliseconds (ms) and is implementation dependent. Some of the most commonly used audio codecs for videoconferencing are listed in the table below.

Codec	Bandwidth	Bit rate	Typical delay
G.711	3 kHz	48, 56, 64 kbit/s	< 1 ms
G.722	7 kHz	48, 56, 64 kbit/s	< 2 ms
G.723.1	3 kHz	5.3, 6.4 kbit/s	< 100 ms
G.728	3 kHz	16 kbit/s	< 2 ms
G.729	3 kHz	8 kbit/s	< 50 ms

It can be clearly seen that compression efficiency (low bit rate) comes at the expense of an increase in delay. G.711 is the oldest of the codecs listed in the table and, as such, is the lowest common denominator. Most users will prefer to use G.722 which is the only codec to provide an audio bandwidth of 7 kHz, which gives more natural sounding speech. All the other codecs provide only 3 kHz, which is equivalent to phone quality speech. If low bit rate is essential, one of the codecs G.723.1, G.728 or G.729 must be used. All the codecs listed in the previous table are supported by the H.323 standard, although only G.711 is mandatory.

Some of the codecs listed are also used for streaming along with other codecs not used for videoconferencing. One of the most popular codecs for audio streaming is MPEG-1 audio layer 3 (MP3) which is suitable for music.

5.2.2 Video codecs

Video signals used in standard domestic analogue television transmission conform to standards such as PAL, NTSC and other less common standards including SECAM. These analogue signals can be digitized and then compressed using a codec. Compression levels are usually more than 100:1, and several tricks are needed in order to achieve this level and still get an output that resembles the original input. Here we will take a phenomenological approach and not worry so much about the details of what goes on behind the scenes when a codec does its work. The most important characteristics of video codecs are resolution, frame rate, bit rate and – for videoconferencing – low delay. There are other characteristics as well, such as color depth, sampling rate, chroma sub-sampling, interlaced vs. progressive scan etc., but these will not concern us here.

The different resolution levels of digital video are usually expressed in terms of the Common Intermediate Format (CIF) which was devised to support both PAL and NTSC. The spacial resolution of CIF (352 × 288 pixels) is based on PAL and the time resolution (29.97 Hz) is based on NTSC. The different resolutions available in CIF and CIF-derived formats are shown in the table below. Except for SQCIF all these are related to each other by a factor of two in each spatial dimension.

Format	16CIF	4CIF	CIF	QCIF	SQCIF
Resolution	1408 × 1152	704 × 576	352 × 288	176 × 144	128 × 96

Practically all videoconferencing systems support the use of H.261 and most also support H.263, which are the two commonly used codecs for videoconferencing. H.262, more commonly known as MPEG-2, is used only in the H.310 standard, and by some non-standard videoconferencing technologies. H.261 is the oldest standard and it is limited to using CIF and QCIF. H.263 was developed as an extension to H.261 specifically for low bit rates, but is an improvement over H.261 at higher bit rates as well. H.263 supports SQCIF, QCIF, CIF, 4CIF and 16CIF, although videoconferencing terminals in common use normally only support QCIF and CIF. At the same resolution H.263 should always be preferred over H.261.

H.261 and H.263 do not specify a particular bit rate or frame rate, except that the maximum frame rate is 30 frames per second. The frame rate can thus be used to adjust the bit rate, and of course a higher resolution also results in a higher bit rate.

The latest standard in video codecs is H.264 which is expected to provide significant improvements over H.263. Support for H.264 is being added to the H.323 standard as well as in newer videoconferencing terminals.

Another important family of codecs are MPEG-1, MPEG-2 and MPEG-4. MPEG-1 can be used for streaming but is mostly used for download and for CD-ROM delivery. The Video CD standard is based on MPEG-1. MPEG-2 is used mainly for digital satellite TV and DVD, but also by some high-end streaming servers. MPEG-4 is expected to have a major impact on streaming both for low bandwidth mobile devices and in broadband environments. MPEG-4 is the basis of the ISMA standard for streaming, and also the 3GPP standard. MPEG-4 is much more than a collection of codecs, rather it is a whole multimedia framework including object coding, mixed media, interactivity, virtual reality, digital rights management and much much more. Video codecs available in MPEG-4 are H.263 and H.264.

Apart from the standardized codecs many proprietary codecs are used for streaming. RealNetworks have their RealVideo, Microsoft have their Windows Media and Apple has historically been tied to Sorensen Video.

5.3 VIDEOCONFERENCING

Videoconferencing is the general term used to cover synchronous audiovisual communication between two or more people. It can be thought of as a telephone conversation with video added but it is also possible to use other media, such as text conversation (chat), drawing (shared electronic whiteboard) and general application sharing. In the simplest case of two communicating parties, videoconferencing is point-to-point, but when three or more parties are communicating it is referred to as multipoint.

Videoconferencing systems are usually classified as being either personal or group systems. As the name implies, group systems are for more than one person and they are often located in meeting rooms, but they can also be roll-about systems that can be used anywhere they are needed.

Group systems are usually based on dedicated hardware (the codec) and attached accessories (screens, cameras, microphones, speakers, document cameras etc.). Some group systems are based on the PC architecture with appropriate custom hardware installed.

Personal systems, or desktop systems, are intended for single users, and are usually PC-based. PC-based systems can use software only or be hardware assisted (either a PCI board or USB attached). There are also some appliance-based personal systems, which consist of dedicated hardware, just like group systems. The main advantage of PC-based systems is the possibility of integrating with other applications such as chat, whiteboard and application sharing, while the main advantages of the appliance-based systems are performance and stability.

5.3.1 Overview of videoconferencing

In the simplest case, videoconferencing involves two locations communicating directly with each other. Each location consists of a device that has audio and video inputs and outputs, is capable of coding and decoding audio and video data, and receiving and transmitting the coded audiovisual content over the network. This device is usually called a 'terminal', codec, 'client' or 'endpoint'. This terminal can be implemented in software, hardware or a combination of both.

User location and address resolution

An important aspect of videoconferencing is the seemingly trivial task of calling the person or terminal that we wish to communicate with. This task can be split into two: first obtain the 'address' and then call the user at that address. The analogy to this in the public switched-telephone network would be to look up a number in the phone book and then dial the digits found. In the case of videoconferencing there may or may not be a directory ('phone book') in which to look up the user. This situation is similar to e-mail, where there does not always exist a directory in which users can be looked up, although such directories are often available within an organization. Directories can be accessed either through LDAP or through a Web-based interface.

When the address of the user has been obtained, it can be used to call the user from a terminal. In some cases, such as ISDN, the address is identical to the network level address, but in most cases another level of translation or address resolution is needed. In H.323, address resolution is performed by a so-called gatekeeper, and in SIP it is performed by a so-called SIP proxy. Once the user's terminal has been configured correctly to use a gatekeeper or proxy, the process of address resolution is completely automatic.

Multipoint videoconferencing

When three or more sites participate in a videoconference they do not usually send and receive the audio/video streams to each other directly. One reason for not sending and receiving streams directly between all participating terminals is that the total number of streams in this scheme is proportional to the square of the number of participants, thus limiting the scalability of such a scheme. The other reason is that each individual terminal would need a way of either mixing or switching between the different streams, thus increasing the complexity of the terminal. For these reasons multipoint videoconferencing usually entails using a central node to which all the participating terminals connect, thus lowering the total number of streams to a number being proportional only to the number of sites. Such a device is called a 'reflector' or 'multipoint control unit' (MCU). A videoconference between the four terminals using an MCU to mix and switch the audio and video is shown schematically in Figure 5.2.

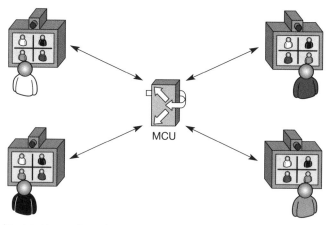

Fig. 5.2 Multipoint videoconferencing

An alternative solution to multipoint videoconferencing is to use multicast, whereby each terminal sends only one copy of its audio and video, but receives audio/video streams from each of the other terminals. This works because the routers in the network do the necessary splitting of the streams.

5.3.2 Problems with NAT and firewalls

Firewall/NAT issues

Users of videoconferencing often run into problems with firewalls and devices that perform Network Address Translation (NAT) – a process which maps private IP adresses, only reachable within an organization, to public IP adresses that are globally reachable, and vice versa.

The problem with firewalls is that their job is to block unwanted traffic, and videoconferencing traffic often falls into the unwanted category. Enabling videoconferencing through a firewall may thus be as easy as asking the firewall administrator to allow this traffic. Some firewalls, however, have problems recognizing legitimate videoconferencing traffic because the protocols are more complicated than most other protocols that a firewall has to handle. A typical videoconference call starts out with one or more TCP connections that serve to set up the call. The terminals use this initial connection to negotiate their capabilities and exchange information about which ports to use for the audio and video data streams. These streams are typically RTP streams which are transported using UDP. Now, if the firewall has not been able to follow the messages exchanged by the two terminals during the call set-up phase, it will block these UDP connections and no audio or video can pass the firewall. Sometimes the firewall will allow outgoing streams and block incoming streams, resulting in a one-way videoconference.

NAT is used in many places to alleviate the scarcity of public IPv4 addresses. The basic problem with NAT is that systems with a private IP address are not reachable from the outside. Clearly a videoconferencing system is not of much use if it cannot be reached by other videoconferencing systems. The obvious solution would be to give all videoconferencing terminals public IP addresses, but sometimes this may not be possible – for example, if all desktop users must be able to use a software videoconferencing endpoint. In such cases the NAT problem can be solved in different ways (outside the scope of this text).

Useful sources of information can be found at:

- Wainhouse Research: 'Traversing Firewalls and NATs With Voice and Video Over IP' **http://www.wainhouse.com/files/papers/WR_trans_firewalls_nats.pdf**
- RADVISION: 'Traversal of IP voice and video data through firewalls and NATs' **http://www.h323forum.org/papers/firewall_nat_traversal.pdf**

5.3.3 Videoconferencing standards

There is no single standard for videoconferencing, but the International Telecommunication Union (ITU) has produced a set of standards through its Sector (ITU-T) which specifies requirements for videoconferencing equipment on different types of network. In particular the ITU-T H-series of recommendations that deal with 'audiovisual and multimedia systems' contain several important standards used in videoconferencing, some of which are shown in the table overleaf.

Name	Title
H.310	Broadband audiovisual communication systems and terminals
H.320	Narrow-band visual telephone systems and terminal equipment
H.321	Adaptation of H.320 visual telephone terminals to B-ISDN environments
H.322	Visual telephone systems and terminal equipment for local area networks which provide a guaranteed quality of service
H.323	Packet-based multimedia communications systems
H.324	Terminal for low bit-rate multimedia communication
T.120	Data protocols for multimedia conferencing

Of all the standards only H.320 and H.323 are in widespread use and the others will not be described here. H.320 is used on the ISDN network and H.323 is used on IP networks, such as the Internet. All the standards in the H.32x family are what might be called 'umbrella' standards, since they reference many other H-series standards, other ITU-T standards and even IETF standards. T.120 is a protocol for data conferencing often used in conjunction with H.320 and H.323.

Another body which has produced standards for use in videoconferencing is the IETF. Rather than producing a standard that specifies the workings of different videoconferencing components, the IETF have produced standards that cover all the issues relevant for such components. Especially relevant is the work of the IETF working groups on 'audio/video transport', 'Multiparty Multimedia Session Control' and 'Session Initiation Protocol'.

SIP is the IETF protocol that comes closest to describing components for videoconferencing, and it leverages many other IETF protocols, such as SDP and RTP. The Session Announcement Protocol (SAP) is used for setting up videoconferences on the multicast backbone (MBone) using, for instance, the freely available MBone tools, which have become a de facto standard.

In the following sections the most common and important standards will be described – T.120, H.320, H.323, SIP, and the MBone tools.

T.120

T.120 is not a videoconferencing standard but a standard for dataconferencing. It is used in conjunction with videoconferencing standards in the H.32x family to enable joint video and data conferencing. Most PC-based H.320 and H.323 systems have support for the T.120 standard, which is independent of the underlying network protocols.

T.120 provides such services as still image exchange and annotation (shared whiteboard), file transfer, text chat and application sharing. The most advanced of these services is application sharing, which allows a user at one terminal to share an arbitrary application – e.g. a word processor – with all the other participants in the conference. This means that the application's window will be visible at all the other terminals, and will be updated when any changes are made. Additionally, any of the remote users can request permission to temporarily take control of the application, for example, to add a paragraph to the document opened in a word processing application.

H.320

The first widespread use of videoconferencing came in the early 1990s as a result of the acceptance of the ITU-T's H.320 standard by equipment manufacturers. This resulted in interoperability between different brands and lower prices for equipment, both of which resulted in increasing use.

H.320 is a standard for videoconferencing on ISDN which is still widely used despite the fact that ISDN bandwidth is costly compared to IP bandwidth. The main advantage of ISDN is that it offers quality-of-service, since it is a circuit-switched technology. Today's IP networks, on the other hand, offer a much greater bandwidth at a much lower cost. There are still many H.320 systems in use and interoperability with this standard may be an issue for some users. Interoperability can be accomplished either by having a terminal that supports both H.320 and H.323 or by using a gateway that is attached to both the IP and the ISDN network, and can translate between H.320 and H.323. Many terminals are mixed H.320/H.323 terminals, and some of the high-end models have built-in MCUs that allow them to act as a bridge between H.320 and H.323.

Audio coding in the H.320 standard is done using one of G.711, G.722 or G.728. Support for G.711 is mandatory, whereas support for G.722 and G.728 is optional. G.711 provides telephone quality audio at up to 64 kbit/s, whereas G.722 – a higher quality codec – provides 'natural speech' quality at the same bit rate. G.728 gives roughly the same quality audio as G.711, but at a fraction of the bandwidth, 16 kbit/s, which is very useful for low bit-rate calls.

Video coding in H.320 is done using either H.261 or H.263. Only H.261 is mandatory, and the resolution can be either QCIF or CIF, with only QCIF being mandatory. H.263 is superior to H.261 at all bit rates and should thus be preferred over H.261.

Multipoint calls in H.320 are accomplished by using an MCU which all terminals dial. The MCU mixes/switches the incoming audio and video, so that all terminals can hear and see (a subset of) the other participants.

H.323

The H.323 standard is, in many ways, similar to H.320, but where H.320 was designed for ISDN, H.323 is designed to work on non-guaranteed quality-of-service packet switched networks, which – although not dictated by the standard – translates to TCP/IP and Ethernet for the vast majority of terminals. The fact that H.323 shares many properties with H.320 makes interworking between the two protocols much easier, and this is reflected in the fact that many hardware based H.323 terminals are also H.320 terminals.

H.323 terminals can call each other by using the network layer address (i.e. the IP address) but H.323 provides for more convenient ways of addressing other terminals through the use of a so-called gatekeeper. A gatekeeper is an entity that provides address translation from numbers or aliases to network addresses, as well as controlling access and performing bandwidth management. When a terminal comes online it registers with a gatekeeper, and other terminals or gatekeepers can now look up the terminal's network address in the gatekeeper. This is completely transparent to the user who just dials a number or enters an alias. When using gatekeepers it is possible to maintain a numbering hierarchy that is independent of the network addresses (IP addresses), and which can therefore be persistent even when IP numbers are changed, such as in the case of using DHCP.

Multipoint conferencing in H.323 is accomplished by using an MCU which mixes or switches the audio and video from the participating terminals. The MCU is usually a dedicated piece of hardware or software, but some terminals have a built-in MCU.

Audio coding in H.323 uses G.711, G.722 or G.728 as does H.320, but H.323 also allows for the additional codecs G.723.1 and G.729. These are low bit-rate codecs (5.3 or 6.4 and 8 kbit/s respectively) developed for wireless/mobile networks and POTS, but also useful in low bit-rate applications such as Internet VoIP. All terminals must support G.711 and most terminals also support G.722.

Video coding in H.323 uses either H.261 or H.263. Video is not mandatory, but if present H.261 must be supported in QCIF resolution. Most terminals support both H.261 and the more efficient H.263 in both QCIF and CIF. H.263 allows for even higher resolutions, such as 4CIF and 16CIF, but these are not widely supported. A second version of H.263, sometimes called H.263+, is also supported by most newer terminals.

See also H.322 in Section 5.5.5.

SIP

Session Initiation Protocol is aimed at providing user location, user availability, user capabilities and call setup. SIP provides many of the features that H.323 does but the SIP architecture is different. At present SIP is used mostly for VoIP rather than videoconferencing, but this may change as SIP usage increases.

In SIP terminology the terminal is called a user agent, but it is also commonly referred to as a client, or simply a phone. User agents can be implemented in software or in hardware (such as IP phones). SIP users are located by an SIP URL, which looks just like an e-mail address. One user can contact another directly, but the common scenario is that an SIP proxy server is used. The proxy server plays a role similar to that of the gatekeeper in H.323, viz. user location and address resolution.

SIP is a text-based protocol similar to HTTP, and it uses the Session Description Protocol (SDP) in the payload to describe user capabilities, i.e. which codecs are supported by the user agent.

Microsoft's Windows Messenger is an SIP user agent with support for both audio, video, chat and application sharing. It is Microsoft's successor to the H.323-based NetMeeting.

For more information look also at SIP in Section 5.5.6.

Useful sources of information can be found at:

- Columbia University SIP page **http://www.cs.columbia.edu/sip/**
- iptel.org **http://www.iptel.org/**
- SIP Forum **http://www.sipforum.com/**
- IETF SIP working group **http://www.ietf.org/html.charters/sip-charter.html**
- MSN Messenger **http://messenger.msn.com**

MBone

The Multicast Backbone conferencing application is not so much a formal standard as a de facto standard which uses many of the IETF standards to provide a videoconferencing solution.

MBone is an overlay network that connects multicast-enabled islands to each other using tunnels. Over time many of these islands have grown and merged, so that native multicast (i.e. multicast without the use of tunnels) is now available on many national research and education networks (NREN). Multicast may or may not be available on campus level LANs depending on whether or not the necessary local configurations have been made. But those who have access to MBone can have multicast based multipoint videoconferencing by using the MBone conferencing applications – the so-called MBone tools. The MBone tools are a collection of separate applications – each with its own specific purpose – which together provide the necessary functionality for videoconferencing. Instead of using servers for setting up the call and for multipoint conferencing, the MBone is used as a medium both for the call set-up and for transporting the media streams. Call set-up is done simply by announcing a session (a meeting) on a well-known multicast IP address. By listening to this well-known address it is possible to get a listing of all available sessions. Sessions can be limited in scope to the institution or region, and participation and privacy can be limited by using passwords and encryption.

The tool that manages session announcement and also starts the other necessary tools when joining a session is the Session Directory Tool (SDR). SDR listens for announcements on the IP address associated with the DNS name `sap.mcast.net` and displays these in a way readable to the user. Announcements are made using the application level protocol called Session Announcement Protocol (SAP), using Session Description Protocol (SDP) in the payload. The SDP content contains all the relevant information needed to join a particular session, such as the IP address and port numbers for the different media, the codecs to be used etc.

The videoconferencing tool (VIC) is the application that displays the remote video locally, and encodes and transmits the local video. Because all participants transmit their video, it is possible to see each of the other participants in a separate window, or VIC can take cues from the audio tool, making it possible to use voice-switched video in one or more windows. VIC supports several video codecs including H.261, H.263 and H.263+.

The Robust Audio Tool (RAT) handles the audioconferencing part, which consists of mixing all the incoming audio streams and transmitting the audio from the local user. RAT can also display a quality matrix that shows the amount of packet loss between different users. RAT supports different audio codecs such as G.711, GSM and G.726. It also supports redundant transmission, which makes it resistant to packet loss.

Other tools include a shared electronic whiteboard (WDB, WB) and a Network Text Editor (NTE). The newer versions of most of the MBone tools include support for IPv6.

Useful sources of information can be found at:

- MBone Conferencing Applications **http://www-mice.cs.ucl.ac.uk/multimedia/software**
- Marratech **http://www.marratech.com/**

- Virtual Rooms Videoconferencing System (VRVS) **http://www.vrvs.org**
- Access Grid **http://www.accessgrid.org**

5.3.4 Resources

Software clients

- NetMeeting **http://www.microsoft.com/windows/netmeeting/**
- GnomeMeeting **http://www.gnomemeeting.org/**
- SGImeeting **http://www.sgi.com/software/sgimeeting/**,
- SunForum **http://www.sun.com/desktop/products/software/sunforum/**,
- Videolink Pro **http://www.smithmicro.com/videolinkpro/videolinkpromac.tpl**

Hardware terminals

- Polycom **http://www.polycom.com**
- SONY **http://www.sony.com/videoconference**
- TANDBERG **http://www.tandberg.net**
- VCON **http://www.vcon.com**
- VTEL **http://www.vtel.com**

Other relevant Web sites

- H.323 Forum Web site **http://www.h323forum.org**
- ViDeNet **http://www.vide.net**
- Global Dialling Scheme **http://www.wvn.ac.uk/support/h323address.htm**
- Internet2 Commons **http://commons.internet2.edu**

5.3.5 Videoconferencing networks

User location and call routing are important concepts in any videoconferencing architecture, so for videoconferencing to become as ubiquitous as e-mail or the public switched-telephone network an extra level of infrastructure (open and accessible to anyone) is necessary. There is no common name for such an infrastructure, but videoconferencing network will be used to cover this functionality.

As long as there is no single standard for videoconferencing on the Internet it is difficult to imagine a single system or 'network' that can play the same role for videoconferencing that the public switched-telephone system plays for ordinary telephony, or ISDN for H.320 based videoconferencing. But at least one can image a system for each of the prevalent standards – H.323, MBone tools and SIP. In fact such systems already exist in some form, although they have not achieved full coverage yet. For H.323, ViDeNet and the Global Dialling Scheme provide global user location and call routing. For the MBone tools and, to some extent, also H.323, the Virtual Rooms Videoconferencing System (VRVS) provides similar capabilities.

Some day H.323, SIP and other voice and video over IP protocols might work seamlessly on the Internet without the need for any overlay networks like those described here. It should be possible to leverage technologies such as the H.323 and SIP URL schemes along with DNS to locate the appropriate gatekeeper or SIP proxy, but the practical issues regarding implementing such a scheme, at least for H.323, are still not solved.

ViDeNet and Global Dialling Scheme

ViDeNet is a network of interconnected H.323 gatekeepers which makes it possible for a terminal connected to a gatekeeper in a ViDeNet zone to dial any other terminal or MCU in a ViDeNet zone directly. ViDeNet is open to everyone, so it is truly global in scope. One of the most crucial aspects of ViDeNet is the dialling scheme or numbering plan, which determines what the number used to dial a terminal or MCU looks like, and how calls are routed between the gatekeepers. The initial dialling scheme used by ViDeNet had scalability and manageability problems, so in 2002 ViDeNet adopted the Global Dialling Scheme (GDS) – a numbering plan developed by HEAnet, UKERNA and SURFnet. Since ViDeNet's adoption of GDS the two have essentially merged, at least from a user's perspective.

GDS has a global gatekeeper at the root (or top) of its gatekeeper hierarchy, with national gatekeepers one level down, and finally institutional gatekeepers. The global gatekeeper consists of several physical gatekeepers placed in Europe, Australia and the US, providing redundancy and resilience. The national gatekeepers can also consist of multiple physical gatekeepers.

In addition to the basic infrastructure consisting of the numbering plan and gatekeeper hierarchy ViDeNet also provides a directory where users can register their terminals and search for other users. There are also tools to assist gatekeeper administrators.

Useful sources of information are:

- ViDeNet **http://www.vide.net**
- Global Dialling Scheme **http://www.wvn.ac.uk/support/h323address.htm**
- Videoconferencing Cookbook **http://www.videnet.gatech.edu/cookbook**

VRVS

The Virtual Rooms Videoconferencing System provides an infrastructure for videoconferencing using a heterogeneous set of technologies including MBone tools, H.323, QuickTime, Java Media Framework and some hardware based MPEG-2 codecs. VRVS is based on the metaphor of virtual rooms, which are similar to an MCU conference in H.323. The virtual rooms are supported by an infrastructure of reflectors distributed among many countries in several continents. The user interface to VRVS is Web based, and includes a directory to search for users and a system to book virtual rooms. VRVS can also be used for point-to-point calls, in which case no booking is necessary.

VRVS was developed by Caltech in support of the high-energy physics community, but it has also been put at the disposal of other scientific communities, and registration is open to everyone.

Initially VRVS supported only the MBone tools, but support for various other clients, such as H.323, QuickTime Player and a Java client, has been added over time, but with limited functionality relative to the MBone tools. In addition to video and audio, VRVS also supports chat, synchronized Web browsing and application sharing.

A useful source of information is to be found at **http://www.vrvs.org**.

5.4 STREAMING

Streaming media is a means for carrying out one-way communication using audio, video and other media, such as text and still images. The user can potentially interact with the media, making it possible to create an interactive rich media experience. The most common use of streaming media is probably Internet radio stations, but a large amount of academic content, mostly in the form of lectures, is also available as streaming video.

Streaming refers to the process of transferring and playing multimedia content from a server to a client player over a network without the need for any intermediate storage on the client system. This is in contrast to downloading the media files to the hard disk on the client system, and then playing them. An intermediate solution, whereby the media starts to play before the download operation has finished, is known as progressive download. Although this is not – technically speaking – streaming media, it may look the same to the end user under some conditions.

Streaming has some benefits over download and progressive download, both from the user's point of view and from the content provider's point of view. First of all there is no need to wait for the (potentially very large) media files to be downloaded to the client system. Apart from making the content available almost instantly it also means that even diskless clients (such as TV set-top boxes) can play streaming media content, and it is possible to tune in to Internet radio and TV stations continually broadcasting. The main advantage of true streaming over progressive download is that the client receives data in a smooth stream, and that client and server can implement intelligent bandwidth management (in case of congestion) and intelligent retransmission (in case of packet loss). Without the benefit of these features, progressive download often suffers from the 'stop and go' syndrome where the player has to wait for some more of the media file to be downloaded before being able to continue playing. It is also important to some content providers that streaming media is not easily saved on the client computer, with the potential risk of being distributed without the knowledge and consent of the content provider.

Streaming media can originate from either a live source (such as a camera) or from media files held in storage on the server. In the former case it is referred to as 'live streaming' and in the latter it is called 'on-demand streaming' (or 'video-on-demand' in the case of video). The major difference between live and on-demand streaming (apart from the very definition) is that a live stream is usually being watched by a large number of clients concurrently, whereas on-demand streams are usually being watched by individual clients at different times. Even if the same media file is being watched on-demand by many different viewers at the same time, chances are that not many of them will have started at the same time and the different clients are therefore not watching it in sync with each other.

On-demand streaming also gives the viewer the opportunity to navigate through the media, either simply by fast-forwarding, pausing, playing etc. or by interacting with elements of the media that link to other parts of the media or different media files. An intermediate mode of transmission is also possible – that of scheduled transmission of stored media files. This mode of delivery is similar to the way a pre-recorded TV programme is broadcast, and in essence it is just like a live stream, except that the input comes from storage rather than a live source.

5.4.1 The technology behind streaming

The main components of any streaming media technology are encoder, server and client. This conceptual architecture is shown in Figure 5.3. The case of live streaming is depicted in the upper part of the figure, while the case of on-demand streaming or scheduled broadcasting is depicted in the lower part. The path of the audio/visual data stream has been shown by arrows, and the control data connections are shown as bidirectional dashed arrows.

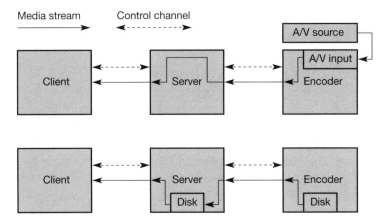

Fig. 5.3 Conceptual streaming architecture

In the case of live streaming, the data passes from a source (e.g. camera and microphone) to the encoder which converts the audio and video data into a digitally coded, compressed and packetized form suited for streaming over a data network. The data is then streamed to the server which in turn splits the stream and passes one stream on to each client (in the case of unicast streaming). Each link in this chain introduces a delay because data is temporarily held in buffers before being passed on to the next link. All these buffers may add quite a significant delay, but this is usually not of any concern since streaming is a one-way communication technology.

In the case of on-demand streaming, the source is usually some form of pre-recorded content which is compressed to a file by the encoder and uploaded (rather than streamed) to the server. This file can then be requested by clients and streamed on-demand from the server.

As mentioned earlier, live streaming and scheduled broadcasting share the common feature of many clients receiving identical streams at the same time. This feature makes these modes of streaming highly suitable for the use of IP multicast, a technique whereby one single stream can be sent from the server and simultaneously be received by an unlimited number of clients. Multicast works by letting the routers that interconnect different parts of the network split the stream, so that any link between routers carries at most only one copy of the stream.

When a live stream is served to the clients via normal point-to-point unicast connections, the server has to produce a number of streams equal to the number of clients. In this case the limit to how many clients can watch the stream is set by the capacity of the server and the capacity of the network to which it is attached.

Unfortunately, multicast is not in widespread use outside academic and research networks.

5.4.2 Streaming media standards

Streaming media is poorly standardized compared to, for example, the World Wide Web which is a single technology (despite the occasional reliance on a particular browser's technology). In the world of streaming media we are not (yet) able to choose a single client for all the different streaming servers, but are instead forced to use the particular client that has been made for the particular server from which we wish to view content. This is despite the fact that all the necessary components are standardized and even used (but in slightly different ways) by all of the major streaming media technologies. Recently an attempt has been made by the Internet Streaming Media Alliance (ISMA) to standardize on a single way of combining these technologies. Whether this standard will become the dominant way to access streaming media remains to be seen.

Some of the standards used in streaming media are:

- **Session Description Protocol** (SDP) a protocol designed for describing multimedia sessions, such as the streaming of a media file.
- **Synchronized Multimedia Integration Language** (SMIL) a markup language (like HTML) used to describe synchronized media, for example a presentation made up of audio, video, still images and text.
- **Real-Time Streaming Protocol** (RTSP) a protocol used for communication between client and server in setting up and controlling a streaming media session.
- **Real-time Transport Protocol** (RTP) a protocol used to transfer audio and video in real time from the server to the client.
- **Internet Streaming Media Alliance** specification (ISMA) a standard specifying a complete streaming media solution based on MPEG-4.

5.4.3 Resources

Streaming media players

- QuickTime Player **http://www.apple.com/quicktime/**
- RealPlayer **http://www.real.com/**
- Windows Media Player **http://www.microsoft.com/windows/ windowsmedia/download/AllDownloads.aspx?display=en&eqstechnology=**

- Kasenna Broadband Player **http://www.kasenna.com**

- Envivio TV MPEG-4 plug-in **http://envivio.com/index.html**

- Mplayer – streaming media player for Linux Streaming Servers/technologies
  http://www.mplayergq.hu/homepage/index.html

Streaming servers/technologies

- RealNetworks **http://www.realnetworks.com/**

- Windows Media **http://www.microsoft.com/windows/windowsmedia/**
  default.aspx

- QuickTime format **http://www.apple.com/quicktime**

- Internet Streaming Media Alliance **http://www.isma.tv/**

- Kasenna **http://www.kasenna.com/**

- MPEG4IP **http://mpeg4ip.sourceforge.net/**

- Cisco IP/TV **http://www.cisco.com/warp/public/cc/pd/mxsv/iptv3400/**

- VideoLAN **http://www.videolan.org**

- IBM VideoCharger **http://www-306.ibm.com/software/data/videocharger/**

5.5 VoIP AND IP TELEPHONY

VoIP and Internet telephony both refer to communications services carried over IP (Internet Protocol) rather than over the public switched telephone network (PSTN). It is worth noting that although similar issues are faced by these technologies, the approaches taken have some fundamental differences.

VoIP and Internet telephony are designed for different network sizes. The former focuses on LANs and has no intention of completely replacing the PSTN service, while the latter is designed to scale over the whole Internet. It should offer an alternative to PSTN in the near future.

In order to send a stream of voice-generated packets over the Internet, the basic steps to be performed are:

- conversion of the analogue voice signal to digital format (using some coding scheme, for example codecs from the G.7xx family (see the table overleaf);

- translation of the digital signal into IP packets;

- transmission of these IP packets over the Internet.

Encoding / compression	Bit rate
G.711 PCM A-Law/u-Law	64 kbps (DS0)
G.726 ADPCM	16, 24, 32, 40 kbps
G.727 E-ADPCM	16, 24, 32, 40 kbps
G.729 CS-ACELP	8 kbps
G.728 LD-CELP	16 kbps
G.723.1 CELP	6.3/5.3 kbps variable

In addition to the basic steps above, the use of communications services over the Internet requires other fundamental issues to be addressed. For example:

- audio codecs (out of the scope of a VoIP/IP telephony architecture);
- signalling protocols;
- directory services.

For communications services to be successful, there should be an easy way of setting up and tearing down a call so the user does not need a full knowledge of all the parameters involved. Making basic calls should be just like placing a PSTN call (i.e. dialling a number on a PSTN phone) and therefore a robust application level signalling protocol is needed. Directory services are an important element in enabling the widespread adoption of VoIP services. The problems to be solved in order to have a successful two-way communication service are:

- voice quality (it must be comparable to the PSTN voice quality);
- IP network performance;
- signalling (it must be user-transparent);
- PSTN-VoIP services interworking (in this case billing services are also foreseen as a requirement);
- management of security access control.

5.5.1 VoIP: the forerunner of Internet telephony

The transport of Voice over IP is progressing rapidly. The essential elements of the service are to turn analogue speech into a digital representation and then transport the signal in IP packets to the recipient, wherever they may be on the Internet.

There are still some problems relating to quality, reliability, security and location services. These issues are easily solvable when both users are located on a simple LAN. When considering quality, there are fewer constraints on a LAN as the availablity of large bandwidth (10, 100 or 1000 Mbps) allows the user to achieve the required performance. Narrow bandwidth leads to packet losses and packet queuing resulting in delay and delay jitter, so attempts to communicate with insufficient available bandwidth are to be avoided if high quality is to be achieved. The same considerations apply to reliability. Narrowing the available bandwidth and increasing the round trip delay of packets travelling from one end user to another decreases the service reliability.

In a well-configured LAN, bandwidth and round trip delays are not a problem. However, security is still an issue even over a LAN because privacy has always to be assured. Such problems are outside the scope of VoIP/IP telephony itself and are solved by 'classic' IP security solutions. The use of directory services is not mandatory to VoIP because of the small size of the network addressed. Corporations adopting a VoIP solution may maintain a separate VoIP phone list consisting of IP addresses for all employees. In a VoIP environment there should be a way of reaching the external world (even if it is not mandatory). This is achievable using IP-PSTN gateways (see Figure 5.4). A gateway is a device through which the interconnection of two different technologies is achieved.

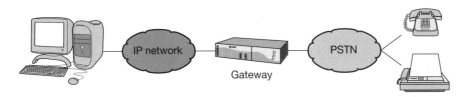

Fig. 5.4 IP-PSTN gateways

While it is not able to replace the classic PSTN completely because of the problems previously detailed, the technology is suitable for:

● enabling users to save on long-distance calls (in a network where different sites of the company are spread in geographic different locations);

● enabling the adoption of value-added services (video, shared applications, whiteboards, Web call centres etc.);

● paving the way to the integration of voice-video and data services/applications.

5.5.2 IP telephony: a possible replacement for PSTN

The IP telephony service is intended to replace the PSTN once reliability, security and a good level of quality of service have been achieved. In the transition period, IP telephony and PSTN will co-exist before a complete replacement takes place. The quality parameters involve delay, jitter and packet losses. Unfortunately, the present Internet is not able to guarantee the required level of service in terms of these parameters. For this reason two-way communications may be disturbed by gaps or periods of silence and, moreover, there may be a clipped-speech effect. In order for VoIP to support a reliable IP telephony service with global coverage, the following issues need to be addressed.

- **Scalability** serving millions of users is mandatory (the classic telephony service providers have millions of users). Current VoIP/PSTN gateways can serve only a few users simultaneously.
- **Transparent integration** (with PSTN) the users must have the chance to access the PSTN seamlessly, otherwise the necessary transition period from a mixed IP telephony-PSTN system will not be feasible.
- **Availability** the traditional PSTN has extremely high availability. Most commercially available IP telephony solutions do not have comprehensive fault-recovery mechanisms aimed at maximizing availability to such a high degree.

In order to overcome the VoIP limitations, IP telephony gateways are usually constructed from three functional elements.

- **Media gateway** (MG)
  - provides translations between circuit-switched networks and packet-switched networks in terms of media flows;
  - sends notification to the MGC about endpoint events;
  - executes commands from the MGCs.
- **Media gateway controller or call agent** (MGC)
  - provides call signalling, control and processing intelligence to the gateway;
  - sends and receives commands to/from the gateway.
- **Signalling gateway** (SG)
  - provides signalling translations between circuit-switched networks and packet-switched networks.

This solution allows the issues of scalability, transparent integration and availability to be resolved. Scalability is resolved because control and signalling functionalities are separated from each other. The SGs and MGCs are thus able to integrate transparently with the PSTN. Moreover, an MG may be controlled by several MGCs with a backup MGC provided in order to increase availability. Another possible solution, which may be coupled with the previous, is to use a signalling proxy server in order to keep the media and signalling flows separate, enabling a differentiated and stricter control on those flows.

The Media Gateway Control Protocol (MGCP) was defined by the IETF RFC 2705 – MGCP Version 1.0. More information can be found at: **ftp://ftp.rfc-editor.org/in-notes/rfc2705.txt**. The MGCP is a master/slave protocol for controlling telephony gateways from MGCs. It assumes limited intelligence at the edge (endpoints) and intelligence at the core (call agent). MGCP differs slightly from SIP and H.323, as detailed in the standards section of the GNRT (Guide to Network Resource Tools – **http://gnrt.terena.np**). MGCP does not replace SIP or H.323 but interoperates with them in order to achieve a complete IP telephony architecture.

5.5.3 IP network for the support of VoIP/IP telephony

Whereas a LAN is sufficient for successfully deploying VoIP (VoIP is considered to be a LAN telephony technology), it fails to support the introduction of IP telephony because of the issues described above. In order to support an IP telephony architecture, IP networks have to be engineered with:

- a sufficiently large bandwidth availability;
- a management system (network nodes configuration, performance monitoring, flow, dynamic management);
- quality of service protocols such as Resource Reservation Protocol (RSVP);
- architectural models such as Integrated Services (IntServ), Differentiated Services (DiffServ) and Multiprotocol Label Switching (MPLS).

A naive implementation of a viable VoIP system can be constructed by over-provisioning the bandwidth on the links, but is rather wasteful in terms of unused capacity, which must be paid for.

5.5.4 Standards

The main outcomes of the standardization efforts in the field of telephony over the Internet have been two distinct architectures. VoIP/IP telephony defined as recommendation H.323 by ITU-T (concerned with international standardization of telecommunications) and SIP from the IETF. Both protocols provide mechanisms for establishing and tearing down a call; moreover they detail the reference server architecture for the deployment of a two-way communication service. A third standard, MGCP, for VoIP has already been described above. Before going into details about the signalling protocols it is worth noting that voice conversion is standardized by the codec recommendations. A summary of the standard codecs of the G.7xx family is given in the table below.

Encoding/compression	Bit rate
G.711 PCM A-Law/ u-Law	64 kbps (DS0)
G.726 ADPCM	16, 24, 32, 40 kbps
G.727 E-ADPCM	16, 24, 32, 40 kbps
G.729 CS-ACELP	8 kbps
G.728 LD-CELP	16 kbps
G.723.1 CELP	6.3/5.3 kpbs variable

5.5.5 H.323

H.323 is an 'umbrella' recommendation defined by the ITU-T Study Group 16. It is described as an 'umbrella' because H.323 provides a framework within which the component parts of the required system are defined in a series of supplementary recommendations (see the table below).

The H.323 recommendation describes terminals and other entities that provide multimedia communications services over packet based networks (PBN) which themselves may not provide a guaranteed quality of service. H.323 is capable of supporting real-time audio, video and/or data communications.

Name	The description of protocols
H.323	Specification of the architecture
H.225	Call control (RAS), call setup (Q.931-like protocol) and packetization and synchronization of media stream
H.235	Security protocol for authentication, integrity, privacy etc.
H.245	Capability exchange communication and mode switching
H.450	Supplementary services including call holding, transfer, forwarding etc.
H.246	Interoperability with circuit-switched services
H.332	For large-size conferencing
H.26x	Video codecs (H.261, H.263)
G.7xx	Audio codecs (G.711, G.723, G.729 etc.)

Figure 5.5 below shows the H.323 protocol stack in order to clarify which protocols are carried over the TCP protocol and which are carried using the User Datagram Protocol (UDP).

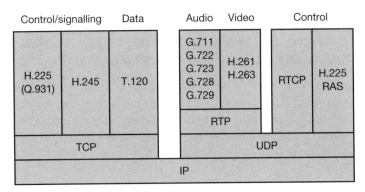

Fig. 5.5 H.323 architecture

The elements of the H.323 architecture are given below.

- **Terminals** the client endpoints that must support at least H.225 call and control channel signalling, RTP/RTCP protocols for media packets and audio codecs (video codecs and data transmission support are optional).

- **Gateways** the physical devices responsible for interconnecting a packet switched network (for example, an IP network) and a circuit-switched network (for example, a PSTN network) that also provide transmission formats, communication procedures or codec translation.

- **Gatekeepers** optional but if present in an H.323 system, all H.323 endpoints must register with the gatekeeper and receive permission before making a call. Gatekeepers may provide address translation, admission control, bandwidth control, zone management, call control signalling, call authorization and bandwidth/call management.

- **MCUs** provide the support for conferencing services with three or more endpoints:
  - multipoint controllers (MCs) – provide control functions;
  - multipoint processors (MPs) – receive and process audio, video and/or data streams.

See also H.323 in Section 5.3.3.

5.5.6 SIP

This is an application layer signalling protocol that defines the initiation, modification and termination of interactive multimedia communication sessions between users. It is an IETF standard developed by the Multiparty Multimedia Session Control (mmusic) group and defined in RFC 2543 SIP: Session Initiation Protocol **ftp://ftp.rfc-editor.org/in-notes/rfc2543.txt**.

It is a text-based client/server protocol, inheriting much functionality from HTTP1.1. It is useful to use HTTP 1.1 functionality when integration between SIP and the Web is needed. SIP is designed to use both UDP and TCP protocols; however, the protocol reliability is granted independently from the transport protocol used. The protocol functionalities can be resumed in:

● user location
● user capabilities
● user availability
● call setup
● call handling.

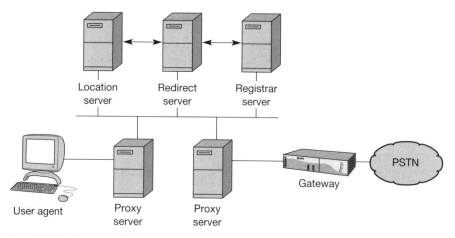

Fig. 5.6 SIP reference architecture

SIP has a distributed server reference architecture as depicted in Figure 5.6. The main architectural elements are:

● **User agent client** (UAC) the end-user system sending SIP requests (initiating or terminating a call);

- **User agent server** (UAS) the end-user system handling call requests (receiving or terminating a call);
- **User agent** (UA) the combination of UAC and UAS;
- **Proxy server** (PS) a network server handling UA requests and responses in proxy mode (acting as both a server and a client to make requests on behalf of other clients);
- **Redirect server** (RS) a network server handling user location services in redirect mode (unlike the PS that initiates its own SIP request);
- **Registar server** a network server able to accept UA registrations;
- **Location server** a network server able to provide user location services (in order to obtain information about a called party's possible location).

The location service itself is out of the scope of the SIP protocol. It is provided by other solutions, for example the RFC 1777 Lightweight Directory Service Protocol (LDSP) **ftp://ftp.rfc-editor.org/in-notes/rfc1777.txt**.

This has been replaced by RFC 3494 Lightweight Directory Access Protocol version2 (LDAPv2) **ftp://ftp.rfc-editor.org/in-notes/rfc3494.txt**.

The definition of gateways is also outside the scope of the SIP architecture, even if they are needed when interfacing with PSTN services.

The SIP address is identified by a SIP URL, in the format `user@host` (e.g. `myname@myhost.domain:port`).

Moreover, SIP I is a very light protocol with very few basic operations that include:

- `INVITE` invitation to a communication session;
- `BYE` termination of user communication session;
- `CANCEL` cancel of a pending request;
- `OPTIONS` (self-explanations);
- `ACK` acknowledgment (it carries with it a number in order to correlate request and response);
- `REGISTER` registering a user to a service.

In addition to the basic methods, the data field of an SIP message is text-based and uses RFC 2327 Session Description Protocol **ftp://ftp.rfc-editor.org/in-notes/rfc2327.txt**.

The additional capabilities that can be provided by the SIP protocol are:

- multiple calls (multiparty conferencing);
- multicast signalling;

- security (using existing mechanisms);
- stateless/stateful scalability (the SIP server may decide how many data are to be kept as state information);
- third-party call control.

5.5.7 H.323 or SIP?

Both protocols are sufficient for standard VoIP solutions, but they are not enough for the successful deployment of an IP telephony architecture. As described above, a more complete infrastructure has to be developed using other protocols. Both H.323 and SIP protocols have pros and cons and new solutions/proposals are continuously being developed in order to improve them. For a more detailed comparison of them, see the links in the section that follows.

5.5.8 Links

- Useful discussion forum (information on protocols and products available) can be reviewed at the H323forum: **http://www.h323forum.org** and the SIPforum: **http://www.sipforum.org**
- H.323 clients and servers may be found at the Open H.323 Web site (Linux/Windows clients and server): **http://www.openH323.org**
- Netmeeting home page (Windows client working with OpenH323 clients and servers) at **http://www.microsoft.com/windows/netmeeting**
- Gnomemeeting home page (Linux client working with OpenH323 clients and servers and with Netmeeting) at **http://www.gnomemeeting.org**
- SIP clients and servers may be found at the Vovida home page (refer to Vocal System for Linux clients and servers, a detailed description of protocols can be found as well): **http://www.vovida.org**
- MSN Messenger home page (MSN is a standard SIP client when the Communications Services option is turned on): **http://messenger.msn.com**
- VoIP clients (not following the described standards) can be found at the UCL Network and Multimedia Research Group home page (those tools are more complicated to use but they provide finer parameter tuning with respect to the user needs): **http://www-mice.cs.ucl.ac.uk/multimedia/software**
- For more information on H.323 please refer to:
  - ITU-T **http://www.itu.int/itudoc/itu-t/rec/index.html**
  - Packetizer **http://www.packetizer.com**
  - Open H.323 **http://www.openH323.org**

- For more information on SIP please refer to:
  - IETF **http://www.ietf.org/html.charters/sip-charter.html**
  - Henning Schulzrinne's SIP page **http://www.cs.columbia.edu/~hgs/sip**
- For more information on MGCP refer to the IETF Web site at **http://www.ietf.org/rfc/rfc2705.txt?number=2705**

5.6 GRID

Increasing demands on bandwidth and memory to run 'heavyweight' applications have driven the distributed computing community to devise effective and competitive solutions to the problem. GRID computing exploits the spare or unused processing capacity of networked computers to solve problems that stand-alone machines would be unable to deal with. The GRID therefore transforms this network solution into a unique and ultimately flexible environment.

In real terms, a grid solution could offer the facility for an organization with huge remote datasets to manipulate data using a third party's computing resources in real time – for example, during downtime in different time zones.

GRID can therefore be defined as a type of parallel and distributed system that enables the sharing, selection and aggregation of resources distributed across 'multiple' domains. Sharing in a grid environment is not related only to file exchange, but it is meant to give direct access to data, software and processors. In order for users from different organizations to use a computing grid in a secure way, they must belong to a virtual organization.

Useful links can be found at:

- Global Grid Forum **http://www.ggf.org/**
- **http://www.gridcomputingplanet.com/features/article.php/2234691**
- **http://www.nesc.ac.uk**
- **http://www.ucisa.ac.uk/events/2003/conference/papers/3-pap-hey.htm**
- **http://www.terena.nl/tech/grid/**
- The EGEE Project **http://public.en-egee.org/**

6

MAIL, NEWS AND FTP

This chapter describes the various tools and technologies that people can use to communicate on the Internet, without requiring the simultaneous presence of the parties involved in the communication. This type of communication is described as 'asynchronous' and is also referred to as a 'store and forward' service. Mail and news are examples.

6.1 E-MAIL

Electronic mail (referred to simply as e-mail) can be described as the electronic equivalent of the traditional mail service. The latter can be used to send text messages and also audio/video tapes, parcels or a mixture of messages and objects. E-mail can also send text messages, audio and video multimedia content, and other file types can be sent as an attachment. E-mail mainly involves communication between humans, but it can also be communication between humans and machines, or between machines.

E-mail is convenient, quick and cheap. People who are new to the Internet often think that the network is equivalent to 'the Web', but after they have been using their network connection for a few weeks they all tend to describe the Internet as 'e-mail and the Web', in that order. E-mail also provides an effective mechanism for the distribution of information to many people simultaneously, for example through mailing lists.

If the analogy of e-mail with the traditional mail model is developed, many familiar functions can be recognized. Traditional mail involves pen, paper, envelope, the recipient's address, a return address, a stamp, a posting or mail box and a postal service to route letters around the world. Receiving letters involves a home mailbox to accept new letters, a post-stamp that shows the sending date and the recipient uses a knife to open the envelope (and perhaps a pair of reading glasses).

With Internet e-mail there are message composition tools instead of pen and paper, an address book to pick up the recipient's address and an 'envelope' that is written automatically. Usually stamps are not needed to pay for service but there are post-stamps with sending and receiving dates and times. There is a 'box' for mail submission and there is a routing service, which is simpler (and faster) than that for traditional mail. There is an incoming mailbox to check for new mail (with flags and audio indication of new message arrival), there are simple display tools (and display helper tools for messages which otherwise would be difficult to read).

The Internet e-mail model can be described in detail by studying Figure 6.1. It illustrates a simple case of an e-mail transaction from originator to recipient.

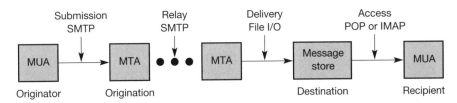

Fig. 6.1 A schematic model for e-mail transmission

The user at the originator side uses an e-mail programme called a Mail User Agent (MUA), and submits a message to the origination host. That host looks up the e-mail routing information to find the destination host to which it should connect and send the message. The destination host receives the message and writes it into its local 'message store', more precisely into the e-mail recipient's mailbox. These tasks of sending e-mail at origination host and receiving at destination host are performed by a programme called Mail Transfer Agent (MTA).

At the receiving side there is another MUA program that checks the mailbox on the message store (periodically or on request by the recipient user) and retrieves the message(s). MUAs are usually specific e-mail programmes installed on a computer (like Program for Internet News and E-mail, Eudora, Pegasus Mail, Microsoft Outlook, Netscape Messenger etc.). Web browsers can also be used to send and receive e-mail at Web sites that offer such a service. These Web interfaces are often implemented as scripts that run both inside a local browser and on the remote Web server. Together they perform the functions of the traditional MUA, in talking to the origination host and the message store. Even if they generally provide less functionality than stand-alone MUAs (especially when files have to be stored, retrieved and attached to the message), they can help in accessing e-mail from places where only a Web interface is available (for example a Web kiosk in an airport lounge or hotel).

The sending and the receiving end-points in Figure 6.1 are humans in most cases. However, the sender and/or the recipient might be an automated process – for example, a monitoring system which sends alarm e-mail messages or an 'order entry system' that receives purchase requests via e-mail.

From the user's perspective the MUA is responsible for most of what happens to an e-mail, i.e. sending and receiving. The part in the middle of the transaction, transmission and delivery, is done by MTAs and is generally transparent to users. The MTA is usually configured by the organization or ISP mail system administrator and need not concern the end user.

The other acronyms used in Figure 6.1 are the names of the protocols used during the various operations:

- **SMTP** Simple Mail Transfer Protocol is the set of commands and information used to communicate between the originating MUA and the MTAs in order to have a message delivered to its final destination;
- **POP** Post Office Protocol is the oldest (and less rich in functionality) access protocol, that allows the recipient MUA to check the incoming mail on the message store server and retrieve new messages to the local recipient machine, sometimes leaving a copy on the POP server. Further processing of retrieved messages occurs on the local machine, for example messages can be deleted or saved in local mailboxes, also called 'mail folders'.
- **IMAP** Internet Message Access Protocol is the most recent protocol that expands POP functionality, allowing the recipient MUA to manage message folders remotely on the IMAP server.

E-mail is one of the oldest services on the Internet and its message format (as well as its protocols) is quite simple – it is composed of ASCII text 'headers' followed by ASCII text 'bodyparts'; the latter being a simple text or a complex multipart body composed using the standard Multipurpose Internet Mail Extensions (MIME) message format.

6.1.1 Becoming an e-mail user

Using e-mail requires access to a computer connected to the Internet and an MUA, either pre-installed or installed by the user. Alternatively, a Web browser can be used to access a Web-based e-mail service such as Hotmail **http://www.hotmail.com**.

Furthermore the e-mail user needs to register with their organization, or with an ISP, in order to get an e-mail address and space for hosting a mailbox.

6.1.2 E-mail addresses

Each person's e-mail address must be unique across the whole Internet. It takes the form of mailname@domain (for example, `john.allan@sons.org.uk`).

The domain element ('sons.org.uk' in the above example) is usually determined by the connecting organization or ISP, and serves as the identifier of the 'network place' inside the organization or ISP where the message store resides. The mailname element ('john.allen' in the above example) is sometimes determined automatically from the user's own name or computer user-id. Alternatively, the user may be allowed to determine their own mailname string, provided somebody else is not already using that string in the same domain. In all cases, a mailname is unique inside any domain, and a domain is unique within the Internet. Note that e-mail addresses are case insensitive, thus `'john.allan@sons.org.uk'` and `'John.ALLAN@Sons.ORG.uk'` are processed as identical e-mail addresses. The use of the period ('.') as a separator between firstname and lastname is not a mandatory requirement but is a widely adopted convention that provides clarity to the human reader.

A last point to remember about e-mail addresses is that even if all possible character sets are used to write the content of e-mail messages (if the MUA and computer interface support them), the mailname can only use a limited subset of ASCII characters. Self-restricting the choice to A–Z, 0–9, periods ('.') and hyphens ('–') should ensure the creation of a valid e-mail address. Some other characters could also be used, provided they are encoded with some complex techniques. The character set allowed for the domain element of the address is an even more restricted subset of ASCII, but the organization or ISP will have already taken care of configuring a valid name.

The existence of the special e-mail address `postmaster@domain` is mandatory within each domain. Its use is restricted to the administrative maintenance of mail services. Typically it is used by other e-mail administrators to report e-mail problems and make mail-related requests.

6.1.3 Finding other people's e-mail addresses

Finding e-mail addresses is not always straightforward. There is no single globally comprehensive directory of e-mail addresses. See also Section 1.2.

E-mail aliases

In some cases a user might be allowed to have 'e-mail aliases' – several e-mail addresses all corresponding to the same mailbox on the same message store. For example `j.allan@sons.org.uk` or `secretariat@sons.org.uk` might be set up as aliases of `john.allan@sons.org.uk`. The effect of the aliases is that e-mail sent to any of the three e-mail addresses will be transparently directed to the mailbox of `john.allan@sons.org.uk`.

In some special cases, when an organization is known by more than one name, multiple domains might correspond to the same message store (i.e. the domain is aliased). Aliases are normally set up by mail system administrators, thus a user should refer to them in order to have them set up.

6.1.4 Mailbox forwarding

If a user is registered as an e-mail user with more than one organization or ISP, they will have more than one mailbox (and thus more than one e-mail address). These may be managed separately or, in some cases, it may be possible to redirect e-mail messages automatically from one mailbox to another. This redirection of mail is called e-mail forwarding. It might be included as a user-controlled mailbox feature, or in some cases it is controlled by the mail system administrator.

When using e-mail forwarding between different mailboxes, the creation of forwarding loops between two, or even more, mailboxes should be carefully avoided. If forwarding is set from mailbox A to mailbox B, then mailbox B should not set forwarding back to mailbox A.

6.1.5 Configuration parameters in MUA

The MUA takes care of performing tasks on behalf of the user. The user may be required to undertake some basic configuration and set some personal preferences.

Configuring an e-mail address (the one which will appear as the sender) is very important. In some cases this address is automatically generated by some utility present on the computer (especially if there is more than one user of the machine), but normally this is information directly inserted into the MUA. Users should be very careful when typing it in – if a wrong sender address is provided, nobody will ever be able to reply to messages.

The MUA usually also needs to know the SMTP server to which outgoing e-mail messages are submitted. In some cases this is configured by the e-mail system administrator, but normally this is not the case. The SMTP server usually belongs to the user's own organization, LAN or domain. SMTP servers are configured to accept submissions only from a restricted group of MUAs, and to reject anything else. When using a system other than their own, guests usually need to edit this information to the local SMTP server where they are temporarily hosted.

To access incoming messages, the MUA must know the name of the server where the message store is. This is usually called the POP or IMAP configuration. Moreover, to access the mailbox the user needs to supply a user-id name and password. For security reasons, the password should not be stored in the saved configuration, but instead should be typed in every time e-mail is accessed. Remember that the password provides exclusive access to the mailbox, but this does not mean security. Passwords and messages will travel 'in-the-clear' (i.e. unencrypted) along this path and could be intercepted by anyone, unless specific secure communication methods between the MUA and message store are adopted. See also Section 4.2.

Many mail systems provide a choice between POP and IMAP access. The selection made determines which additional features can be expected when accessing the message store. POP allows the incoming new messages to be downloaded from the message store server. The folder for incoming messages is normally named inbox and in case of POP there is one inbox located at the message store and one on the local computer. Normally, messages are deleted from the message store 'inbox' immediately after they have been downloaded to the local inbox. In some cases there is the option to leave the mail on the server, which, if activated, will keep a copy of the incoming messages on the message store as well. With POP, e-mail folders are handled locally on the user's computer.

IMAP offers the same kind of access to the incoming messages folder, but additionally it allows many folders to be kept and managed directly on the message store, so full collections of folders can be handled easily on different servers, local or remote, and the functionality provided is definitely enhanced. Keeping folders on a central server is also a very good choice if they have to be read from different computers. Message store servers are often provided with services which include regular disk backup, so having a copy of your messages on a managed server is a good way of protecting the integrity of your message collection. In addition, IMAP servers often offer encrypted (and thus secure) connections between MUA and message store providing a further level of privacy to the user. As a consequence of these advanced capabilities, IMAP is recommended as the access protocol of first choice, in preference to POP.

6.1.6 Message composition

Historically, Internet e-mail consisted of plain ASCII text, and this is still the minimal common ground, as established by the standard (Request for Comment RFC 822). To be sure that messages will be correctly received and displayed by any recipient, this minimal feature profile should be adopted, at least for the first attempt at sending an e-mail. The additional features that a recipient can handle can be established later.

With MIME (see Section 6.1.11) the features of message content can be enhanced in almost any way imaginable – fonts, colours, formatting, video, audio etc. There are, however, some guidelines that should be followed to avoid problems and help in successful transmission of the content.

- Do not send HTML-only messages (this feature can be configured in the MUA preferences) but, if there is a real need to send HTML, send at least both HTML and plain text alternative bodyparts. Many users do not like receiving HTML, or their MUA requires complex operations to display it.

- When sending simple text, for example, there is no need for special formatting, so do not use a word processor to compose it. The recipient might not have the same application to open it, or would have other problems in handling and replying to it. For simple text always use the MUA message composition internal tools. It is easier, faster and more standard. If there is a need to send word processor documents, attach them to the e-mail as formatted documents, always adding a simple text explanation in the message to tell the recipient what they are.

- When an MUA is requested to 'reply-to' a message, it will automatically give you a copy of the incoming message, usually indented and highlighted with a prefix marker such as the '>' character in the left hand margin. Do not automatically quote the complete message, just the relevant portions – delete irrelevant portions from the quote so as to make the message shorter and more intelligible to the recipient.

- There are conventions for expressing some feelings – upper-case text is considered as 'shouting', and 'smileys' or 'emoticons' can help in expressing ideas more clearly.

- Adding a 'signature' to messages (containing the information that would go on a business card) is an option for consideration.

It is possible to save copies of outgoing messages, but usually this has to be configured by the user. The options are normally 'all outgoing mail is saved automatically' or 'you manually send yourself a copy explicitly using the cc: (carbon copy), or fcc: (file carbon copy) options on a per message basis'.

Finally, security is also possible when sending e-mail messages. The use of Pretty Good Privacy (PGP) or Secure/Multipurpose Internet Mail Extensions (S/MIME) can be used to sign and/or encrypt messages before sending them. Most modern MUAs support both techniques.

See also Section 4.2.3.

6.1.7 Sending e-mail

Once a message is sent, it is (almost) immediately delivered to the recipient. Thus there is no way of stopping what has been sent. Only if the message cannot be immediately delivered to the remote site will it be queued at the sender's side (or at some intermediate MTA), usually for a maximum 2 or 3 days, and delivery will be retried periodically. After the expiration of this period, if delivery is still unsuccessful an error message is sent back to the originator. The conventional sender name of the error message is 'Mailer-daemon' or 'Postmaster'. Delays are possible for various reasons, such as network congestion, routing failures and network outages. Some of the tools listed in Chapter 7 can be used to try to investigate these delays. Other delays in delivery include, for instance, problems at the originating and/or remote MTA, at the recipient mailbox etc.

How does the sender know if a message has been delivered? Unless the MUA, the whole chain of MTAs and the recipient MUA support the 'receipts' service, there is no automatic way of knowing. Usually, when an error occurs the sender should expect an e-mail back with the error description. When 'silence' occurs after sending an e-mail, it is reasonable to expect that a correct delivery has taken place. If the e-mail services you and the recipient are using support receipts, this will give a positive indication of correct delivery.

6.1.8 Receiving e-mail

Many e-mail users receive many messages each day. A good practice is to organize mail messages that you have received in folders (for example, by sender or by project). Keeping all messages in a single huge inbox folder will very soon make finding information problematic, and sometimes create problems for the MUA. Users should keep track of their mailbox status, especially if it has size limitations.

Subscribing to mailing lists should also be handled carefully – some of them deliver hundreds of messages per day and leaving a mailbox unattended for a few days in such a situation might create serious problems. See Section 6.2.

In order to handle incoming messages, most MUAs provide filtering features (or there are external tools like Procmail on UNIX-like systems) that allow automated actions on messages before they are seen by the end user. A common use of filters includes separating messages into different folders by sender or by subject, and automated detection of unsolicited commercial e-mail (UCE) and spam messages (see also Section 4.10).

The MUA might also support security features for receiving messages, i.e. verifying the integrity of messages and the identity of the senders, or decrypting messages that only the recipient should be able to read. In fact, if no security options are used, recipients should be very careful in trusting the origin of messages – forging sender addresses and whole messages is easy, even for those without specific technical knowledge. Only PGP or S/MIME can avoid this unpleasant situation.

Finally, remember that e-mail senders expect recipients to respond to messages directed explicitly to them. Having a mailbox but not reading messages, or reading but not responding, is bad practice and will cause annoyance.

6.1.9 Transmission of files

E-mail allows for the fast and easy transmission of any sort of document or computer file, for example images, word processor formatted documents, spreadsheets or anything else which might be on a computer as a file.

When using modern MUAs, sending files by e-mail is a matter of selecting the menu option for attaching a document (hence the name 'attachment'). The MUA normally takes care of the process of converting the document by encoding it into plain text (ASCII) format automatically. This is a preliminary operation to sending documents via Internet e-mail because not all mail servers, through which the message might go, can handle binary formats. Word-processed documents, spreadsheets, images and other binary files need to be encoded into plain text before sending. Encoding usually implies an increase in size of the attached document and this must be taken into account, as many mail systems impose a size limit on the mailbox or on a single message. Normally the increase on encoding is between 50 and 100 percent of the original file size.

There are a number of ways in which encoding in ASCII may be achieved, including Base64 and the older non-standard BinHex, UUEncode etc.

File encoding: Base64, UUEncode, BinHex

Base64 encoding is a standard, often used inside MIME multimedia messages for binary files, or for files that do not fit well into the ASCII character set. As a standard, it is deployed on all existing operating systems and there are also a number of stand-alone encoders/decoders that help in handling this format. In fact this is the only method of encoding that ensures interworking of all standard MUAs on the Internet.

UUEncode is a method of encoding binary files to plain text. UUEncode originates from UNIX systems, though software for other platforms is also available. UUEncode (and UUDecode) is incorporated into a number of mail packages. Exchanges between different systems using UUEncode may not be entirely reliable as it has not been completely standardized, and thus the resulting decoded file might not be identical to the one sent, resulting in it being unusable by the recipient.

BinHex originated with Apple Macs and is primarily handled by many Mac applications, and also some PC applications such as Microsoft Internet Explorer and Netscape Navigator. BinHex should only be used if MIME is not available, or if there are specific reasons to use it when sending attached files. Using BinHex may result in similar problems resulting from using UUEncode.

Conversion between different file formats

The same conversion algorithm that has been applied to the document on the sender side (encoding) must be performed on the recipient side (decoding) in order to obtain the original content. Dedicated conversion software is available for a number of platforms. When a message with an attached encoded document is received, the recipient's MUA steps in, taking care of decoding, saving and displaying the document.

Commonly, a message that has an attachment will include an icon or other indication. The user can select and display the file with a simple mouse click or by pressing the 'Enter' key after positioning the cursor on the file name.

If the MUA does not have the required decoding facility (or if it has not been instructed about how to handle such a file format) it will simply save the file to some default directory leaving the user to locate and open the appropriate decoding application. This is cumbersome and unfamiliar to many users, so it should be avoided. Before sending files, first establish that the recipient's mail program can handle the intended format. A simple question like 'Is your mail program MIME compliant?' can avoid headaches.

Size of files and compression

One important issue to consider when sending large files attached to e-mail message is the 'size limitation' which many mail system administrators set on their mail servers. In fact, many mail systems (MTAs) will not let a message pass if it is bigger that a certain limit, and this limit is usually not very high – common size limits range from 1 to 10 megabytes.

Some MTAs can handle large transmissions but it is not uncommon for large files or messages (for example above 500 kb) sent by e-mail to be broken down into smaller chunks automatically. While a sophisticated MUA on the recipient side may handle reconstituting these adequately, a safer option for large files is to reduce the size by compressing them before attachment.

The same considerations as for encoding apply to files that are compressed – make sure the recipient will be able to decompress files by using a decompression programme.

A better option for sending large files is to make them available through File Transfer Protocol (FTP) rather than e-mail. The file can be deposited at the remote FTP site, or made available at the local FTP site for the recipient to pick it up. More information about FTP can be found in Section 6.4. Remember that e-mail is NOT the primary tool for sending files around the Internet!

6.1.10 Transmission of viruses

Exchanging files by e-mail is one of the great conveniences of the Internet. It is not, however, without its down side – specifically, the transmission of viruses that may reside in seemingly innocuous documents such as word-processed files. Viruses and worms are computer programmes that replicate themselves and (try to) infect large number of computers where, once activated, they can act destructively. A virus can be transmitted to a computer each time a file transfer is involved, in many cases by innocent parties exchanging files by e-mail.

From the user's mailbox the virus or worm can be easily spread to other e-mail users listed in the address book, if the MUA is vulnerable to such operations. The Melissa virus, for example, extended the insidious effects of the macro virus genre by propagating itself through further multiple automatic e-mail transmissions of an infected document, using the Microsoft Outlook address book to generate a list of recipients. Many other similar viruses exist nowadays (see also Section 4.9).

The arrival of a virus file in a mailbox does not imply that the computer is infected. It is opening and executing the file that starts the viral activity. If adequate precautions are taken before opening the infected file, the virus chain can be stopped. However, many modern MUAs open all attachments automatically in order to facilitate the user in reading them. For example, when Microsoft Outlook receives an infected file, the worm will take advantage of a vulnerability that allows the attachment to autoexecute when the e-mail is read or previewed.

As a minimal precaution, never configure mail programmes to open any attached file automatically. The user should decide if the origin of the message is trustworthy and should always be allowed the choice of saving the file on disk and examining it with appropriate antivirus software. In some cases the mail system administrator might also have installed an automated antivirus utility on the message store. In such a case a message containing a file infected by a virus should be detected automatically and the virus or the entire file removed before it can be retrieved from the mailbox – informing the intended recipient that this happened. However, new viruses might exist which the centralized antivirus mail software does not identify, so always apply the above minimal precautions when handling files received via e-mail.

Further online resources about computer viruses are available from **http://www.cert.org/other_sources/viruses.html**.

It is important not to propagate another example of viral activity, the so-called 'chain letters', which instruct the recipient to forward them to all their friends. These are usually hoaxes with false content or promises. They are not harmful but their negative effects are the waste of resources, user and network time and computer space. For more information see **http://hoaxbusters.ciac.org**.

6.1.11 Multipurpose Internet Mail Extensions

Encoding methods (like Base64), used as a standard for incorporating files for transmission via e-mail, have already been introduced. This is just one aspect of multimedia e-mail services. Other aspects include the use of non-ASCII character sets, the presence of 'alternate' message body parts etc. The standard method for supporting these services is MIME, a protocol specification that allows Internet mail to carry the full set of multimedia messages and contents, by determining the content type precisely. MIME is now incorporated into most MUAs. With a MIME compliant MUA, information is added to the headers of a message specifying the type of content included and how the content is to be processed. There is no need for users to 'negotiate' the contents format and send additional information on how to interpret it. Various types of content can be specified via MIME, including binary data, images, audio and video files, alternate national language versions of the message content, or alternate plain text and HTML versions of the same content.

EXAMPLES *MIME examples*

If the message is a piece of text in the Croatian language, which uses the ISO-8859-2 character set, the mailer inserts a line in the header of the message:

```
Content-type: text/plain; charset=iso-8859-2
```

In this example the notation 'iso-8859-2' is a registered MIME name for a character set supporting most of the central and east European national languages. If the receiving MUA supports this character set, it will successfully display the text of the message using the appropriate characters of the Croatian language. The content-type defaults for MIME are:

```
Content-type: text/plain; charset=us-ascii
```

As another example, if a GIF file is included, the mailer inserts a line like this in the header of the message:

```
Content-Type:Image/Gif
```

The information 'Content-Type:Image/Gif' instructs the receiving MUA how to display the image received, using the appropriate tools.

As previously mentioned, MIME usually uses Base64 for encoding binary files. This may be indicated in the header with a line like this:

```
Content-Transfer-Encoding: base64
```

Quoted-Printable is the encoding technique most appropriate for ASCII files with a small section of non-ASCII characters (for instance, accented letters in different languages). If the receiving mailer is MIME compliant, it will correctly interpret the lines in the header and decode and display, or save the file appropriately.

As MIME is the only encoding method that is a standard, always try to use it to send e-mail messages in situations where plain ASCII is not enough or there is a need to enclose non-ASCII files.

6.2 MAILING LISTS

Mailing lists enable people with a common interest to exchange views, circulate news and announcements, make documents available to each other and pool their expertise. The discussion on a mailing list normally focuses on a single subject, though this subject may be fairly broad, encompassing many subtopics. A mailing list is a typical service that a working group sets up as its main tool for discussion and working together.

Mailing lists have proved to be such a productive tool that it might even be that the members of the group do not need to meet physically at all!

Quite often a mailing list archive, accessible via e-mail (or quite commonly via a Web interface) is often found associated with a mailing list.

Further information about mailing lists can be found in Chapter 1.

6.2.1 How do mailing lists work?

The facility to send one message to multiple recipients is common to all e-mail programs. Multiple e-mail addresses can be grouped under one collective name, often referred to as an alias. This means that the local mail program can provide a sort of home-made mailing list, with addresses being manually added and removed from the alias. However, these home-made lists have limited capabilities and should not be used for large numbers of addresses (typically larger than 10–15 recipients per list) as they can result in problems and errors.

Users should note that the list of recipients on the home-made mailing list is known only at the home computer of the creator, thus it is only usable by the user of the local machine, not by any others on the list. Other features of a real mailing list are equally unavailable – for example, replying to all the persons in the group would require enumerating them all in the reply, or creating another alias on other sender computer which will not be synchronized with the original alias list.

Dedicated mailing list manager software running on a server offers, on the other hand, the greatest functionality and capability for the management of large-scale mailing lists. Most mailing lists are managed by one of the highly developed mailing list managers (MLMs) such as LISTSERV, Majordomo, Listproc and Mailbase.

MLM software may provide some or all of the following functions:

- automated processing of subscriptions;
- distribution of messages;
- making available files associated with the list, such as the monthly archives of messages;
- searching and indexing of message archives via the Web or commands sent by e-mail.

While an MLM's main functionality is to distribute messages via e-mail (from one to many persons), its other administrative services listed above are also activated and controlled via e-mail, by sending commands in appropriately formatted e-mail messages.

Each mailing list will have at least one person responsible for the operation of the list. This is the so-called list owner. The list owner will see that the list runs smoothly, provide any necessary information files, answer questions from members and so on. Some lists are open for subscription to anyone. Others are closed, in which case the list owner will probably invite selected individuals to join the list and subscribe them manually. Individuals have to agree before they are placed on a mailing list, and have the right to request to be unsubscribed and stop receiving mailings at any time. On a closed mailing list, in some cases, only people belonging to the list are allowed to post messages, while non-members trying to post to the list address would either receive an error notification or a message from the list MLM software informing them that their message has been submitted to the list owner for approval. Sometimes both non-member and member postings are sent to a moderator for approval before they are redistributed to the list members. In such a case, the list is called a 'moderated' list. There are, of course, various degrees of openness and closedness in mailing lists, and inquiries about the status of a mailing list should always be made before subscribing.

It is important to note that there are different e-mail addresses associated with one mailing list:

- the list address itself, for postings to all list members;
- the administrative address, for help, subscription etc. (usually managed automatically by the MLM);
- the list owner address (human);
- the moderator address (human).

6.2.2 Setting up a mailing list

There are thousands of mailing lists on a vast variety of topics. Refer to Section 1.3.1 for sources to search for mailing lists on a specific topic. If interested parties cannot find a list on the topic of their interest, they might consider setting up a list themselves. They will have to choose the MLM to use for the list, depending on the server platform on which they wish to install it. Some of the MLMs are commercial products, like LISTSERV, while others are public domain software, like Majordomo. Depending on the specific choice, they should of course consult the specific documentation for each MLM for setting up a mailing list. For example, for guidelines on running a LISTSERV list there is a List Owner's Manual for LISTSERV at **http://www.lsoft.com/manuals/ownerindex.html**.

Joining a mailing list is very simple. Send an e-mail message containing a 'subscribe' or 'join' command to the administrative address of the list. This usually looks like:

```
subscribe <listname> <YourFirstName> <YourLastName>
```

Substitute as appropriate between the angle brackets but, of course, also adapt the syntax to the specific MLM running the list. The sender's e-mail address will be taken from the headers of the subscribe message, and usually need not be set explicitly in the subscribe command. A good start, even before sending the subscribe message, might be to send a message to the administrative e-mail address of the list containing both subject and the first and only line in the body part the text 'HELP'. Usually, the sender will receive a short summary of available commands and information on how to subscribe and carry out other operations on the list. A subscribe message with the correct syntax usually receives a reply informing the sender that they are now subscribed to the list.

It is important to remember that the subscribe message, and other administrative messages, should go to the administrative address, not to the list itself. With an automated mailing list, administrative messages are processed automatically by the MLM. If such messages are sent to the list itself, they will normally be distributed to every subscriber of the list which, besides generating a certain amount of irritation, wastes everyone's time including the sender's, as the message will not have achieved the intended objective. Some mailing lists may have a moderator who weeds out unsuitable messages (such as 'subscribe') before they are distributed to the list, or possibly a smart MLM will reject such messages but this cannot be assumed.

Here are some examples of administrative addresses:

- LISTSERV@terena.nl
- mailbase@mailbase.ac.uk
- Majordomo@garr.it

And some examples of list addresses:

- child-health@mailbase.ac.uk
- chat-developers@ucla.edu
- ietf-announce@ietf.org

In some cases, the subscribe and other commands can also be handled via a Web-based interface, which might facilitate actions by offering point and click buttons and fields to fill in. However, this is not generally true, and there is no common template for these Web-based MLM command interfaces.

6.2.3 MLM commands

MLMs respond to commands in e-mail messages. Commonly, they will handle commands to:

- subscribe to a list;
- leave a list (unsubscribe);
- receive a list in digest format;
- suspend mail temporarily;
- obtain a list of subscribers;
- obtain a list of archive files;
- search and retrieve archive files.

Consult your MLM's help file for information on the commands available.

6.2.4 Handling mailing list correspondence

Some lists are very active and generate many messages each day. With others, weeks may go by without any traffic. Subscribers need to learn to cope with the mail that a list generates. When there is a lot of incoming mail, users need to be discriminating about what they read and what they retain. The initial filtering of messages can be done by scanning the subject fields and deleting those they recognize as irrelevant. If their mail program has a filtering capability, they can configure it to sort (and delete) nominated categories of incoming mail. Whichever filtering process is used, they will need to act decisively on the messages that remain, deciding which messages should be discarded, which acted on and which retained for reference, following up accordingly. They should set up a logical filing system for retained messages. Later, when information is needed, it is useful to be able to refer to all the correspondence on one particular subject. Belonging to a mailing list should encourage everyone to effectively perform the actions they, as an e-mail user, should do anyway in order to benefit from its services.

Also remember that there is a sort of 'common agreement' among e-mail users that requires a request for action or an answer to be followed up. Owning an e-mail address without reading or answering the messages that other users send generates irritation generally and diminishes the advantages of using one of the best Internet tools.

Make use of the facilities that a mailing list provides. For instance, you may perhaps opt for a daily digest of messages (all the messages put together in one message) or suspend the list while on holiday. If the mailing list provides an archive of messages, a user can always refer to that to see what has been missed – the archive for particular periods can be requested with one of the list's mail commands. In fact, with some busy mailing lists regular scanning of the message archive for items of interest may be preferable to subscribing.

For guidelines on mailing list etiquette see Netiquette FYI 28 at **http://www.potaroo.net/ietf/rfc/fyi/fyi28.txt** or Request for Comments (RFC) 1855 Netiquette Guidelines at **ftp://ftp.rfc-editor.org/in-notes/rfc1855.txt**.

One last, but very important, topic about mailing lists – the e-mail address added to a mailing list on joining will usually be the address which appears in the 'From:' line of the subscribe message. Subscribers who have multiple mailboxes and different addresses should be wary. Moreover, if an e-mail address is changed for any reason, remember to remove the subscription (unsubscribe) from all mailing lists. In order to do this, use the same 'From:' address used in the subscribe message or, in case of problems, contact the list owner and ask for the address to be removed or updated directly with the new one. The list owner will probably ask for some information, just to confirm that the request actually comes from the same person whose data are going to be modified, but this little bit of extra work is preferable to leaving addresses on the list which do not exist. Keeping the e-mail environment 'clean' helps the Internet to function correctly and avoids possible irritation for other users and list owners.

6.2.5 Mailing list managers

A mailing list manager (MLM) is a server that manages mailing lists. When a user sends an e-mail to a mailing list the correspondent MLM takes care of forwarding it to all the addresses in the mailing list. The most popular MLMs are LISTSERV and Majordomo.

LISTSERV

LISTSERV, from L-Soft International, is a system for the creation, management and control of electronic mailing lists. It is one of the two most widely deployed mailing list manager packages on the Internet and millions of LISTSERV list messages are sent each day. LISTSERV offers a great deal of functionality to support the administration of its mailing lists and to give users a range of options covering the way in which they receive list messages, files and information and request database searches.

LISTSERV lists are maintained by LISTSERV servers (listservers). For each list that it maintains, a listserver will manage the subscriber list, distribute list messages, make associated documents available, log e-mail traffic, archive messages and also carry out database searches of archives and files in response to e-mail commands.

There are versions of LISTSERV for various operating systems, like VM, OpenVMS, UNIX, and various Windows types. There is also a free version, named LISTSERV Lite, which is available for small-scale non-profit mailing list management (up to ten mailing lists).

Sending commands to LISTSERV

All LISTSERV functions (from straightforward subscribe and unsubscribe commands through to complex database searching functions) can be accessed through e-mail commands placed in the body of the message.

Always remember that e-mail commands go to the LISTSERV e-mail address, not to the mailing list address. If commands relate to a particular list, it is preferable to send e-mail commands to the specific listserver that manages that list, if the address is known. Otherwise, try using the general LISTSERV address, `LISTSERV@LISTSERV.NET`.

This address may be used to forward your message to the correct server. This address can also be used for any information requests, such as Help or Info. This automatic search for the correct server is unique among MLMs, and dates back to the old times when the Internet, as we know it now, was not yet in existence. However, nowadays all existing LISTSERV installations are no longer coordinated with the others and a query to the general address might fail to gather the requested information.

A LISTSERV administrative e-mail address takes the form of `LISTSERV@domain` where the 'domain' is the same as the domain part of the mailing lists managed by that installation. `LISTSERV@ACSU.BUFFALO.EDU` is, for example, the LISTSERV installation at 'ACSU.BUFFALO.EDU', and all mailing lists managed by it will have addresses like: `listname@ACSU.BUFFALO.EDU` (for example `NETTRAIN@ACSU.BUFFALO.EDU`).

However, with the most recent versions of the LISTSERV software, it is possible to access some LISTSERV functions via the Web, for instance to read message archives and subscribe to the lists.

When a LISTSERV server receives an e-mail command, it will ignore the 'Subject:' line of the mail header, so commands must be in the body of the message. Several commands can be sent to LISTSERV in the same mail message, with each command on a separate line. Here is an example of an e-mail sent (using Pine MUA) to the general address asking for the 'HELP' file.

```
PINE 4.44 COMPOSE MESSAGE Folder: INBOX 18 Messages
To: listserv@listserv.net
Cc:
Attachment:
Subject: this line is ignored, and I can also leave it
blank!
----- Message Text -----
HELP

^G Get Help ^X Send ^R Rich Hdr ^Y PrvPg/Top ^K Cut Line
^O Postpone
^C Cancel ^D Del Char ^J Attach ^V NxtPg/End ^U UnDel
Line ^T To AddrBk
```

Subscribing and unsubscribing to a public mailing list

Anyone with access to e-mail can join a public LISTSERV list. For example, to subscribe to the mailing list named 'NETTRAIN' existing on the listserver named 'ACSU.BUFFALO.EDU', simply send a message to the address LISTSERV@ACSU.BUFFALO.EDU and in the first and only line of the message text write SUBSCRIBE NETTRAIN Mary Smith. This command tells LISTSERV that the subscriber wishes to have 'Mary Smith' associated to their e-mail address as a personal name in the subscribers list.

To remove an e-mail address from a mailing list, the command to send is UNSUBSCRIBE, inserting the appropriate list name.

How to find the appropriate LISTSERV mailing list

A distributed database of information about most of the publicly accessible LISTSERV lists is automatically generated and maintained by a number of LISTSERV installations around the Internet. The chance of finding something relevant is probably quite high, given that there are currently more than 110 000 public lists coordinated via LISTSERV. The lists can be searched via the WWW at the CataList Reference Web site maintained by L-Soft at **http://www.lsoft.com/lists/listref.html**

Browsing through the list of lists provides a broad picture of the scale and variety of LISTSERV lists. It is also possible to search for LISTSERV lists by topic, get details on each list, browse message archives and even subscribe.

All this information can, of course, be accessed via e-mail. Any listserver will provide a list of the lists it maintains in response to an e-mail containing the word 'LIST'. To obtain a list of LISTSERV lists dealing with a particular topic, make a keyword search of the global list of lists using LIST GLOBAL keyword.

However, remember again that some restrictions are introduced concerning the availability of information on LISTSERV-managed mailing lists. In fact to prevent this useful mechanism for finding information being turned into a paradise for e-mail spammers, a number of automated checks exist, blocking queries or postings which seem to be too large for a normal use of the service.

Other tools, like Web searching tools, can identify mailing lists that might be of interest. Remember that many of the major mailing lists on the Internet are managed via Majordomo. Hence limiting a search to LISTSERV is definitely a restriction to be avoided.

Some other useful LISTSERV commands

Here is a short list of the most useful of the other commands that can be sent to LISTSERV.

- REVIEW F=MAIL send a list of subscribers belonging to the mailing list. 'F' is the format requested. Other format options include MIME/text, MIME/Appl and UUEncode.
- LISTS send a list of lists maintained by the server.
- LIST GLOBAL send a list of LISTSERV lists (from any co-ordinated server) with this keyword in the description.
- INDEX send a list of archive files for this list.
- GET F=MAIL GET filename filetype <options> will get the file specified in the filename and file type input. Files can in fact be stored at a listserver and made available for retrieval by users. There are two types of files stored – miscellaneous files relevant to the list deposited by the list owner or administrator, and archives of e-mail distributed to the list.
- SET when someone joins a list, LISTSERV adds information about their name and e-mail address to its membership database and assigns a default set of list options, unless they specify otherwise. This command enables these options to to be changed. There are additional options on most commands.

EXAMPLES   *Some LISTSERV examples*

- Suppose you wish to subscribe to the 'NETTRAIN' list at 'UVBM.BUFFALO.CC.EDU'. Your full name is Mark P. Waugh. Then you will send the command LISTSERV@UVBM.BUFFALO.CC.EDU SUBSCRIBE NETTRAIN Mark P. Waugh.
- Suppose you wish to leave the 'INFO-MAC' mailing list (to which you have already subscribed) at the node 'CEARN.cern.ch'. The command: UNSUBSCRIBE INFO-MAC should be sent to the LISTSERV@CEARN.cern.ch that manages the INFO-MAC list.

- To leave all the LISTSERV lists you belong to, send the command `UNSUBSCRIBE * NETWIDE` to your nearest (or any) LISTSERV.

- Suppose you wish to receive a listing of all mailing lists that have the text 'europe' in their name or title. Send the command `LIST GLOBAL EUROPE` to your nearest (or any) LISTSERV server.

- If you want to stop receiving mail from all the lists at 'SEARN.sunet.se' to which you belong, send the following command `SET * NOMAIL` to LISTSERV@SEARN.sunet.se.

- If you wish to retrieve the file 'PCPROG ZIP' from a filelist, in XXE file format, send the command `GET PCPROG ZIP F=XXE` to the LISTSERV server that holds the file.

Finding more information on LISTSERV

All of L-Soft's manuals for LISTSERV are available on the Web at **http://www.lsoft.com/manuals/**.

Majordomo

The other major MLM used on the Internet to manage mailing lists is Majordomo. This is freeware, very well maintained and with good documentation and support via the mailing lists of users and developers. Nearly all the features provided by LISTSERV are also provided by Majordomo, although the commands to access them have different syntax. One major difference is that Majordomo does not provide the equivalent of the general LISTSERV address and all its related features, like global search or global management.

Majordomo lists are maintained by Majordomo servers, which handle all functionalities. A number of Web interfaces and archive tools exist which work well with Majordomo.

Majordomo exists on UNIX and is written entirely as a script (in Perl). Thus if an operating system can run Perl then it can also run Majordomo. Most of the information, documentation and support for running and using Majordomo is available from **http://www.greatcircle.com/majordomo/**.

Sending commands to Majordomo

All Majordomo functions can be accessed through e-mail commands that are placed in the body of the message, and again it should be remembered that e-mail commands go to the Majordomo e-mail address, not to the mailing list address.

A Majordomo e-mail address takes the form `Majordomo@<domain>`, where `<domain>` is the same as the domain part of the mailing lists managed by that installation. 'Majordomo@garr.it' is the installation at 'garr.it', and all mailing lists managed by it will have addresses like <listname>@garr.it (for example, announces@garr.it). With Majordomo it is also possible to access some of the functions via the Web, for instance reading message archives and subscribing:

Majordomo will ignore the 'Subject': line of the mail messages sent to its e-mail address, so commands must be in the body of the message. Several commands can be sent in the same mail message, with each command on a separate line. Here is an example of an e-mail sent (using PINE) to the Majordomo address asking for the 'HELP' file.

```
PINE 4.44 COMPOSE MESSAGE Folder: INBOX 23 Messages
To: Majordomo@garr.it
Cc:
Attchmnt:
Subject: this line is unimportant!
----- Message Text -----
help


^G Get Help ^X Send ^R Rich Hdr ^Y PrvPg/Top ^K Cut Line
^O Postpone
^C Cancel ^D Del Char ^J Attach ^V NxtPg/End ^U UnDel
Line ^T To AddrBk
```

Subscribing and unsubscribing to a public Majordomo mailing list

Anyone with access to e-mail can join a public Majordomo list. For example, to subscribe to the mailing list named 'Public-news' existing on the server named 'garr.it', send a message to the address Majordomo@garr.it and in the first and only line of the message text write SUBSCRIBE Public-news.

Receiving the above command, Majordomo subscribes the address that appears in the 'From:' line of the message. Depending on the configuration that was given by the list owner, in some cases the subscriber can also tell Majordomo which e-mail address to subscribe (for example 'John.Smith@mydom.com') overriding the one appearing in the 'From:' line. To obtain this, add the e-mail address to the end of the command SUBSCRIBE:

```
SUBSCRIBE Public-news John.Smith@mydom.com
```

To remove an e-mail address from a mailing list, the command to send is UNSUBSCRIBE <listname>, replacing <listname> with the actual name of the list.

If the address that needs to be unsubscribed is different from the one appearing in the 'From:' field of the e-mail (and if the list owner enabled this feature), specify the address at the end of the line UNSUBSCRIBE <listname> <address>.

For example `UNSUBSCRIBE Public-news John.Smith@mydom.com`.

How to find the appropriate Majordomo mailing list

Majordomo does not have the equivalent of the `LIST GLOBAL` command of LISTSERV so other tools, like Web searching tools, have to be used to identify the mailing list a subscriber might be interested in. Remember that many of the major mailing lists in the Internet are managed via Majordomo.

Some useful Majordomo commands

Here is a short list of other useful commands that can be sent to Majordomo.

- `WHO <listname>` send a list of subscribers belonging to the mailing list.
- `INFO <listname>` send me information about the `<listname>` mailing list. This command will send the special file that the list owner composed to describe the mailing list.
- `LISTS` send a list of lists maintained by the server.
- `WHICH` send the list of lists where my e-mail address is subscribed.
- `INDEX <listname>` send a list of archive files for this list.
- `GET <listname> <filename><filetype>` send me this archive file named belonging to listname.

Some Majordomo examples

EXAMPLES

- To subscribe to the 'Public-news' list at 'garr.it', send the command `SUBSCRIBE Public-news` to Majordomo@garr.it.
- To leave the INFO-VMS mailing at the node lists.cern.ch, send the command `UNSUBSCRIBE INFO-VMS` to Majordomo@lists.cern.ch which manages the INFO-VMS.
- To leave all the Majordomo lists on a specific Majordomo server, send the command `UNSUBSCRIBE *`.
- To retrieve the file 'Public-news.9902' (very likely the February 1999 archive of the Public-news mailing list) send the command `GET Public-news Public-news.9902` to the Majordomo server that holds this file.
- To contact the manager of the Majordomo installation at 'garr.it', send the enquiry to `Majordomo-owner@garr.it` and the e-mail will be directed to the appropriate individual.
- To contact the owner of the 'Public-news' mailing list, again running at 'garr.it', send the enquiry to `Public-news-owner@garr.it` and again the e-mail will be automatically forwarded to the appropriate individual.

Web and archive tools for Majordomo

There are a number of Web based interfaces for Majordomo. One of the most commonly used freeware Web interfaces is MajorCool, which can be found at **http://www.conveyanced.com/MajorCool**.

To handle a Majordomo (or virtually any) e-mail archive via the Web, use MHonArch which is available at **http://www.oac.uci.edu/indiv/ehood/ mhonarc.html**.

These are just two examples. Searching around the Web will provide a large number of additional tools that can be used in conjunction with Majordomo and other mailing list managers.

Finding more information on Majordomo

All Majordomo documentation manuals are available on the Web at **http://www.greatcircle.com/majordomo**.

6.3 USENET NEWS

Usenet News, also known as News, is a forum for group discussion, providing distribution and archiving of messages (also called articles) posted to topic-based newsgroups. There are tens of thousands of newsgroups on almost any subject you can think of. The main broad categories for organization of newsgroups are:

- alt (alternative);
- comp (computing;)
- misc (miscellaneous);
- news (related to the News system itself);
- rec (recreational);
- sci (science);
- soc (social);
- talk (just a talking forum).

Within each of these categories is a hierarchical ranking of subcategories. Furthermore, main national hierarchies (e.g. hr for Croatian news tree) exist. Discussions in groups that belong to these hierarchies are usually led in the national language of that news tree.

News is an old Internet service still used for group asynchronous communication, although communities created around a newsgroup are less tightly knit than is the case with mailing lists.

Usenet newsgroups are propagated around the world through a system of newsfeeds to News hosts. With over 30 000 newsgroups currently in existence and the sum total of daily postings amounting to hundreds of megabytes, it is not surprising that organizations running News hosts commonly opt for limited newsfeeds, comprising just a selection of newsgroups. For the same reason, messages may be stored for only a few days, before they are discarded to make room for fresh News.

6.3.1 Accessing Usenet News

Newsgroups can be read at thousands of sites (News servers) around the world. From the user's point of view, one of the major differences between mailing lists and News is that mailing list messages arrive in a mailbox whereas newsgroup messages wait for the reader to come to them. In that sense, reading News is more similar to accessing information via Web browsing than to reading e-mail. However, while the information on the Web is specific to the server visited, the information in newsgroups is the same, whichever server is accessed.

Users read messages using a newsreader program. Some WWW browsers come with a built-in newsreader or a dedicated newsreader program may be used. Also some MUAs, like PINE, have a built-in newsreader.

The newsreader accesses the local (or remote) News host using Network News Transfer Protocol (NNTP) enabling as many newsgroups and their contents as required to be pulled down. The newsreader keeps track of which articles in each newsgroup have been read, so the next time the same newsgroup is accessed, these can easily be skipped. If a newsgroup that the human reader is interested in is not taken at their site, a request for it can be placed with the local News administrator. If a reader does not know if their site has News access, check with the local computer support staff. If there is no local News access, there are also publicly accessible newsgroup archives on the Web through **http://groups.google.com/**.

6.3.2 News coverage

Users sending a News message post it to a particular newsgroup. In addition to the main categories mentioned above, there are categories based on particular subject areas (for example bionet, biz and vmsnet), geographical areas, organizations or commercial interests. A fee is usually charged for access to commercial newsgroups. There are newsgroups on subjects ranging from education for the disabled to *Star Trek*, and from environmental science to politics in the former Soviet Union. The quality of the discussion in newsgroups may be excellent, but this is not guaranteed. Some newsgroups have a moderator who scans the messages for the group and decides which are appropriate for distribution.

Newsgroups can provide a useful source of information and help on technical topics, for example on software bugs. They commonly offer an associated list of frequently asked questions (FAQ) to avoid saturating the group with repetitions of the same questions. If the FAQ cannot answer a question, users can post it to the newsgroup and an expert somewhere in the world can often supply the answer.

New News users are encouraged to check the following newsgroups:

- news.announce.newusers;
- news.newusers;
- news.* (how to find a News group that interests you);
- *. answers (usually has FAQs).

For a detailed explanation see the article *What_is_Usenet?* in one of the following periodical postings:

- news.announce.newusers;
- news.admin.misc;
- news.answers. (This is a special-purpose News group dedicated to holding the range of FAQ documents from all newsgroups.)

A searchable archive of all the FAQs from news.answers is available from the Internet FAQ archive at **http://www.faqs.org/faqs/**.

Most, if not all, newsreaders provide the same basic functions:

- selecting a newsgroup of interest – newsreading software will make these groups immediately accessible, so that their contents can be read quickly and easily;
- subscribing to newsgroups;
- unsubscribing from newsgroups – removing groups from an easy access list;
- reading newsgroup postings – newsreaders display new messages or postings and keep track of which postings have and have not been read;
- tracking the threads of discussion – replies to a posting are grouped with the original posting, so that the human reader can follow the messages within a newsgroup which are part of a particular discussion or topic;

- posting to newsgroups – readers can participate in group discussions and know where to send their postings, which will appear, after some time, as a News article world-wide;

- responding to a posting – readers can send a response to the newsgroup (often called follow-up) or privately to the author of a posting (often called reply).

For information about News tools and information for users see the Swiss Education and Research Network (SWITCH), NetNews Homepage at **http://www.switch.ch/netnews/netnews.html**.

Usenet news is also the Internet service where the concept of 'correct user behaviour on the network' (also known as netiquette) was first developed. Thus, before becoming an active News user who posts articles, have a look at the summary of nettiquette do's and don'ts at **http://www.ietf.org/rfc/rfc1855.txt**.

6.3.3 Newsreader programs

While in the past stand-alone newsreader programmes were often used, it is now common to obtain this functionality by using Web browsers such as Netscape and Internet Explorer, which include newsreading software and support News protocol. For instance, Microsoft Internet Explorer uses Outlook Express to view and post to News.

The first step in accessing News is to download the list of available newsgroups. This can be a very large list depending on the News host. The user then selects the newsgroups to which they wish to subscribe. Thereafter these will be the ones that will be downloaded by default. With a subscription in place, the user can now access the articles that are currently held for each of the newsgroups, read them and post new articles.

Similarly, those who use the PINE mail user agent for their e-mail can also use it for reading favourite newsgroups in a totally transparent way. They will see the list of newgroups, read news and post answers exactly as they would normally read e-mail.

As previously mentioned, those without a newsreader can access the service and participate in the News discussions on **http://groups.google.com**. This service, in addition to containing searchable archives of postings from more than 30 000 newsgroups, offers a Web interface to News. Registered users can participate in discussion needing only a Web browser.

6.4 TRANSFERRING FILES

FTP is the traditional facility for transferring files between host computers on the Internet. It really refers to a type of communications protocol, that is a set of communicating conventions used by the computers involved in a transaction, although people often use the term FTP to mean the FTP software (described below) that uses this protocol. FTP, like other older protocols on the Internet (for example telnet), has some security problems as it might send user passwords 'in clear' around the network. For such reasons we suggest that you use, whenever available, more secure methods for file transfer, like Secure CoPy (SCP) or Secure FTP (SFTP).

6.4.1 FTP software

FTP software is normally already available on any host connected to the Internet, and is also freely available for most operating systems and platforms on the Internet. In addition, the FTP protocol is incorporated into other types of programs, including WWW browsers and Web authoring programs, that can also be used to transfer files. A login and password may be required to establish an FTP connection to a privately operated remote computer, although many public archives permit 'anonymous' FTP access by anyone, i.e. without specifying any real password. As previously mentioned, the use of the FTP software should be limited to these public archives. For security reasons, SCP or SFTP should be used for accessing private FTP servers.

6.4.2 Using FTP Software

The major use of FTP is clear from its name – it is a tool for transferring files over the Internet, both between individual users and between users and some public services. Security will generally be provided by the use of a password. From the user's perspective file transfer is possible in two directions, sending and receiving – also called uploading and downloading respectively – between the client computer and a remote FTP server. The description in this section is limited to the two most common uses of FTP – retrieving software from public archives, and uploading Web documents to a Web server.

Retrieving (downloading) files

In some cases, an FTP link on a Web page may provide a direct link to a file which can be downloaded. If this is provided, the user can click on the link, and may be unaware that transfer by FTP is taking place, apart from for the fact that clicking to the link does not display a new Web page, but prompts the user about saving a file on the local disk.

Alternatively, a reference to a file on a public FTP site which takes the form: `ftp://domain/path/filename` can be typed into the address bar of your Web browser. This tells the browser all it needs to know to retrieve the file. An example of what a user might type into the browser address bar is: `ftp://ftp.nic.it/rfc/rfc1405.txt`. This action will initiate downloading the file named 'rfc1405.txt', located in directory '/rfc' from the host named 'ftp.nic.it', using FTP protocol, with an 'anonymous' login and dummy password.

While it is most likely that FTP operations are encountered starting from Web browser sessions, the traditional use of FTP is via dedicated FTP software. Some examples follow:

- The command line based FTP program, where `ftp` is typed at the prompt – the utility used on UNIX (including Linux and Mac OS X) and from the command prompt MS-DOS window in Windows.
- WS_FTP for Windows, a graphics based FTP.
- Fetch for Apple Mac running the old Apple Mac OS prior to version X.

These clients provide more flexibility and control. For instance, such packages normally allow the retrieval of multiple files in one transaction, or the viewing of a list of existing files on the remote server. Using the dedicated command line FTP client to download the same file as in the above example, the command sequence will be (user input is in bold typeface):

```
ftp ftp.nic.it
Connected to ftp.nic.it.
220 ftp.nic.it ANONYMOUS ONLY FTP (Version 6 mjr) ready.
Name (ftp.nic.it:mary): anonymous
331 Guest login ok, send ident as password.
Password: John@mydomain.com (this is usually not echoed on
the screen)
230 Guest login ok, access restrictions apply.
Remote system type is UNKNOWN.
ftp> cd rfc
250 CWD command successful.
ftp> get rfc1405.txt
local: rfc1405.txt remote: rfc1405.txt
227 Entering Passive Mode (193,205,245,12,7,112)
```

```
200 PORT command successful.
150  Opening  ASCII  mode  data  connection  for  rfc1405.txt
(33885 bytes).
100% |*************************************| 34951 8.45 kb/s
00:00 ETA 226 Transfer complete.
34951 bytes received in 00:04 (8.44 kb/s)
ftp> quit
```

Uploading files to a remote computer

FTP software is often used to transfer files from a local computer to a remote server. For example, Web pages are often composed on a PC and then transferred using FTP to the Web server. Some Web authoring packages include an FTP facility for this purpose. FTP software typically allows the user to list, delete and rename files on the remote computer, and to view and alter remote file permissions.

When logging in to a remote computer to upload files, users need to specify a logon name and password to access a specific file area rather than the general FTP file area which is open to all.

Netscape has a basic FTP upload facility built-in which is used by typing into the address bar `ftp://username@domain/path`. Also the traditional command line FTP allows files to be uploaded (put) onto remote computers. See the examples below for both modes of operation.

6.4.3 General aspects of using FTP

Whichever FTP tool is used, the following are required:

- the name of the host computer (the domain name or IP address);
- the location of file (the path);
- the filename.

When an FTP connection is established using a client program, a username and password will be requested by the remote host. If it is a computer on which the user has an account, they will need to supply their normal username and password. For public FTP sites the following convention is used for guest access:

- log on with the user-id 'anonymous';
- enter your own e-mail address as the password (this is the normal convention not a universal mandatory rule).

Once successfully logged on, the user may then need to specify one of two modes of transfer:

- ASCII (plain text);
- binary.

This setting may need altering if it is discovered that files, once transferred, are unusable at the receiving end. Use the ASCII transfer option for plain-text files such as HTML files, postscript and anything produced with a plain-text editor. Use binary for all other file types such as word-processed, database, spreadsheets, graphics, compressed files and executables. If binary files are transferred in ASCII mode, the transfer may not be successful and the file may be corrupted. Some FTP software can automatically detect and set the necessary transfer mode.

FTP examples

EXAMPLES

Downloading a file from a public FTP archive with a Web browser

The file `wsftp32.zip` is located in the public directory `/pub/mirror/win95/winsock-1/FTP/` on the FTP server `ftp.uni-magdeburg.de`

To FTP it using a Web browser, type the following into the address bar, `ftp://ftp.uni-magdeburg.de/pub/mirror/win95/winsock-1/FTP/ws_ftp32.zip`

Depending on how its preferences have been set, the browser will save the file to disk, unzip it automatically, or ask what user action should be taken.

Using Netscape to upload files

A Web browser can be used to upload files to the user's filespace on a server, providing they do not mind sending their password in a URL. Suppose the username is 'xenon' on the FTP server `sun1.ucs.tam.org` and the user's directory is `/user/xenon`.

In the browser address bar, type `ftp://xenon@sun1.ucs.tam.org/user/xenon`.

There will then be a prompt for a password, and when that has been accepted, there will be a Web page listing the items in that directory. The files can then be transferred into the directory by dragging and dropping their icons into the page. Alternatively this can be done in one step by using `ftp://xenon:password@sun1.ucs.tam.org/user/xenon`.

Using FTP to download / upload files

This uses the traditional FTP command line interface to download/upload files to a
remote computer, for example into an anonymous upload area, or into a specific
user account. It is also simple and straightforward. Here is an example of carryng
out the same operation as above for user 'xenon', but without Netscape.

```
ftp
sun1.ucs.tam.org
Connected to
sun1.ucs.tam.org.
220 sun1.ucs.tam.org
FTP (Version 6.2) ready.
Name (sun1.ucs.tam.org:mary): xenon
331 xenon OK send password.
Password:
yourpassword (this is usually not echoed on the screen)
230 xenon login ok.
Remote system type is Solaris.
ftp> pwd (this is just to check were we are before proceeding)
250 /usr/user/xenon
ftp>get file1.txt (we download from remote computer the
file file1.txt)
local: file1.txt
remote: file1.txt
227 Entering Passive Mode (193,205,245,12,7,112)
200 PORT command successful.
150 Opening ASCII mode data connection for file1.txt
(12538 bytes).
100%
|************************************| 12538 6.45 kb/s
00:00 ETA
226 Transfer complete.
34951 bytes received in 00:02 (7.41 kb/s)
ftp> put newfile1.txt (we upload to the remote computer
the file newfile1.txt)
local: newfile1.txt
remote: newfile1.txt
227 Entering passive mode; use PORT (193,205,245,12,14,222)
150 ASCII Store of /usr/user/xenon/newfile1.txt started.
100% |************************************| 14870
201.81 kb/s --:-- ETA
```

```
226 Transfer completed. 14870 (8) bytes transferred.
14870 bytes sent in 00:00 (59.68 kb/s)
ftp> quit
```

6.4.4 Further information about FTP

There are a number of extensive FTP archives such as: The Swedish University Network's FTP Archive at **http://ftp.sunet.se/**.

The user can also find FTP files using many Web search tools such as:

- AllTheWeb.com **http://www.alltheWeb.com/**
- Filesearching.com **http://www.filesearching.com/**
- TILE.NET/FTP **http://www.tile.net/ftp/**

For further detailed information on FTP commands, refer to Using FTP (Section 6.4.2) in **http://www.ietf.org/rfc/rfc2151.txt** or use the online help included with FTP software.

Accessing heavily used sites

Commonly, FTP sites that are heavily used or that have a widely dispersed user group will be mirrored. This means that the whole structure and contents of the archive will be duplicated elsewhere. This distributes the load on the server, and makes retrieving files more efficient for users. Regular automated updating ensures that the mirror site is in step with the original collection. The UK Mirror Service can be found at: **http://www.mirror.ac.uk/**.

Where there is a choice of sites offering the same software, it is usually a good idea to retrieve from the nearest site. It is faster for the user and good for the network environment. For instance, if the user is in Europe, give preference to a European site over an American one.

7

NETWORK TOOLS FOR USERS

More and more users find themselves in the situation of having to self-administer their own computer. Some general networking knowledge and possession of networking tools can therefore be helpful.

This chapter provides general information about networking concepts such as: network components (switches, routers and so on), the way all the components work together, how hosts can be identified by an IP address and the protocols used. Detailed examples of several TCP/IP tools, including the results of real sessions using them, are also provided. The topics discussed are:

- Ethernet, LAN concepts
- TCP/IP protocol
- Client–server and peer-to-peer model
- DNS
- Network tools: ping, traceroute and others.

7.1 BASIC NETWORKING CONCEPTS

The first time you connect a computer to a new network, you will use some programs to give it a configuration and enable basic network services. On other occasions, your computer might experience network connectivity problems – again you can use some programs to investigate the problem. These programs, named network tools, enable you to set the network parameters, check whether they are working properly, test if other computers (hosts) can be reached by IP address and by name. The tools enable the user to narrow down where problems might be and decide who to contact.

Business computers are typically connected to the Internet through their institution or corporate LAN. Home-based computers establish the connection via a link to an ISP. Additionally, 'nomadic' users utilize 'visitors' networks from a hotel room or from a conference 'terminal room' or even when on the move. In an institution or a corporate LAN, computers are usually configured by the network administrators, who can also provide help and support.

In other situations (home or nomadic) obtaining help from net support staff might not always be a viable or timely solution. Thus, knowing at least some basics about network tools might help users to understand the nature of a network connectivity problem and isolate it; sometimes even solve it, or at least find who to contact, i.e. those responsible for the support of the service that is not functioning.

In order to better interpret the output produced by network tools, knowledge of some network basics is required. So, before dealing with 'how to' use network tools, some idea of what network concepts are about will be introduced.

The global Internet architecture will be briefly presented, without giving details about design or implementation, in order to explain how your desktop computer communicates on the network and, conversely, what might be the problem when it cannot communicate. Basic Internet-related terms and acronyms will be defined along the way.

7.1.1 Network components and structure

A computer network can be defined as a set of nodes and links that provide the data transport infrastructure. Basic building blocks are routers, switches and circuits (lines, links, connections). The way they are interconnected forms the network topology. Smaller networks are (inter)connected to each other, and together they form the Internet network.

The Internet is thus a network of networks. Its global architecture allows for seamless interconnection of different (heterogeneous) networks all of which use the Internet Protocol (IP).

The Internet grew from a small US-based research network interconnecting a scientific research and government wide-area network to a global academic network. Now with commercial development it has grown to its current status, where the interconnected networks of ISPs compose the largest part of the infrastructure.

A distinction can be made between the 'edge' networks, and the 'backbone' networks. Computers (hosts) that are the source or destination of the data are connected to the edge networks (e.g. a campus, a corporate network or via an ISP point-of-presence). The backbone networks that provide the transport function are shared by many edge networks and are made of high bandwidth links and high-speed routers. An edge network is connected to a backbone network through a router, usually one so-called 'upstream' router, and its associated link, called the 'last mile' in the network path.

Backbone networks must offer high grade network performance in order to sustain the cumulative traffic generated by all the edge networks connected to them. However, it is important to consider the 'last mile' link between the backbone and the edge network, as well as the link that connects the user computer to the edge network.

The growth of network traffic nowadays (from text-only mail, telnet or gopher to downloading images, audio and video files, streaming video conferencing or moving huge scientific data sets) not only requires an increase in backbone network capacity, but also those 'last miles' need to be adequately upgraded.

For institution or corporate users, their computers are usually connected to the office LAN via (Fast)Ethernet or wireless services. This already provides high bandwidth 'intranet' access to internal services, as well as bandwidth for access from the LAN to the global Internet. Nevertheless, the 'last mile' (LAN-to-Internet link) needs to be correctly dimensioned. On the other hand, for home-based computers, the 'last mile' problem link to their ISP is more accentuated, since high-speed links can be prohibitively costly. In the past, the choice was between modem and ISDN dial-in connection to the ISP, while at present a shift is happening towards using broadband, xDSL (Digital Subscriber Line) and other high-speed solutions. Where the 'last mile' cannot be potentiated (e.g. for cellular phones as devices to access the network), network traffic needs to be reduced (e.g. WAP protocol to access Web data). The topology of the network is not static – there is constant growth, both of edge networks and backbone networks. So not only is the network itself growing in size, but also the internal interconnectivity of the network is becoming more densely meshed.

The up-to-date view of the network is very complex, and usually the network looks different if you look at it from a different point. This is why the question 'Where do I find a map of the Internet' has no answer! Inside routers, the routing tables hold the information needed to forward the data traffic correctly. However, this is not a full picture of the network, just the minimum information to decide on the next hop along a complex path. Only a few routers inside the backbone have a wider vision of the network connectivity, even if this is, again, not enough to draw a full map.

The path (route) that data takes on its way from source to destination is also dynamic. Usually there are many paths that lead from a given source to a given destination, and the actual path is selected by routers. In the case of connectivity problems in one link, traffic to the same destination can be re-routed through a different path. This is one of the strengths of the Internet, and was also one of its major design goals.

7.1.2 Protocols and standards

The many different networks that make up the Internet are highly interoperable thanks to the fact that all the participating nodes utilize common sets of rules for communication – protocols. Protocols are formal rules of data communication and define both the format of the data and the method by which it is interchanged.

In the Internet network the TCP/IP protocol suite is used. TCP/IP is named after the two most important protocols in the suite – Transmission Control Protocol (TCP) and Internet Protocol (IP). The management of the Internet protocols is taken care of by the Internet Engineering Task Force (IETF), under the guidance of its steering committee, the Internet Engineering Steering Group (IESG) and its architecture board – the Internet Architecture Board (IAB). The IETF is the primary standard–setting body for Internet technologies. For more information see **http://www.ietf.org**.

The specification documents of the Internet protocol suite, as defined by the IETF, are published in the Request For Comments (RFC) document series at **http://www.rfc-editor.org**. Among these, the 'For Your Information' (FYI): **http://www.rfc-editor.org/fyi-index.html** is very useful. FYI contains information that does not deal directly with setting standards; rather, it contains information of a more general nature. The FYI topics range from historical to explanatory to tutorial, and are aimed at the wide spectrum of people who use the Internet.

7.1.3 Client/server and peer-to-peer model

Hosts on the network may have either client or server functions (or both). Client computers do not offer any service to others, they run application programmes that collect data from server(s) and present it to the user. Servers are bigger computers that offer one or more services by continuously running dedicated 'server' programmes (applications) that listen for and respond to clients' requests. Broadly speaking, applications can be anything from e-commerce and shopping, to banking, education, healthcare, and so on. More specifically applications would be various servers – e-mail server, Web server, file transfer, database server and so on. Server computers must be configured to have a well-known address for them to be always accessible.

The other model of communication between computers is peer-to-peer (P2P), where application services do not reside on a server, but hosts communicate directly and exchange information with each other. An example is where each host makes available to the others some files it owns, and at the same time can access files hosted by the others. Another example is distributed videoconferencing, where every user can see all the other participants at the same time.

Protocol layers

There are several theoretical models introducing 'protocol layers' in order to describe the different steps performed during the interaction between an application and its underlying network (see RFC 791 and its updates). A simplified view would define three broad layers only: one for network transport infrastructure; one for the real applications; and the layer in between. The layered structure helps not only in the implementation of the network protocol, but also in the process of fault isolation.

7.1.4 Addressing and routing

IP addressing and routing conventions are part of the IP protocol. Addressing is used to uniquely identify hosts, while routing is used for host-to-host communication in determining the path a packet must take, based on the receiving host IP address. (A 'packet' is a unit for data transmission at the network layer.)

Internet address space is a set of globally (worldwide) unique numbers. The task of assigning addresses is an administrative duty which ensures that no two networks would attempt to use the same network address in the Internet. In order to manage the address space, registration is necessary. The address registrations are undertaken by Regional Internet Registries (RIRs) (see ICANN, **http://www.icann.org**). RIRs are responsible for address allocation and this must be done with care. RIRs keep track of IP number allocation and contact persons; this information is available online in the 'whois' database, which can be interrogated with the `whois` command (see Section 7.2.7) , or via RIRs' Web.

IP address

Users normally refer to machines and services using 'names' (see Section 7.1.10), but when computers make network connections these names are immediately translated to numeric IP addresses, which are used in composing the network packets.

The traditional IP address (also called IPv4, standing for IP version 4) is a 32-bit (4 bytes) number that uniquely identifies a network interface on a host. While a host usually has one network interface (and one IP address), sometimes it is equipped with more network interfaces (multi-homed host). The IPv4 address space is capable of addressing a theoretical maximum of $2^{32} = 4\,294\,967\,296$ distinct IP numbers (hosts).

An IP address is commonly written in the so called Internet standard 'dot notation', as four (decimal) numbers, separated by dots for example 192.87.30.2. Each number can have maximum value of 255.

IP address space thus runs from 0.0.0.0 to 255.255.255.255. Some of the numbers are reserved for special purposes. Others are assigned to customers, usually in blocks/ranges, for example TERENA has the range 192.87.30.0 – 192.87.30.255 (as reported by whois command).

IP has an addressing structure which developed as a two-level hierarchy in both addressing and routing. One part of the address, the network part, identifies a particular network that a host is connected to. The other part, the local part, identifies the particular end host on that network. Internet routing, then, has to deal only with the network part of the address, routing the packet to a router directly connected to the destination network. The local part is not used at all in Internet routing itself, rather it is used to determine the intended host on the destination network.

Historically Internet addresses also had 32 bits – the first 8 bits providing the network part and the remaining 24 bits the local part. With this setup it was possible to address a maximum of 256 networks. These addresses were used for many years, but then it became necessary to adapt the address architecture to allow more networks to be connected.

The IP address space was then segmented in such a way to provide three classes (named A, B and C of size large, medium and small) of network addresses (classful addressing). However, with the accelerating growth of the Internet two problems appeared:

- the rapid depletion of address space, due to the crude classful divisions;
- and the uncontrolled growth of the Internet routing table, due to unaggregated routing information (a large number of routes for a large number of different networks to be reached).

In order to resolve some of the problems of classful addressing, the technique of subnetting was invented. It provided another level of addressing hierarchy by inserting a subnet part into the IP address between the network and local parts.

The length of the subnet part of the IP address is determined by the subnet mask (netmask), which in binary notation has 1s at positions where masking is needed, and 0s at positions that are not masked, but represent the local part of the address. TCP/IP protocol can then easily determine which IP addresses are local (and can be delivered immediately) and which are remote (to be handed to the outbound router). Each computer configured with TCP/IP must now have a subnet mask defined. Computing a subnet mask is usually done by system administrators or ISPs, and you just need to configure it together with the IP address. Netmasks are usually written as four decimal numbers or in hexadecimal notation. An example netmask is 255.255.255.224 (ffffffe0 in hexadecimal).

Later, subnetting was no longer sufficient to keep up with Internet growth and the supernetting technique was introduced, under the name classless inter-domain routing (CIDR). This is, however, totally transparent to users, and there is nothing more than the usual IP address and netmask to configure.

ISPs play an important role in address space distribution – they are delegated large segments of the IP address space, which they then assign to their customers, again in contiguous segments of just about the size necessary for the customer's network.

7.1.5 Routing

Routers connect different networks, forward IP traffic and determine which path it takes. Per-packet processing is performed at routers. The IP header of the packet is examined and routing decisions are made based on the destination IP address and the current state of the network connectivity. The latter is held and constantly maintained by the router, in the form of routing information, which accurately reflects the forwarding state of the network.

For example, routing information for a 'customer' (or 'edge') network describes the reachability of it in the form of the so-called 'routing advertisement', which is propagated throughout the whole Internet. The growth of routing tables is one of the problems in the current IP protocol, which will be resolved in its future version (see Section 7.1.8).

7.1.6 NAT

When a new 'edge' network is to be added to the Internet, it must first obtain and register a range of public, but globally unique IP addresses for its hosts. The size of the registered range must be large enough to accommodate the number of hosts currently used and the possible growth of this number in the near future. However, the range cannot be arbitrarily large, since the total Internet address space would be entirely consumed with such assignments. Additionally, starting with a small range and then requesting the expansion of that range at a later date is not possible. This is because adjacent ranges are not reserved (are not 'waiting'), but are assigned to other 'edge' networks in the meantime. It is possible to apply for an entirely new and larger address range, but this implies renumbering (reconfiguring the IP address) of all network hosts. Renumbering also happens when the ISP providing network backbone connectivity is changed.

Network address translation (NAT) was developed as a short-term solution to the problem of public IP address space consumption. The idea is simple – basically an 'edge' network does not use a large range of public IP addresses, but a range of so-called 'private' addresses that are used internally. Only a small range of public IP addresses is used, for external visibility on the general Internet. The internal range can be as large as a class A network, while the external range can be as small as one single IP address shared by all. The translation between the internal and the external addresses is performed on the edge of the network by a NAT device. The conversion takes place for each IP packet, both incoming and outgoing. The internal addresses are normal IP addresses in all their aspects, but are assigned from a pool of IP addresses reserved for NAT and private IP networks purposes.

There are three private address ranges (as defined by RFC1918), of different size:

- 10.0.0.0 – 10.255.255.255;
- 172.16.0.0 – 172.31.255.255;
- 192.168.0.0 – 192.168.255.255.

If the IP address you are using belongs to one of these ranges, then either you are on a network which does not communicate with the Internet, or you are behind a NAT.

These addresses were allocated for use by private networks that either do not require external access or require limited access to outside services. Enterprises can freely use these addresses to avoid obtaining registered public addresses. But, because private addresses can be used by many within their own realm, they are non-routable over a common infrastructure of the global Internet. When communication between a privately addressed host and a public network (like the Internet) is needed, address translation is required, as described above.

NAT exists in a variety of configurations (static NAT, dynamic NAT, NAPT) depending on how the translation takes place. NAT works by creating bindings between addresses and storing them in a NAT table.

In the simplest case, known as 'static NAT', a one-to-one mapping is defined between public and private addresses. Large networks use this technique, which is not an address sharing solution but is still a way of saving IP addresses that are otherwise wasted in subnets.

More often, a pool of public IP addresses is shared by an entire IP subnet. This is called 'dynamic NAT' since bindings between private and public addresses are created dynamically – when a private host initiates a connection, it is assigned a public address from a pool. Connections may be rejected when the pool is exhausted, if previous connections are not terminated, so access by other clients is blocked. Since public addresses are assigned to internal hosts at unpredictable times and in random order, this solution can not be used for servers that need to be reachable at a known public address (the one associated with its DNS entry) from the general Internet.

A variation of dynamic NAT, known as 'network address port translation' (NAPT), may be used to allow many hosts to share a single IP address. All the outgoing connections from the private hosts are sent out with the same IP address, but with a different outgoing port number (See Section 7.1.10), rewritten in packets by the NAT device. At the same time, a trace is kept in the NAT table specifying for each outgoing port number which host (its internal IP address) initiated which connection (its original port number). For inbound traffic, the NAT device uses the port mapping table to translate from the single external IP address to the clients' real local IP address. In this solution the general Internet has the visibility of one IP address, at which some services on different ports can be offered. But an additional table needs to be maintained – a virtual server table, specifying, for each service port in the incoming connections, the binding to the private IP address of the internal host that is running the service. Alternatively, servers are put on the part of the network that is not behind NAT.

NAT is commonly used by residential users having more than one host, and small businesses that share a single public IP address for outbound traffic, while blocking inbound session requests. NAT can also be used by enterprises wishing to insulate themselves from ISP address changes, or by those wanting to hide private network topology for some reason, for instance for security reasons.

The packet sender and receiver (should) remain unaware that NAT is taking place. However, NAT is not entirely transparent to the remaining network programmes and services. In fact many of these are adversely impacted by NAT. Some NAT-sensitive protocols are Kerberos, X11, remote shell, IPSec but there are many others. Whenever identification of the real single host talking to the network is required, for example, when using network security or dealing with P2P application, NAT cannot be used. Thus, if you experience permanent problems in accessing some network services, or using network security, you should first check if you are behind a NAT by examining your IP address (another possible source of problem might be the presence of a firewall between your network and the Internet).

7.1.7 DHCP

When a computer is connected to a network, networking parameters need to be configured, such as the computer IP address, network mask, address of a default route, and domain name. Each of these items must be supplied before applications can use TCP/IP.

Traditionally these parameters were configured for each computer manually, by inserting the appropriate values in predefined files (or in appropriate fields if a graphical user interface was available).

Dynamic Host Configuration Protocol (DHCP) simplifies loading parameters into the network software and permits completely automated address assignment. It allows a computer to join a new network, obtain a valid IP address and begin using it, all without the end user's or the operator's manual intervention.

A DHCP server is preconfigured to manage a set of addresses and assign them to the clients as requested. Once the DHCP service is set, joining new hosts to the network is handled automatically. This is particularly convenient in 'terminal rooms' for meetings or conferences, where a large number of guest computers need to be configured for networking, or for residential or small office users with xDSL and more than one host on their LAN.

When DHCP allocates an address automatically, the DHCP server does not assign the address forever. Instead, the server specifies a lease with a predefined period during which the address may be used. A computer must extend the lease, or stop using the address, when the lease expires. Next time a computer joins the network, it will not retain the previous IP address, but will be assigned a new one. Consequently, the computer DNS name (the one associated with the IP address) will also be new. As a result, statistics, management or security tools cannot be based on a computer name (nor an IP address), in an environment where DHCP is in use. In practice DHCP is not as disruptive to network services as NAT, but it can introduce some difficulties when you need to identify problems or use some services.

While dynamic assignment of IP addresses is fine for client computers, it is not appropriate for a server, which must be available at a known address (and a known name). DHCP accommodates both types of computers, at the additional cost of operator manual intervention in preparing the entries for hosts that need a permanent address. An administrator can configure a DHCP server to have two types of addresses:

- permanent addresses that are usually assigned to server computers (or to those with a need for a permanent address);

- a pool of addresses to be allocated on demand to all the others. When a computer boots and sends a request to DHCP, the DHCP server consults its database to find configuration information. If the database contains a specific entry for the computer, the DHCP server returns the configuration information from the entry. If no entry exists for the computer, the server selects the next IP address from the pool and assigns it to the computer.

7.1.8 IPv6

The current Internet Protocol, known as IPv4, has served well for over 20 years but it is reaching the limits of its design. It is difficult to configure, it is running out of addressing space and it provides no features for site renumbering to allow for an easy change of ISP, among other limitations. Various mechanisms have been developed to alleviate these problems (for example DHCP and NAT), but each has its own set of limitations.

The new IP version 6 (IPv6) brings a larger address space (and a new notation for it) plus more efficient routing, simpler configuration and built-in IP security.

The larger 128-bit IPv6 address (versus the 32-bit IPv4 address) allows more flexibility in designing new addressing architectures, as well as providing large enough address space for predicted future growth of the Internet and Internet-related technologies. The IPv6 address space is capable of addressing 2^{128} distinct IP numbers.

It is very likely that IPv6 addresses will first appear in devices which we currently would not normally call 'a network host', but which require an IP address and use the Internet as a communication system. Such a device is nearly any object you can think of, ranging from your microwave oven, to a surveillance video camera, or your car engine central monitoring system to your mobile communication device, all talking to servers or sharing information as P2P. Of course, computers and traditional network nodes will also use IPv6, as soon as their edge network and backbone support it.

From a user's perspective, however, IPv6 can be considered to be just a different version of the IP address to be used, and in some cases as an additional 'option qualifier' to be included when you are using network tools.

7.1.9 Network performance and problems

The Internet is stable and robust, but there are situations when connectivity is interrupted or is slow. Users then experience delays or timeouts in accessing remote services. However, there are situations where the destination server itself (e.g. Web site) can be overloaded and unresponsive, even though the network in between has adequate resources to manage the traffic load.

The main reason why network performance problems occur (apart from major breakdown of some network equipment), is the fact that a network is a dynamic system, and the delivery times of packets depend on the current traffic (much the same as the road system can not guarantee arrival time for a car, since it depends on the traffic it finds along the way).

Packets in the network are mostly delivered on a 'best effort' basis at the highest possible rate that the network can sustain, but they can also be dropped/discarded by the network. Congestion situations are handled by dropping excess packets at overloaded routers that have no more space in their transmission queue. This packet loss is sensed on the sender side and is interpreted as a performance signal, so the dropped packet gets retransmitted and the sending rate gets reduced.

Fortunately, the Internet has been designed to cope with many of the possible problems and to sense current network load conditions and dynamically adapt to them (for example, send packets along an alternative route or slow down the rate with which data is 'injected' into the network etc.).

Bandwidth (in bytes/second) is a static characteristic of a given network link. However, the round trip time (RTT) (in seconds) of the packets (sometimes called delay, or link latency) over the same link can change dynamically, depending on the current load caused by cumulative traffic over a given link and also on the destination host processing load, which may vary.

Tools presented later in this chapter will help in diagnosing situations where network performance is degraded and in understanding the nature and the location of the problem.

7.1.10 Naming systems

Names are used for identification. In a computer communications network, identifiers can refer to a variety of objects – hardware (hosts and their network interfaces), software services, persons, Web pages, files etc. All the participants involved in the communication need to be identified precisely, in order to be reached by the data. Thus, computers have IP addresses and hostnames as identifiers; software services are identified by the well-known port numbers; persons are identified by their login/usernames, their mailbox name or by a digital certificate; resources on the Web are identified by their URL etc. More generically, any object can be identified by its 'distinguished name' (DN), stored in a directory.

The various identifiers have different naming conventions (format and interpretation). Here we will discuss ports, DNS and URLs, while mail addresses are explained in Section 6.1.2.

Network services, ports

Just as TCP/IP hosts have a unique IP address, applications on the host are associated with an address, called a port. In this way many different services can be offered at the same IP address – the host can run a number of applications (server processes), each listening on its own port. A remote application is thus uniquely identified by the IP address port number couple. Although users will rarely see port numbers in the commands or applications they use, port numbers are present in the network packets and, thanks to port number specification, the data will be transported to and from the correct application. Some of the well-known TCP port numbers are:

Port number	Service
25	SMTP
110	POP3
143	IMAP
80	http
443	https
21	ftp
23	telnet
22	ssh
43	whois
119	nntp
79	finger
389	pdap

DNS

Although IP addresses alone would suffice as a means of referring to accessible sites on the Internet, they are not user-friendly (especially if you consider the new IPv6 128-bit addresses). Easier-to-remember identifiers have been introduced – the host names, along with a service that holds the mapping between the names and the corresponding IP addresses, the naming service. Additionally, names are grouped in domains for more easily distributed management and to create a globally unique public name space. This Internet naming service is known as the Domain Name System (DNS).

The DNS namespace is composed of a set of hierarchical domains arranged like the branches of an inverted tree. From one common 'root' a limited number of top-level domains branch into further subdomains at lower hierarchy levels. The 'name tree' makes every domain name unique in the entire tree.

A name, according to DNS conventions, is written as a series of labels (strings) separated by dots, starting from the most specific subdomain and continuing towards the parent domains higher in the hierarchy to the top-level domain (TLD), ending at the final dot which stands for the 'root' domain, the parent of all TLDS.

Examples of subdomain and domain names:

- terena.nl.
- ietf.org.
- ts.infn.it.
- nl. (country code TLD for The Netherlands)
- it. (ccTLD for Italy)
- org. (gTLD, general TLD)
- com. (gTLD)
- edu. (gTLD)
- biz. (recently introduced gTLD)

When the trailing dot is present, the name is said to be a 'fully qualified domain name' (FQDN). If the name supplied does not have the trailing dot, the 'default domain' name is appended to it before making the first query. Only if this fails will the DNS software make other attempts, at last adding only the final dot. However, in day-to-day use the final dot is often omitted, although a query to the DNS would find the answer much faster if it were included.

There is one TLD reserved for each country (ccTLD). There are also some traditional top-level domains (gTLD) not explicitly tied to any particular country. These include:

- com – commercial establishments;
- edu – North American educational institutions;
- org – not-for-profit organizations;
- gov – american government agencies;
- mil – MILNET hosts;
- int – International organizations;
- net – network backbones.

For information about top-level domains see **http://www.icann.org/tlds/**.

Examples of host names belonging to respective domains:

- www.terena.nl
- ftp.terena.nl
- erasmus.terena.nl

From the management perspective, the naming service is not located at one central site but is run at sites distributed worldwide to which has been delegated the authority for their respective subdomains. 'Authority' means having complete autonomy in creating names in one subdomain (both hostnames and additional subdomains can be added at deeper hierarchy levels), and having responsibility for responding to queries about the given subdomain.

If hosts on your network are going to participate in DNS, you must obtain and register a unique domain name and activate a server to support it. The registration is done with the organization that has been delegated the authority for the parent domain of the new domain being registered. For TLDS the authority has been delegated to registries as listed at ICANN, **http://www.icann.org**.

From the technical point of view two features characterize the DNS:

- it is implemented as a distributed database that holds the namespace mappings and associated information in the so-called resource records;
- it is a client–server based model, with a nameserver side (the application that maintains the data) and a resolver side (clients to interrogate the nameserver). Domains are controlled and name translations are performed by DNS servers which provide the resource records from the database in response to queries. At least one nameserver is needed to support each domain – it maintains the domain data and responds to clients about queries specific to that domain. More nameservers for the same domain are needed for service resilience (e.g. the 'root' domain that must always be available currently has 13 name servers).

The interaction between DNS server and resolver is as follows. The resolver part of the DNS runs on individual computers throughout the Internet, and is activated every time some information from DNS is needed. The resolver is configured to interrogate the nearest DNS server for all the queries it might have, which will in turn either give the reply, or interrogate other remote nameservers higher in the hierarchy, starting from the root servers and following the delegation path. There is also a caching mechanism implemented, so answers, once collected, are not discarded but are reused for a period of time.

For an example of how the delegation path is followed by a resolver from root servers to the server for a given domain, see the `dig` command in Section 7.2.5.

The majority of names contained in the DNS database refer to hosts:

- a resource record of type A defines the IP address mapped to the name;
- a resource record of type CNAME maps the canonical name and the alias of a host;
- a resource record of type PTR is a reverse pointer from the IP address to the host name.

Other records in the DNS database are 'structural' and necessary for the functioning of the DNS system itself:

- type SOA holds start-of-authority information;
- type NS defines which hosts are acting as name servers for a domain.

One other widely used resource record type is used in the process of mail delivery ('type MX' records define mail exchangers, i.e. hosts which are acting as mail servers for the domain).

For a non-technical explanation of how domain names work on the Internet see **http://www.internic.net/faqs/authoritative-dns.html**. Standard documents about domain names are: RFC 1034 and RFC 1035.

URL, URI

The World Wide Web is a network of information resources. However, this network is virtual since there are no direct physical connections between the objects on the Web (as there are in the underlying Internet network). There are mechanisms that contribute to make the objects appear to be readily available and connected to each other. One of the key mechanisms is the uniform naming scheme for locating resources on the Web – universal resource identifiers (URI) and their subset uniform resource locators (URLs).

URIs define how objects on the network are named and addressed. They are used to 'locate' resources, by providing an abstract identification of the resource location. Users point the browser at some location using an URI, which allows a Web browser to obtain files from any location on the Internet, using a variety of protocols, including HTTP, FTP, Gopher and others.

Every resource available on the Web – HTML document, image, video clip, program, etc. – has an address that may be encoded by a URI. URIs typically consist of three pieces of information:

- the naming scheme of the mechanism used to access the resource;
- the name of the machine hosting the resource;
- the name of the resource itself, given as a path.

EXAMPLES   Consider the URI that designates the FYI documents start page:

http://www.rfc-editor.org/fyi-index.html

This URI may be read as follows: there is a document available via the http protocol, residing on the host named 'www.rfc-editor.org', accessible via the path '/ fyi-index.html'.

The list below provides information on how the URI format should be interpreted for the protocols most often seen in HTML documents.

- **http://host:port/directory/file-name?searchpart** identifies a WWW server location. Port defaults to 80.
- **ftp://user:password@host:port/directory/file-name** identifies an FTP site. Port defaults to 21. If 'user:password' are omitted, the default is anonymous access to the FTP site.
- **mailto:mailname@domain** identifies an individual's Internet e-mail address.

Finding more information

- The World Wide Web Consortium Introduction to HTML 4.0 includes an introduction to URIs and URLs, at **http://www.w3.org/TR/REC-html40/ intro/intro.html**.
- A complete description of the URI and URL format may be found in RFC 1738 and its updates RFC 1808, RFC 2368 and RFC 2396.

7.2 NETWORK TOOLS

The following sections provide descriptions and detailed examples of several TCP/IP tools, including the results of actual sessions using them. Although the tools were historically intended for network administrators, more and more users find themselves in the situation of having to self-administer their own computers and need to learn how to benefit from using the network tools. Users' computers nowadays are equipped with a variety of operating systems, ranging from different flavours of Microsoft Windows and Apple MacOS, to Unix-like systems, for example, Linux, Mac OS X and others.

For the network tools described here, all these different software platforms will not be covered in detail – the focus will be on each instrument's basic functionality. The examples included are run mostly from a Unix-based platform and should suffice to get the idea of what each tool is meant for. Achieving the same functionality on other platforms should be very similar in most cases. However, for each tool presented, additional indications will be included for platform specifics wherever appropriate.

7.2.1 Troubleshooting a network problem

When you are troubleshooting a TCP/IP networking problem, you should start by checking the TCP/IP configuration on the computer experiencing the problem. With different operating systems, different commands are used to get host computer configuration information (`ifconfig`, `ipconfig`, `winipcfg`, TCP/IP control panel) and sometimes you need more than one command (for example, `ifconfig` plus `netstat`) in order to get the complete picture of the network configuration. If the TCP/IP setup seems to be correct, the next check is the configuration of the DNS servers, which provide name resolution.

If no problems appear in the TCP/IP and DNS configuration checks, the next step is testing the ability to connect to other host computers on the TCP/IP network, e.g. by using `ping`, first with IP addresses rather than with DNS names. The suggested sequence of tests is:

- ping your own host IP address itself;
- ping any other host on the same network next;
- ping your default router to see if it is up;
- ping a host on a remote network to verify that you can communicate through the router.

If the remote host cannot be reached, you might want to further investigate with Traceroute or PathPing. You might want to specify for these tools that no IP addresses should be translated with DNS while doing the initial connectivity tests.

Finally, ping a remote computer by name. If pinging by address succeeds but pinging by name fails, then the problem lies in name-to-address resolution, not network connectivity.

DNS lookup tools (`host`, `dig` and `nslookup`) can be used to check the host's ability to resolve name-to-address mappings, and to verify from which DNS server the host is getting the mapping information.

In summary, in a network troubleshooting procedure one should check the following:

- do you have an IP address?
- can you ping the host itself?
- can you ping others in your local subnet?
- do you have the default router listed in your routing table?
- can you ping the IP address of the default router?
- can you numerically ping something on the other side of the default router?
- is your system correctly pointing to a nameserver?
- can you ping the IP address of the nameserver?
- can you ping other systems by name?

If all the above network connectivity tests succeed, you can probably reach your destination or safely use network applications, e.g. a Web browser or an MUA (although they might need additional configuration parameters, like 'Web proxy' server configuration, or SMTP/POP/IMAP server addresses) and they should be able to communicate with servers on both local and remote TCP/IP networks, that is on an intranet and on the Internet respectively.

If connectivity tests fail, you can try to contact the network managers in charge of the specific service that is non-operational.

7.2.2 Command line interface

Network tools first appeared as simple text-based commands, with a command line interface (CLI), and many remain as such nowadays, although some of them have graphical or Web-based interfaces added. Not all these utilities are found at all TCP/IP hosts, but they can easily be found or installed on another computer in the same 'edge' network. For example on the same LAN, a server might be found running a multi-user operating system like Unix, Linux, Mac OS X or OpenVMS. Using the tools from such a computer would be equivalent for the purposes of the test execution.

CLI consists of giving text commands at a computer prompt and receiving text-based output. In order to do this, you first need to reach the CLI of a host and you can do this in one of the following ways:

- open a command or 'shell' window on Unix-like platforms, if located at the host's console;
- open a virtual terminal session (telnet or SSH) if located at a remote client;
- open a DOS window (command prompt) on Windows platforms.

Telnet uses TCP/IP virtual terminal protocol. Using telnet, a user can login to another host and appear to be a directly-attached terminal at the remote system. However, telnet use is deprecated for security reasons (passwords at login time travel in clear text through the network, and can be intercepted easily) and you should use SSH instead, whenever available: with SSH everything you type is sent encrypted along the network.

It might happen that some of network tools discussed here are not directly accessible by their name (e.g. on a Unix-like system are not in the user's path for commands), in which case they should be called with a full path name, e.g. `/usr/sbin/ping` instead of `ping`.

While network tools on different operating systems have the same basic functionality as described here, the actual command line may appear slightly different, since command syntax (options and arguments) are not standardized across platforms. The examples in this book focus on functionality and their most frequent way of use, rather than on full command line syntax. The command `man` (manual) on Unix-like systems, or other online help documentation might be helpful in further exploring the details on options for using commands.

To make the examples easier to understand, what the user actually types on the keyboard is shown in **bold**, while the output of the command is in normal typeface.

7.2.3 Connectivity testing tools

The tools `ping`, `traceroute` and `pathping` are intended for use in network testing, measurement and management. They should be used primarily for manual fault isolation. Because of the load they could impose on the network, it is unwise to use them during normal operations or from automated scripts. For this same reason it might be that they are not in a user's execution path by default, or even that their execution is disabled for all except the privileged user, e.g. a network administrator.

ping

Ping is a simple utility that sends probe packets (echo messages) to a destination host and reports on its reachability, along with the RTT. It uses the Internet Control Message Protocol and is responsible for detecting network error conditions and reporting on them. Ping can report on dropped packets (those arriving too quickly to be processed) and on connectivity failure (when a destination host can't be reached). For the explanation of why packets can get dropped or why RTTs to the same destination vary, see Section 7.1.9. The network host where `ping` sends its probe packets can be specified either by name or by IP address. For example, **ping erasmus.terena.nl** might geneate the response `erasmus.terena.nl is alive`. In this simple case, `ping` has sent just a few test packets and the host has responded. Otherwise, after a timeout, `ping` would have replied `no answer from host`.

However in most existing implementations the default behaviour of `ping` would be to continuously probe the destination addresses and print one line of output for every response that it receives. The packet's sequence number and the RTT are printed for every successful probe. No output line is produced if there is no response. On some platforms the 'Request Timed Out' message is displayed for such probes. If the remote system being pinged is across a high-delay link, such as a satellite link, responses may take longer to be returned, so you should specify a longer timeout. `ping` terminates after a predefined number of probes (e.g. five in Windows) or when the user interrupts it (normally with a Control-C). On termination, Ping computes RTT and packet loss statistics and displays a summary.

In the next example there is no packet loss, since there are no missing sequence numbers (`icmp_seq`). RTT times are different because of the dynamic nature of the network and its traffic.

EXAMPLES

```
ping erasmus.terena.nl
PING erasmus.terena.nl: 56 data bytes
64 bytes from erasmus.terena.nl (192.87.30.2): icmp_seq=0.
time=32. ms
64 bytes from erasmus.terena.nl (192.87.30.2): icmp_seq=1.
time=31. ms
64 bytes from erasmus.terena.nl (192.87.30.2): icmp_seq=2.
time=31. ms
```

```
64 bytes from erasmus.terena.nl (192.87.30.2): icmp_seq=3.
time=32. ms
64 bytes from erasmus.terena.nl (192.87.30.2): icmp_seq=4.
time=32. ms
64 bytes from erasmus.terena.nl (192.87.30.2): icmp_seq=5.
time=32. ms
64 bytes from erasmus.terena.nl (192.87.30.2): icmp_seq=6.
time=31. ms
^C
> ----erasmus.terena.nl PING Statistics----
7 packets transmitted, 7 packets received, 0% packet loss
round-trip (ms) min/avg/max = 31/31/32
```

In the next example, RTTS are longer, and there is some packet loss (no responses to packets from 3 to 12).

ping www.ietf.org
```
PING www.ietf.org: 56 data bytes
64 bytes  from  www.ietf.org  (132.151.6.21):  icmp_seq=0.
time=135. ms
64 bytes  from  www.ietf.org  (132.151.6.21):  icmp_seq=1.
time=258. ms
64 bytes  from  www.ietf.org  (132.151.6.21):  icmp_seq=2.
time=234. ms
64 bytes  from  www.ietf.org  (132.151.6.21):  icmp_seq=13.
time=119. ms
64 bytes  from  www.ietf.org  (132.151.6.21):  icmp_seq=14.
time=120. ms
64 bytes  from  www.ietf.org  (132.151.6.21):  icmp_seq=15.
time=120. ms
64 bytes  from  www.ietf.org  (132.151.6.21):  icmp_seq=16.
time=116. ms
64 bytes  from  www.ietf.org  (132.151.6.21):  icmp_seq=17.
time=118. ms
^C
----www.ietf.org PING Statistics----
18 packets transmitted, 8 packets received, 55% packet loss
round-trip (ms) min/avg/max = 116/152/258
```

If you make the test with a host which is far away (with respect to networks), you can see that the RTT is much longer:

ping dns5.cnnic.net.cn.
```
64 bytes from 61.139.76.53: icmp_seq=0. time=1598. ms
```

Availability

The `ping` command is installed by default on Unix systems (including Linux and Mac OS X) and on all Windows versions. On older MacOS systems a graphical equivalent named 'MacTCP Ping' exists. Ping is also available on the Web as a service. See for example **http://www.net.cmu.edu/cgi-bin/netops.cgi** (sends ten pings, and reports the times and min/max/avg summary statistics) or **http://www.uia.ac.be/cc/ping.html** (indicates whether the target host is alive or not).

`traceroute`

ping can be used for a fast check of the reachability of a host but it does not show where on the network path the problem might be, for example, where the slow or overloaded links are. For this analysis use `Traceroute`. Almost every device on the Internet supports ICMP and responds to `ping` packets, but note that some network administrators might disable the response to `ping`. Thus while a 'positive' reply from `ping` means a definite confirmation of a host being reachable, a 'negative' reply does not automatically imply that the host is unreachable. That is why using further tools is advisable when investigating possible problems.

The utility `traceroute` allows users to map the route that packets would take from their local host to another Internet host. It traces the route by sending probe packets to all the routers in the path between the source and destination, and displays the round-trip delay associated with each attempt. For more information about routing see Section 7.1.4.

The `Traceroute` tool is often used as a debugging aid, in order to find a routing or link problem. Note that it reports the route at the time of the test execution and reflects the destination reachability at that moment. It is advisable to run `traceroute` (to a couple of important remote sites) when there are no connectivity problems and save the information for reference. When problems arise, `traceroute` can be run again and its output compared with the stable situation. The minimum requirement is that you should know your default router (on your LAN) and the router next to it (at your ISP site), since they represent the 'last mile' for all your network traffic to and from the Internet.

The route is traced by first sending packets with a short time-to-live (TTL) – these expire at first router and get back to Traceroute where the name of the router so discovered is recorded. Packets are then sent out with longer TTLs and they expire at routers further away in the path. `traceroute` attempts to contact each router along the path until it either gets to the host, or it hits the maximum number of hops (default is 30).

At each attempt three probes are sent, and a line printed showing the address of the router reached (by default hostname is resolved as well), and the RTT of each probe. If there is no response within a timeout interval, a * is printed for that probe. Probes can also result in some kind of unreachability condition, in which case a specific code (!H, !N, !S, !T, !U etc.) is printed for that probe. Destination networks can result in being unreachable for a variety of reasons, see Section 7.1.9.

In the following example, `traceroute` is tracking the route to host 'erasmus.terena.nl'. The following shows the 12-hop path that a packet would follow from the host where the command was issued to the host 'erasmus.terena.nl'. The packet must travel through 11 intermediate routers the first of which is the host's default router. First hops have short RTTs, while on the internal university campus network. The eighth hop is a long link (over the ocean), so the time is necessarily longer than the others. At the tenth hop there are two very long RTTs, but they do not influence the final RTT to reach the destination host. The eleventh hop shows the IP number of the ISP TERENA is connected to, Surfnet.

EXAMPLES

```
traceroute erasmus.terena.nl
traceroute to erasmus.terena.nl  (192.87.30.2),  30  hops
max, 40 byte packets
```

1 CAMPUS-VL4.GW.CMU.NET (128.2.4.1) 1.079 ms 0.822 ms 0.712 ms

2 CORE255-VL255.GW.CMU.NET (128.2.255.12) 0.921 ms 0.740 ms 0.740 ms

3 HYPER-VL502.GW.CMU.NET (128.2.33.233) 1.434 ms 1.089 ms 0.962 ms

4 bar-cmu-ge-4-0-0-1.psc.net (192.88.115.185) 2.539 ms 1.212 ms 0.958 ms

5 beast-bar-g4-0-1.psc.net (192.88.115.18) 3.734 ms 0.871 ms 0.677 ms

6 abilene-psc.abilene.ucaid.edu (192.88.115.124) 10.365 ms 10.303 ms 10.423 ms

7 nycmng-washng.abilene.ucaid.edu (198.32.8.84) 14.737 ms 29.410 ms 27.179 ms

8 surfnet-nycmng.abilene.ucaid.edu (198.32.8.105) 103.969 ms 104.041 ms 103.799 ms

9 PO13-0.CR1.Amsterdam1.surf.net (145.145.166.61) 104.464 ms 104.009 ms 104.964 ms

10 PO0-0.AR5.Amsterdam1.surf.net (145.145.162.2) 297.593 ms 183.256 ms 257.072 ms

11 145.145.18.46 (145.145.18.46) 104.573 ms 104.492 ms 104.471 ms

12 erasmus.terena.nl (192.87.30.2) 106.568 ms 103.761 ms 106.556 ms

You can use the `traceroute` command to determine where the packets are stopped on the network. In the following partial example, the destination host is not reachable, and Traceroute prints

```
'*' or error code !H at 7th router in the path:
7 * 213.244.164.42 (213.244.164.42) 37.576 ms !H 42.247 ms !H
```

Availability

`traceroute` is installed by default on Unix-like systems. On Windows it is called 'tracert'. A graphical equivalent exists for older versions of MacOS.

The `traceroute` tool is available on the Web as a service at numerous sites. Unfortunately, these servers trace the route from their host to a host that the user chooses, rather than from the user's host to the target. Nevertheless, interesting route information can be found at **http://www.net.cmu.edu/cgi-bin/netops.cgi**, or at **http://www.traceroute.org** which holds a rich list of `traceroute` servers (often called 'looking glass' servers) from around the world.

pathping

If you are having delays on the route to some destination on the Internet, you can use the `pathping` command to attempt to see where the problem is. `pathping` combines some of the functionality of both the `ping` and `traceroute` (`tracert`) commands.

`Pathping` output will first show the hops (routers) you go through to get to the destination IP address (the equivalent of the `traceroute` functionality). Then it will send packets to every router on a path for a set period of time, and finally will compute statistics based on the packets returned from each router.

`Pathping` is useful because it allows you to see the amount of loss that occurs at any router and along any link. Hence, you can determine which routers or links might be having network problems.

EXAMPLE

```
pathping -n erasmus.terena.nl
Tracing route to erasmus.terena.nl [192.87.30.2]
over a maximum of 30 hops:
0 128.2.4.1
1 128.2.255.12
2 128.2.33.233
3 192.88.115.185
4 192.88.115.18
```

```
5 192.88.115.124
6 198.32.8.84
7 198.32.8.105
8 145.145.166.61
9 145.145.162.2
10 145.145.18.46
11 192.87.30.2
Computing statistics for 125 seconds...
Source to Here This Node/Link
Hop RTT Lost/Sent = Pct Lost/Sent = Pct Address
0 128.2.4.1
0/ 100 = 0% |
1 0.92ms 0/ 100 = 0% 0/ 100 = 0% 128.2.255.12
0/ 100 = 0% |
2 1.08ms 0/ 100 = 0% 0/ 100 = 0% 128.2.33.233
0/ 100 = 0% |
3 1.21ms 0/ 100 = 0% 0/ 100 = 0% 192.88.115.185
0/ 100 = 0% |
4 0.87ms 0/ 100 = 0% 0/ 100 = 0% 192.88.115.18
0/ 100 = 0% |
5 10.36ms 2/ 100 = 2% 0/ 100 = 0% 192.88.115.124
0/ 100 = 0% |
6 27.17ms 0/ 100 = 0% 0/ 100 = 0% 198.32.8.84
0/ 100 = 0% |
7 103.96ms 5/ 100 = 5% 0/ 100 = 0% 198.32.8.105
22/ 100 = 22% |
8 104.46ms 12/ 100 = 12% 0/ 100 = 0% 145.145.166.61
0/ 100 = 0% |
9 183.25ms 10/ 100 = 10% 1/ 100 = 1% 145.145.162.2
0/ 100 = 0% |
10 104.57ms 16/ 100 = 16% 0/ 100 = 0% 145.145.18.46
0/ 100 = 0% |
11 103.73ms 14/ 100 = 14% 0/ 100 = 0% 192.87.30.2
Trace complete.
```

In the sample report above, the 'This Node/Link', 'Lost/Sent = Pct' and 'Address' columns show that the link between 198.32.8.105 and 145.145.166.61 is dropping 22 per cent of the packets. The router at hop 9 is also dropping packets addressed to it, but this loss does not affect its ability to forward traffic that is not addressed to it.

The loss rates displayed for the links, identified as a vertical bar (|) in the 'Address' column, indicate that link congestion is causing the loss of packets being forwarded on that path. The loss rates displayed for routers indicate that these routers might be overloaded.

Availability

pathping exists on Windows 2000 and XP. For more details see: **http://www.microsoft.com/windows2000/en/server/help/pathping.htm**.

7.2.4 Tools for host network configuration

ifconfig

As already mentioned, on different operating systems different commands are used to get or set host computer network configuration information. The Ifconfig command, characteristic for Unix and Unix-like operating systems, will be used here for example purposes. Hints for other platforms are included at the end of the section.

In any case, the most important parameters to check, in order to ensure host basic network connectivity, are its IP address, subnet mask and the default router (sometimes incorrectly called the default gateway). If DHCP is used on your network, then DHCP setup should be considered among the basic parameters mentioned above.

Ifconfig (interface configuration) is used to display or configure host network interface parameters. For more information about network interfaces, IP addresses and netmasks (see Section 7.1.4). The command ifconfig is used to assign an IP address to a network interface and to configure other network interface parameters. The ifconfig command is normally used at boot time to define the address of each interface present on a machine; it may also be used at a later time to redefine an interface address or other operating parameters. If no option is specified, ifconfig displays the current configuration for a network interface. Attention has to be paid to whether or not the interface has the correct IP address ('inet' field) and network mask ('netmask' field). There are additional options for ifconfig to control the DHCP configuration of the interface.

EXAMPLES   To print out the information for all interfaces on the host, use the following command:

```
ifconfig -a
lo0: flags=1000849 mtu 8232 index 1 inet 127.0.0.1 netmask
ff000000
eri0: flags=1000843 mtu 1500 index 2 inet 216.57.215.93
netmask fffffe0 broadcast 216.57.215.95
```

Two interfaces are shown – lo0 and eri0, both up and running. lo0 is a software 'interface' (stands for 'loopback' interface) with the IP address 127.0.0.1, and is reserved for the communication with the host itself (localhost). eri0 is a hardware network interface with the IP address 216.57.215.93 and the netmask of ffffffe0 (hexadecimal notation).

The values ifconfig uses for each interface configuration are usually specified through a graphical interface or a menu-driven installation system which stores the parameters in files, from where they are read by ifconfig at each reboot of the host. Files typically involved are /etc/hosts and /etc/netmasks.

Availability

Ifconfig is usually present on Unix-like systems. On platforms in the **Windows** family of operating systems, the command to use in order to review the network configuration is not standardized and depends on the version of the operating system you are using. On newer versions (NT and after) use the ipconfig command with the /all option, which will produce a detailed configuration report for all interfaces. For older Windows 9x computers, use the winipcfg command instead.

Another way to show and repair IP configuration in Windows XP is to open **'Network Connections'** on the start menu and right click the connection that you want to check, and then choose **'Status'**.

On the **MacOS**, prior to Mac OS X, you can use the TCP/IP control panel to review or set the TCP/IP configuration, including IP address, netmask, default router and DNS configuration.

On some platforms there is the option to have more than one TCP/IP configuration for a host, each with its own set of parameters referred to by a common name. This is useful for portable computers, which often change the network they are attached to (e.g. office LAN, home dial-in connection, guest DHCP at conference etc.). So it is a matter of simply selecting a different configuration set, in order to activate new network parameters – a reboot is usually not necessary.

netstat

To complete the picture of a host's TCP/IP configuration, routing parameters also need to be checked. This can be done by the netstat utility, which can report on routing table entries. netstat can show various other parameters regarding host network status but here we shall discuss only interface status (netstat -i) in addition to routing table (netstat -r).

When `netstat` is invoked to report on a host's routing table (`netstat -r`), it will list from the table the available routes and their status. Each route consists of a destination host or network, and a gateway/router to use in forwarding packets to that destination.

In the example below three entries from a routing table are reported.

- The first entry describes how to reach other hosts on the same LAN (subnet 216.57.215.64): directly from this host (216.57.215.93) via its hardware network interface `eri0`.

- The second entry describes how to reach all other destinations, not covered by routing table entries: by sending to (default) router 216.57.215.65.

- The last routing table entry describes how to reach the host itself (localhost): via software interface `lo0`.

```
netstat -nr
```

Routing Table:

Destination	Gateway	Flags	Ref	Use	Interface
-------------	---------	-----	----	----------------	
----	----	--	--	--	--
216.57.215.64	216.57.215.93	U	1	5173	eri0
default	216.57.215.65	UG	1	14134	
127.0.0.1	127.0.0.1	UH	2	130734	lo0

Option `-n` is used to request a numerical report – that is IP addresses only, no DNS mapping to host names takes place.

Destination 'default' (the default route) specifies the host on the local subnet that provides physical connection to remote networks, and is used by default when TCP/IP needs to communicate with computers on other subnets. The host that provides routing is usually a dedicated hardware device, called a router, but the same function could also be implemented in software on a general purpose host. Although routing tables can be populated dynamically, hosts on LANs usually have only one statically configured route, pointing to the default router. In this case routing tables are populated via the `route` command that reads its parameters from a system file (typically `/etc/defaultrouter`) at each reboot of the host.

In the other example below `netstat` is used to show the network interface status (`netstat -i`), which can be useful in a troubleshooting procedure. Examining

whether input and output packet counters on the network interface are growing
before and after you issue some network commands that cause traffic, will reveal
whether the host is successfully communicating through the network interface.
The command `netstat -i` produces a list of interfaces that are used for IP traffic
consisting of the interface name, MTU (maximum transmission unit), the network
to which the interface is attached, addresses for each interface, and counters
associated with the interface. The counters show the number of input packets,
input errors, output packets, output errors and collisions respectively.

EXAMPLES

Hardware interface `eri0` has the IP address 217.57.215.93, receives and sends
packets regularly, with no collisions, and there was one output error.

```
netstat -ni
```

Name	Mtu	Net/Dest	Address	Ipkts	Ierrs
lo0	8232	127.0.0.0	127.0.0.1	458268	0
eri0	1500	216.57.215.64	217.57.215.93	8630680	0

Opkts	Oerrs	Collis	Queue
458268	0	0	0
6334123	1	0	0

Availability

The `netstat` utility is installed by default on Unix-like systems. The `netstat -r`
functionality is equivalent on Unix and Windows platforms. To see the current
default router (default gateway) setting on a Windows system use `ipconfig`
`/all`; for older Windows 9x computers use `winipcfg`. On older MacOS systems
use the TCP/IP control panel. The command `route` is available on Unix and
Windows NT, 2000 and XP to handle the routing. Interface status can be reported
via Netstat on Windows systems as well, by using `netstat -e`. This (as well as
other netstat options) differs from UNIX to Windows platforms.

Additionally, a list of all active TCP/IP connections can be examined via Netstat
(addresses and port numbers are reported) plus all TCP and UDP ports the
computer listens on. In Windows XPs additional options of Netstat will display the
process id for the process that uses the connection. On Unix this functionality
can be achieved with a separate utility (`lsof` – list open files and sockets for
a process).

7.2.5 DNS lookup tools

To search the Internet domain namespace effectively, it helps to know its hierarchical structure and some details about DNS database organization (resource records types) – see Section 7.1.10.

Lookup tools are to used to examine entries in the DNS database for matches to a particular host or domain name. An entry (record in the database) maps a resource name to some value. One common use is to determine the value of a host system IP address from its name.

All the three tools presented here, `host`, `dig` and `nslookup`, have similar functionality. They differ in the ease of use and presentation of results. Historically, `nslookup` was the first tool used to query the DNS and is still installed by default on many systems. The utilities `host` and `dig` appeared later – they are easier to use with more flexibility and clarity of output.

The DNS is a distributed database thus, unless the tool is explicitly told to query a specific name server, it will try the default name server configured for the host where you run it. More than one DNS server my be specified, if the first one fails. The file typically involved in DNS configuration on a Unix system is `/etc/resolv.conf`, while on other platforms DNS configuration is usually found together with basic TCP/IP parameters, like IP address etc.

Tools, by default, issue the query looking for a 'resource record of type A', i.e. given a host name they look for its IP address. To obtain information about other resource records (SOA, NS, A, CNAME, MX, PTR etc.), you need to set the query type explicitly.

Name servers can be requested to dump all the resource records from a domain database, that is to list the contents of the whole domain. The operation is also called 'zone transfer'. While the DNS data is public by its service nature, disclosing all the information about a domain in one simple operation is regarded as a security risk, so zone transfer is often prohibited administratively.

Several sites provide DNS information via the Web, obviating the need for a user to have a local DNS client such as `nslookup` – for example **http://www.Webmaster-toolkit.com/dig.shtml**. A comprehensive listing of DNS-related tools can be found at **http://www.dns.net/dnsrd/tools.html**, including online tools.

host

`host` is a simple utility for performing DNS lookups. It is normally used to discover a host name from an IP address or vice versa.

The `host` command invocation is followed on the command line by the name that is to be looked up, and by default `host` will query for A records. If you insert a dotted-decimal address instead of the name, `host` will, by default, query for the name corresponding to the address, e.g. perform a 'reverse lookup' using PTR records.

To set the query to a specific type, you use the `-t` option on the command invocation. To perform a zone transfer for a full domain, use a query of type AXFR.

```
host www.terena.nl
```
```
www.terena.nl is an alias for godzilla.terena.nl.
godzilla.terena.nl has address 192.87.30.5
```

A lookup for which IP address is mapped to the DNS name 'www.terena.nl' reveals two pieces of information: there is no direct mapping from www.terena.nl to an IP number, but it is an alias for the host named 'godzilla.terena.nl.', which does have an IP number.

```
host 192.87.30.5
```
```
5.30.87.192.in-addr.arpa  domain  name  pointer  godzilla.
terena.nl.
```

A reverse lookup of which DNS name is associated with the IP address 192.87.30.5 (PTR record) leads back to 'godzilla.terena.nl'. In these two examples, direct mapping (name to IP) and reverse mapping (IP to name) are equivalent, which is not always and necessarily the case. On many occasions reverse mapping is missing, and this is particularly true for addresses which are dynamically assigned. Also note that the DNS answer to a PTR query displays the IP address in reverse order, appending 'in-addr.arpa' to it. This also reveals the structure of the IP address reverse tree in DNS, and the historical name 'arpa', which was the name of the first section of the Internet.

```
host-t soa terena.nl
```
```
terena.nl    SOA    ns1.terena.nl.    hostmaster.terena.nl.
2002102201 28000 3600 604800 86400
```

A query of the record type SOA (start-of-authority) for the domain 'terena.nl' shows several important items. The primary authoritative server for the domain is 'ns1.terena.nl', and a human operator, who can be contacted regarding DNS related problems, is e-mail address 'hostmaster@terena.nl'. (@ is represented with a dot for historical reasons). The database for the domain is at its serial (version) number 2002102201 (usually encoding, somehow, the date of the last update), and finally by some timing information.

```
host -t mx terena.nl.
terena.nl mail is handled by 10 erasmus.terena.nl.
```

A query of the record type MX (mail exchanger) shows that the 'host erasmus.terena.nl' is designated to handle all the mail for the domain 'terena.nl'.

```
host erasmus.terena.nl.
erasmus.terena.nl has address 192.87.30.2
```

This simple query of the record type A finds the IP address for the host 'erasmus.terena.nl'.

Availability

The Host utility is included in the BIND software distribution, in the `contrib` directory (**http://www.isc.org/products/BIND**).

dig

`dig` is a flexible and comprehensive tool for interrogating DNS name servers.

EXAMPLES

A typical invocation of `dig` is shown in the following example. In the output, lines starting with ';' are comments added by `dig` for clarity and they do not make up part of the data received as reply to a query. 'ANSWER SECTION' presents the reply data as it is stored in the remote DNS server database. Here again, as in the example for the `host` utility, we learn that DNS name 'www.terena.nl'. has one record associated, of type `CNAME` and is mapped to the value 'spinoza.terena.nl'.

The name 'spinoza.terena.nl.' has one resource record of type A (for address). Additionally, in the 'AUTHORITY SECTION', two records of type NS are listed, showing which name servers are authoritative for this zone, 'ns1.terena.nl' and 'ns1.surfnet.nl'. As is often the case, additional ('secondary') name servers for a domain are hosted at some organizations outside the LAN, for service resilience. If the entire LAN becomes unreachable from the Internet, the DNS information about the domain is still serviced by the secondary name server. TERENA has one secondary name server at the 'surfnet' site.

```
dig www.terena.nl.
; <<>> DiG 9.2.1 <<>> www.terena.nl.
;; global options: printcmd
;; Got answer:
;; ->>HEADER<<- opcode: QUERY, status: NOERROR, id: 30164
;; flags: qr aa rd ra: QUERY: 1, ANSWER: 2, AUTHORITY: 2,
ADDITIONAL : 1
```

```
;; QUESTION SECTION:
;www.terena.nl.        IN     A

;; ANSWER SECTION:
www.terena.nl.        86400 IN     CNAME    spinoza.terena.nl.
spinoza.terena.nl.    86400 In     A        192.87.30.5

;; AUTHORITY SECTION:
terena.nl.            86400 IN     NS       ns1.surfnet.nl.
terena.nl.            86400 IN     NS       ns1.terena.nl.

;; ADDITIONAL SECTION:
ns1.tenena.nl.        86400 IN     A        192.37.30.2

;; Query time: 18 msec
;; SERVER: 192.87.30.2#53(192.87.30.2)
;; WHEN: Wed Sep 17 13:08:26 2003
;; MSG SIZE  rcvd: 129
```

In a previous example (see page 225) the answer was received from the name server on the local machine (127.0.0.1), where dig is running. This name server is just caching DNS responses and is not authoritative for the domain terena.nl, so perhaps it has some outdated information.

Now we interrogate, directly, the name server authoritative for the domain, the server ns1.surfnet.nl., by using the syntax dig@server:

dig @ns1.terena.nl. www.terena.nl

```
www.terena.nl. 86400 IN CNAME spinoza.terena.nl.
spinoza.terena.nl. 86400 IN A 192.87.30.5
terena.nl. 86400 IN NS ns1.surfnet.nl.
terena.nl. 86400 IN NS ns1.terena.nl.
ns1.terena.nl. 86400 IN A 192.87.30.2
;; SERVER: 192.87.30.2#53(ns1.terena.nl.)
```

We receive the same answer (comments deleted), so the local copy in cache is correct and valid.

A query type other than the default A resource record can be specified by adding the appropriate acronym after the name. Zone transfers can be performed by specifying a type 'AXFR'. For example, to query for the MX resource record of the domain terena.nl, use the command dig terena.nl mx.

The `dig` utility has a number of invocation options. One interesting option regarding the delegation path is `+trace`. It activates tracing of the delegation path for the name being looked up – it shows you, starting from the root name servers, the hierarchy of DNS servers involved in answering your query. In fact when tracing is enabled, `dig` makes iterative queries to resolve the name being looked up. It will follow referrals from the root servers, showing the answer from each server that was used to resolve the query.

The example below shows the delegation path for the domain 'terena.nl'. Additionally, it can be seen that the 'root' domain (marked with the '.') is serviced by 13 name servers (`A.ROOT-SERVERS.NET`, etc.), the country Netherlands nl. domain is serviced by six name servers, and the TERENA domain 'terena.nl' is supported by two authoritative name servers. Each of the `dig` queries was obtained from one of the several authoritative servers, i.e. the initial reply was obtained from `I.ROOT-SERVERS.NET`.

```
dig +trace terena.nl
; <<>> DiG 9.2.1 <<>> +trace terena.nl.
;; global options: printcmd
. 33591 IN NS I.ROOT-SERVERS.NET.
. 33591 IN NS J.ROOT-SERVERS.NET.
. 33591 IN NS K.ROOT-SERVERS.NET.
. 33591 IN NS L.ROOT-SERVERS.NET.
. 33591 IN NS M.ROOT-SERVERS.NET.
. 33591 IN NS A.ROOT-SERVERS.NET.
. 33591 IN NS B.ROOT-SERVERS.NET.
. 33591 IN NS C.ROOT-SERVERS.NET.
. 33591 IN NS D.ROOT-SERVERS.NET.
. 33591 IN NS E.ROOT-SERVERS.NET.
. 33591 IN NS F.ROOT-SERVERS.NET.
. 33591 IN NS G.ROOT-SERVERS.NET.
. 33591 IN NS H.ROOT-SERVERS.NET.
;; Received 244 bytes from 127.0.0.1#53(127.0.0.1) in 6 ms
nl. 172800 IN NS AUTH02.NS.UU.NET.
nl. 172800 IN NS NS2.NIC.FR.
nl. 172800 IN NS NS.DOMAIN-REGISTRY.nl.
nl. 172800 IN NS NS.RIPE.NET.
nl. 172800 IN NS SUNIC.SUNET.SE.
nl. 172800 IN NS NS2.DOMAIN-REGISTRY.nl.
;; Received 278 bytes from 192.36.148.17#53(I.ROOT-SERVERS.NET)
in 89 ms terena.nl. 345600 IN NS ns1.terena.nl.
```

```
terena.nl. 345600 IN NS ns1.surfnet.nl.
;; Received 103 bytes from 198.6.1.82#53(AUTH02.NS.UU.NET)
in 142 ms
terena.nl.       86400      IN      SOA      ns1.terena.nl.
hostmaster.terena.nl. 2003010101 28000 3600 604800 86400
;; Received 78 bytes from 192.87.30.2#53(ns1.terena.nl) in
44 ms
```

Availability

The dig utility is part of the BIND distribution (**http://www.isc.org/products/BIND**).

nslookup

The nslookup tool is typically used to query name servers interactively, although it can be used non-interactively by specifying the whole query on the command line. Interactive mode is selected when no arguments are supplied on the command line. To exit from an interactive nslookup session, type Control-D or type the command 'exit' followed by <RETURN>. To learn about the commands embedded in nslookup type 'help'.

To request information about a particular name, just type it at the nslookup prompt '>' followed by <RETURN>. Initially the query type is set to A, so information returned for a host is its IP address. To get other information, you should change the query type to one of supported query types: A, SOA, NS, MX etc. by using the command set querytype=value.

To request a listing of all information in a domain (zone transfer), use the ls command.

The following example makes the same queries as in the example for the host utility. The user enters the type required when prompted with '>'. The output from nslookup is more verbose than that of host.

EXAMPLES

nslookup > www.terena.nl

```
Server: 127.0.0.1
Address: 127.0.0.1#53
Non-authoritative answer:
www.terena.nl canonical name = spinoza.terena.nl.
Name: spinoza.terena.nl.
Address: 192.87.30.5
> set type=ptr
```

```
> 192.87.30.5

Server: 127.0.0.1
Address: 127.0.0.1#53
Non-authoritative answer:
5.30.87.192.in-addr.arpa name = spinoza.terena.nl.
Authoritative answers can be found from:
30.87.192.in-addr.arpa nameserver = ns0.terena.nl.
30.87.192.in-addr.arpa nameserver = ns1.terena.nl.
30.87.192.in-addr.arpa nameserver = ns1.surfnet.nl.
ns1.terena.nl internet address = 192.87.30.2
ns1.surfnet.nl internet address = 192.87.106.101

> set type=soa
> terena.nl.

Server: 127.0.0.1
Address: 127.0.0.1#53
Non-authoritative answer:
terena.nl
origin = ns1.terena.nl.
mail addr = hostmaster.terena.nl.
serial = 2002111912
refresh = 28000
retry = 3600
expire = 604800
minimum = 86400
Authoritative answers can be found from:
terena.nl nameserver = ns1.surfnet.nl.
terena.nl nameserver = ns1.terena.nl.
ns1.terena.nl internet address = 192.87.30.2
ns1.surfnet.nl internet address = 192.87.106.101

> set type=mx
> terena.nl

Server: 127.0.0.1
Address: 127.0.0.1#53
Non-authoritative answer:
terena.nl mail exchanger = 10 erasmus.terena.nl.
Authoritative answers can be found from:
terena.nl nameserver = ns1.terena.nl.
terena.nl nameserver = ns1.surfnet.nl.
erasmus.terena.nl internet address = 192.87.30.2
```

```
ns1.terena.nl. internet address = 192.87.30.2
ns1.surfnet.nl. internet address = 192.87.106.101

> set type=any
> erasmus.terena.nl.

Server: 127.0.0.1
Address: 127.0.0.1#53
Non-authoritative answer:
Name: erasmus.terena.nl.
Address: 192.87.30.2
Authoritative answers can be found from:
terena.nl nameserver = ns1.terena.nl.
terena.nl nameserver = ns1.surfnet.nl.
ns1.terena.nl internet address = 192.87.30.2
ns1.surfnet.nl internet address = 192.87.106.101
> exit
```

Examples of non-interactive `nslookup` command invocations are:

- `nslookup www.terena.nl.`

- `nslookup 192.87.30.5`

- `nslookup -type=mx www.terena.nl.`

Availability

The `nslookup` utility is installed by default on Unix-like and Windows systems.

7.2.6 Finding contact network managers

When network problems appear, there are persons in charge, for different services, who can be contacted. Local institution network administrators or your ISP help desk are the most obvious choices. Depending on the nature of the problem, they, or users themselves, should contact remote network managers.

- For problems regarding e-mail at remote 'domain' contact `postmaster@domain`. This is a standard, mandatory address – each domain should have it configured, read and followed-up.

- For security problems involving remote 'domain' try to contact `abuse@domain`. This is a widely adopted (but not standard) address.

- For DNS problems contact the e-mail address listed in the SOA record for the 'domain', which can be obtained with a simple DNS query (see the example included with the `host` command in Section 7.2.5). The address might be 'hostmaster@domain' or 'domainmaster@domain' or 'root@domain', none of which is standard, so the safest solution is to query the DNS for the 'domain' SOA record and use the e-mail address included there. Remember that the @ sign is not present, but is implied at the position of the first dot. Alternatively, the contact person address registered in the whois database for the domain might be used (see Section 7.2.7).

- For problems involving IP addresses contact the e-mail address for the tech-c or admin-c person listed in the whois database (see the example below).

- For problems regarding a Web site at remote 'domain' try to contact **Webmaster@domain**. This is a widely adopted (but not standard) address.

7.2.7 Whois

When an organization registers a new DNS domain or a new IP address range, the registration data, including the organization name and its contact persons, are usually included in public databases maintained by the registration service. A number of separate databases are maintained – for IP numbers, for gTLDs and for ccTLDs. These databases are called 'Whois', as is the tool and the protocol to access them. A Web-to-whois gateway is commonly available.

At the time of writing, three whois servers cover all IP numbers assignments (see Section 7.1.4):

- **American Registry for Internet Numbers** **http://www.arin.net/whois/index.html**
- **European IP Address Allocations** **whois.ripe.net**
- **Asia Pacific IP Address Allocations** **whois.apnic.net**

The respective Web servers are at:

- **http://www.arin.net/whois/index.html**
- **http://www.ripe.net/db/whois/whois.html**
- **http://www.apnic.net**

For some of the gTLD names (.COM, .NET, .ORG, .EDU) and Registrars (see the Accredited Registrar Directory at **http://www.internic.net/regist.html**) the whois server at **rs.internic.net** (or via Web at **http://www.internic.net/whois.html**) directly maintained the Registry database until some time ago. Currently this database contains the information about which other whois server you should query to obtain the detailed information – with a manual two-step operation you can get the information anyhow (see the example below).

For information about ccTLD names, the situation is variable by country. In many countries there are whois servers for their Registry database, like in Italy at 'whois.nic.it', but in order to discover if and where there is such a whois server, you should start from the information about the ccTLD itself, which you can access via **http://www.iana.org/cctld/cctld-whois.htm**.

There are also a number of whois servers which you can access via Web, like the one at IANA (**http://whois.iana.org/**) or at nic.it (**http://www.nic.it/RA/database/viaWhois.html**).

EXAMPLES

Suppose you encounter some problems with the traffic originating from the IP address 192.87.30.5. If, by using DNS lookup tools, you cannot find to whom this address belongs (domain terena.nl), you might want to find out who registered the IP address itself.

As there is no way to guess its geographical location from the IP address, you should try a whois query to one of the three IP-related whois servers, and if you get no answer then you should try the others.

The reply extracted from the whois database (shown partially below) reveals that TERENA Secretariat has registered the range of '255' IP numbers (inetnum field), that the administrative contact person (admin-c field) is designated by the nic-hdl key 'TH378-RIPE', and that the technical contact person (tech-c) is the same as admin-c (which is not always the case).

When there are network problems in which these IP numbers are involved, one of tech-c or admin-c persons can be contacted, depending on the nature of the problem. Further down in the example all the details about the person 'TH378-RIPE' can be found, along with the phone number and e-mail address.

```
whois -h whois.ripe.net 192.87.30.5
```

```
inetnum:      192.87.30.0 - 192.87.30.255
netname:      TERENP-SEC-LAN
descr:        TERENA Secretariat
country:      NL
admin-c:      TH378-RIPE
tech-c:       TH378-RIPE
```

```
status:          PSSIGNED PP
notify:          info@SURFnet.nl
mnt-by:          SN-LIR-MT
mnt-irt:         irt-CERT-NL
changed:         Erik-Jan.Bos@surfnet.n1 19940816
changed:         valkenburg@terena.n1 19970121
changed:         Derk.Reinders@SURFnet.nl 20010326
changed:         Rogier.Spoor@SURFnet.n1 20020605
source:          RIPE

route:           192.87.0.0/16
descr:           SURFnet CIDR Block IV
origin:          AS1103
notify:          netmaster@surfnet.nl
mnt-by:          PS1103-MNT
mnt-lower:       SN-LIR-MT
changed:         Erik-Jan.Bos@surfnet.nl 19960416
changed.         Wim.Biemolt@surfnet.nl 20011213
source:          RIPE

person:          TERENA Hostmaster
address:         TERENA Secretariat
address:         Singel 468-d
address:         NL-1017 AW Rmsterdam
address:         The Netherlands
phone:           +31 20 530 4488
fax-no:          +31 20 530 4499
e~mail:          hostmaster@terena.n1
nic-hdl:         TH378-RIPE
notify:          info@SURFnet.nl
notify:          hostmaster@terena.nl
mnt-by:          SN-LIR-MT
changed:         valkenburg@terena.nl 19970121
changed:         Derk.Reinders@SURFnet.nl 20010327
source:          RIPE
```

Suppose you are looking for someone responsible for the domain name 'akamai.com' and you need a phone number to contact (with DNS lookup tools you can only find an e-mail address). Then you send your query to the generic gTLDs whois server, 'rs.internic.net', which will point you to the correct whois server, 'whois.opensrs.net', where you will find the full information. With another query to this server, you can discover the phone number and other information. You will also note that the format of the answers which you get from a whois server might be different from server to server, as there is no standard for whois output.

```
whois -h rs.internic.net akamai.com
Whois Server Version 1.3
```

Domain names in the .com and .net domains can now be registered with many different competing registrars. Go to **http://www.internic.net** for detailed information.

```
Domain Name: AKAMAI.COM
Registrar: TUCOWS, INC.
Whois Server: whois.opensrs.net
Referral URL: http://www.opensrs.org
Name Server: YH.AKAMAI.COM
Name Server: YG.AKAMAI.COM
Name Server: YC.AKAMAI.COM
Name Server: USE1.AKAM.NET
Name Server: EUR1.AKAM.NET
Name Server: ASIA2.AKAM.NET
Name Server: NS1-2.AKAM.NET
Name Server: NS1-3.AKAM.NET
Name Server: NS1-42.AKAM.NET
Name Server: EUR2.AKAM.NET
Name Server: NS1-137.AKAM.NET
Name Server: USE3.AKAM.NET
Status: REGISTRAR-LOCK
Updated Date: 29-jul-2003
Creation Date: 17-aug-1998
Expiration Date: 16-aug-2007
>>> Last update of whois database: Wed, 17 Sep 2003
18:19:42 EDT <<<
```

The Registry database contains only .COM, .NET, .ORG, .EDU domains and registrars.

```
whois -h whois.opensrs.net akamai.com
```

```
Registrant:
Akamai Technologies, Inc.
8 Cambridge Center
Cambridge, MA 02142
US
```

```
Domain name: AKAMAI.COM

Administrative Contact:
Hostmaster, Akamai hostmaster-billing@akamai.com
8 Cambridge Center
Cambridge, MA 02142
US
+1.6174443000 Fax: +1.6174443001

Technical Contact:
Hostmaster, Akamai hostmaster-billing@akamai.com
8 Cambridge Center
Cambridge, MA 02142
US
+1.6174443000 Fax: +1.6174443001

Registration Service Provider:
Akamai Technologies, hostmaster@akamai.com
617-444-3000
This company may be contacted for domain login/passwords,
DNS/Nameserver  changes,  and  general  domain  support
questions.

Registrar of Record: TUCOWS, INC.
Record last updated on 29-Jul-2003.
Record expires on 16-Aug-2007.
Record Created on 17-Aug-1998.

Domain servers in listed order:
NS1-2.AKAM.NET 193.108.91.2
NS1-3.AKAM.NET 193.108.91.3
NS1-137.AKAM.NET 193.108.91.137
NS1-42.AKAM.NET 193.108.91.42
EUR1.AKAM.NET 212.187.244.35
EUR2.AKAM.NET 212.187.169.152
USE3.AKAM.NET 80.67.67.182
USE1.AKAM.NET 63.209.170.136
YC.AKAMAI.COM 209.246.46.48
ASIA2.AKAM.NET 193.108.154.70
YG.AKAMAI.COM 63.215.198.86
YH.AKAMAI.COM 63.241.29.188
```

Looking for someone responsible for a domain inside a ccTLD such as 'dfn.de' requires further iterations, but if you can somehow get the name of the whois server for '.de' (for example asking the information from the contact persons listed in the IANA ccTLD registry, and obtaining 'whois.denic.de') then the procedure is straightforward. Unfortunately there is no all-encompassing list of existing whois servers for ccTLDs.

```
whois -h whois.denic.de dfn.de
```

```
% Copyright (c)2002 by DENIC

% % Restricted rights.

% % % Except for agreed Internet operational purposes, no
part of this
% information may be reproduced, stored in a retrieval
system, or
% transmitted, in any form or by any means, electronic,
mechanical,
% recording, or otherwise, without prior permission of the
DENIC
% on behalf of itself and/or the copyright holders. Any use
of this
% material to target advertising or similar activities are
explicitly
% forbidden and will be prosecuted. The DENIC requests to
be notified
% of any such activities or suspicions thereof.

domain: dfn.de
descr: Verein zur Foerderung eines Deutschen Forschungsnetz
e.V.
descr: Anhalter Str. 1
descr: 10963 Berlin
descr: Germany
nserver: deneb.dfn.de 192.76.176.9
nserver: ws-fra1.win-ip.dfn.de 193.174.75.178
nserver: ws-kar1.win-ip.dfn.de 193.174.75.154
nserver: ws-mue1.win-ip.dfn.de 193.174.75.166
nserver: names.zrz.tu-berlin.de
status: connect
changed: 20030604 150152
source: DENIC
```

```
[admin-c]
Type: PERSON
Name: Martin Wilhelm
Address: DFN-Verein
Address: Geschaeftsstelle
Address: Anhalter Strasse 1
City: Berlin
Pcode: 10963
Country: DE
Changed: 20020131 144006
Source: DENIC

[tech-c][zone-c]
Type: PERSON
Name: Karsten Leipold
Address: DFN-Verein
Address: Geschaeftsstelle
Address: Anhalter Strasse 1
City: Berlin
Pcode: 10963
Country: DE
Phone: +49 30 884299 49
Fax: +49 30 884299 20
E-mail: poldi@dfn.de
Changed: 20011119 143132
Source: DENIC

[tech-c][zone-c]
Type: PERSON
Name: Holger Wirtz
Address: DFN-Verein
Address: Geschaeftsstelle
Address: Anhalter Strasse 1
City: Berlin
Pcode: 10963
Country: DE
Phone: +49 30 884299 40
Fax: +49 30 884299 70
E-mail: wirtz@dfn.de
Changed: 20020131 144004
Source: DENIC
```

GLOSSARY

AAA(I) Authentication, authorization, accounting/auditing (infrastructure) is the framework that provides support to identify users (authentication) to allow them to perform some specific tasks (authorization) and to establish the resources that users consume (accounting).

ActiveX A technology developed by Microsoft. With an ActiveX-enabled browser ActiveX controls can be downloaded as part of a Web document to add functionality to the browser (similar to Java applets). In particular, ActiveX enables seamless viewing of Windows files of all types (e.g. spreadsheets) and, in combination with other technologies such as Java and scripting languages, makes possible the development of complex Web applications.

aiff Sound format for Apple Mac. Files are downloaded then played locally. Playable with LiveAudio plug-in which comes with Netscape Navigator 3.0 and higher. Playable in Internet Explorer 3.0+.

AIM AOL Instant Messenger.

API Application program interface – a set of functions or subroutines that a program, or application, can use to tell the operating system to carry out a specific task.

APOP Authenticated Post Office Protocol (see also POP).

ASCII American Standard Code for Information Interchange.

ASF Advanced Streaming Format – Microsoft's streaming format. Can include audio, video, scripts, ActiveX controls and HTML documents. Playable with Windows Media Player (included with Windows 98 and newer).

ASP Active Server Pages – a server-side technology from Microsoft for building dynamic and interactive Web pages. ASP code is embedded in the HTML page.

ASP(2) Application Service Provider – a third-party entity that provides applications to be used by customers.

au Sound format for Unix. Files are downloaded then played locally. Supports 8-bit sound only. Playable with LiveAudio plug-in which comes with Netscape Navigator 3.0 and higher. Internet Explorer 3.0+ supports .au MIME type.

Authentication The process by which one party proves to an independent party its right to assert a given identity.

Authorization The process by which the receiver of a request determines whether the request should be permitted.

Avatar A graphical image of a user, such as used in graphical real-time Chat applications, or a graphical personification of a computer or a computer process, intended to make the computing or network environment a more friendly place.

avi Audio/video interleaved – video file-type used by Video for Windows, Microsoft's multimedia architecture. Playable with Windows Media Player.

B-ISDN Broadband Integrated Services Digital Network.

Backbone These networks provide the transport function. Backbone networks are shared by many edge networks and are made of high bandwidth links and high-speed routers. The edge network is connected to the backbone network again through a router, usually one so-called 'upstream' router and its associated link, called the 'last mile' in the network path.

Bandwidth (This) is a static characteristic of a given network link. However, the round trip time of packets (sometimes called delay or link latency) over the same link can change dynamically, depending on the current load caused by the cumulative traffic over a given link and depending also on processing load of the destination host.

Bitmap graphics A type of image format in which an exact pixel-by-pixel mapping of an image is stored for rendering by an output device. Examples of bitmap formats used on the Web include GIF, JPEG and PNG.

CA Certification authority – a trusted third-party entity which creates and assigns certificates. The CA guarantees that the individual granted the unique certificate is, in fact, who he or she claims to be.

Caching The temporary storage of files on a computer to allow fast access of subsequent requests. Web documents retrieved may be stored (cached) for a time so that they can be accessed conveniently if further requests are made for them. Whether or not the most up-to-date copy of the file is retrieved is handled by the caching program, which initially makes a brief check and compares the date of the file at its original location with that of the copy in the cache. If the date of the cached file is the same as the original, then the cached copy is used.

CERN Conseil Europeen pour le Recherche Nucleaire.

CERT Computer Emergency Response Team.

CGI Common Gateway Interface – a server-side technology in which the processing of information takes place at the server end and the results are sent back to the Web browser in a dynamically generated HTML page. CGI enables communication between Web servers and other programs at the server side.

CIDR Classless inter-domain routing.

CIF Common Intermediate Format – a video format used in videoconferencing systems.

Classified directory A catalogue of Internet resources that have been selected and evaluated by humans.

Client–server A model of interaction between computers which is commonly used on the Internet. Users employ client software, such as a Web browser, to request information from servers. Servers, such as WWW servers, supply information in response to requests from clients. The client, normally installed on the user's computer, displays the information for the user. In the client–server model, clients and servers have a special relationship derived from the common use of a well-defined set of communicating conventions (protocol). For example, Web browsers and servers use HTTP.

CMS Content management system.

Codec COmpresser/DECompresser or COder/DECoder – both terms are good descriptions of what a codec does. Its task is to take an uncompressed input and output a compressed (or coded) version of the signal, and to decompress (or decode) a compressed signal to an uncompressed one.

Cookies Provide a means for a Web server to induce a client to store information about itself which can subsequently be called up by the Web server when required. This might be information which the user has supplied about themselves, their preferences or their requirements via forms input. The oft-cited example is the shopping list which might be added to from time to time.

CPIM Common presence and instant messaging.

Crawler A software program that visits Web sites and indexes pages it finds for search engine indexes (also known as spiders and robots).

CRL Certificate revocation list.

CRM Customer relationship management.

CSS Cascading Style Sheet – a simple mechanism for adding style to HTML documents. It is a style sheet language which gives the ability to define a set of stylistic rules that describe how HTML documents will be presented.

DBMS Database management system – a set of programs that allows you to store, modify and extract information from a database.

DCMI Dublin Core Metadata Initiative.

dcr Macromedia Director format. Playable with Macromedia's players.

DES Digital Encryption Standard – a symmetric-key encryption method developed in 1975.

DHCP Dynamic Host Configuration Protocol – simplifies loading parameters into the network software and permits completely automated address assignment. It allows a computer to join a new network, obtain a valid IP address and begin using it, all without either the end user's or the operator's manual intervention.

Digital Certificate – an encrypted file issued by a certification authority, which contains the public key (and other information) of the person the certificate belongs to.

Directory A database with information about organizations, individuals and other resources on the Internet – used as a basis for directory services.

Directory service A directory service locates organizations, individuals and other resources on the Internet (see also White Pages and Yellow Pages).

DN Distingushed name.

DNS Domain name system – the Internet naming service. It is a distributed database which enables mapping between IP adresses and names of the computers (hosts).

doc Common MS format for formatted text files. Used in the MS Office program suite.

DOM Document Object Model – a platform and language neutral interface which allows programs and scripts to dynamically access and update the content, structure and style of documents. The document can be further processed and the results of that processing can be incorporated back into the presented page. (W3C)

DSS Digital signature standard.

DTD Document type definition.

DVD Digital versatile disc or digital video disc.

Dynamic HTML The use of a combination of HTML, JavaScript and stylesheets for interactivity and animation in Web pages.

exe Self-extracting archive for MS Windows. No additional software needed on the MS Windows platform.

Forms Forms (related to Web) are a defined area of an HTML document, such as a box into which the user can input data in order to have it processed by another application, for instance to run a search on a database.

FQDN Fully qualified domain name.

FTP File Transfer Protocol – a protocol for communication between computers on the Internet to allow them to transfer files.

FYI 'For your information' documents are RFC documents which contain information that does not deal with standards. They contain information of a more general nature.

GDS Global dialling scheme.

GIF Graphics Interchange Format – a format for lossless compression of images containing areas of solid colour such as icons, graphs and line-art logos. GIF supports 256 colours (8-bit indexed colour), transparency, interlacing and animation.

Global Grid Forum (GGF) – a forum to support the development, deployment and implementation of Grid technologies. See also **http://www.ggf.org** (GGF documents are available at **http://www.ggf.org/documents/default.htm**).

Grid A parallel and distributed system that enables the sharing, selection and aggregation of resources distributed across 'multiple' domains.

GSM Global system for mobile communication – a digital cellular communications system.

gz Gnu version of zip used on Unix. Use unzip on Unix, MacGZip on Mac, Stuffit Expander for Windows on MS Windows.

H.323 ITU standard for videoconferencing over local area networks and packet-switched networks generally. It is based on a recognized real-time standard and is commonly used with video over the Internet to ensure that users can communicate with each other. The standard applies both to one-to-one and multiparty videoconferences.

Host A computer connected to the network – the actual source or the destination of the data transferred over the network.

hqx Macintosh BinHex file encoded as text. Use Xbin on Unix, Stuffit Expander on Mac, BinHex on MS Windows.

HTML Hypertext Markup Language – the native language of the WWW. HTML enables links to be specified, and also the structure and formatting of Web documents to be defined. HTML documents are written in plain text, but with the addition of tags which describe or define the text they enclose.

HTTP Hypertext Transfer Protocol – the foundation protocol of the WWW. It sets the rules for exchanges between browsers and servers. It provides for the transfer of hypertext and hypermedia, for recognition of file types and other functions.

HTTPS Secure HTTP.

IAB Internet Architecture Board.

IANA Internet Assigned Numbers Authority – is responsible for assigning new Internet-wide IP addresses.

ICANN Internet Corporation for Assigned Names and Numbers.

ICQ 'I seek you' – online instant messaging program.

ID Identifier.

IEC International Electrotechnical Commission.

IEEE Institute of Electrical and Electronics Engineers (standardization is being done by IEEE Standards Association, **http://standards.ieee.org**).

IESG Internet Engineering Steering Group.

IETF Internet Engineering Task Force – the primary standards setting body for Internet technologies. Operates under the guidance of its steering committee IESG and its architecture board IAB.

Imagemap Also known as active map – is a graphic containing active link areas. Instead of the link being from a word or phrase in the document, it is embedded in a defined area of the imagemap. Clicking on that area fetches the referenced document. Imagemaps are often used to provide a graphical entry point to a Web site, though a text-based route through the site should always be given as an alternative.

IMAP Internet Message Access Protocol – a recent protocol which expands POP functionality allowing the recipient program to manage message folders remotely on the IMAP server.

IMPP Instant Messaging and Presence Protocol.

Instant messaging A technology that offers text-based synchronous communication between people. Instant messaging usually refers to communication between two people, whereas chat usually refers to communication between more than two people.

Internet media type See MIME type.

IP address A 32-bit number that uniquely identifies a network interface on a host.

IRC Internet Relay Chat.

IRTF Internet Research Task Force.

ISDN Integrated Services Digital Network – a system of digital telephone connections. It allows multiple digital channels to be operated simultaneously through a single, standard interface.

ISMA Internet Streaming Media Alliance.

ISO International Standards Organization.

ISP Internet service provider.

ITU International Telecommunication Union.

ITU-T Telecommunication Standardization Sector.

JAVA Powerful, cross-platform programming language developed by Sun Microsystems. Java applets (small applications) may be incorporated into Web documents and can be executed securely by any Java-capable browser.

Javascript A client-side scripting language used for writing small programs that are embedded inside a page of HTML.

JID Jabber ID.

JPEG Joint Photographic Experts Group – a format for efficient compression of natural, true-colour items such as photographs or items with subtle colour gradations. JPEG supports up to 16.7 million colours (24-bit colour), variable compression and progressive download. JPEG does not support transparency or animation.

LAN Local area network.

LDAP Lightweight Directory Access Protocol – a standard for building distributed directories and directory services. Developed from X.500.

MAN Metropolitan area network.

MBone The multicast backbone – an overlay network that connects multicast-enabled islands to each other using tunnels.

MCU Multipoint control unit – device in videoconferencing that connects two or more audiovisual terminals together into one single videoconference call.

Meta-search engine A service that searches a number of search engines and repackages the results for the user.

Metadata Data about data – provides information about the networked resource.

MG Media gateway.

MGC Media gateway controller.

MGCP Media Gateway Control Protocol.

mid, midi A music definition language and communications protocol rather than a format, MIDI (Musical Instrument Digital Interface) contains instructions to perform particular commands. Playable with LiveAudio plug-in for Netscape. Automatically playable with sound-enabled versions of Internet Explorer or with Windows Media Player.

MIME Multipurpose Internet Mail Extensions – a protocol specification which allows Internet mail to carry the full set of multimedia messages and contents, by precisely determining the content type.

MIME type Also Internet media type, or content type – the type of the file content specifed according to the MIME standard.

MLM Mailing list manager.

MMS Microsoft Media Server protocol.

mov Format for QuickTime movies. Playable with QuickTime players.

MP3 MPEG Audio Layer 3 – a format that offers 10–20 fold compression of audio allowing the coding of CD-quality sound in relatively small files. This has become the format of choice for delivering audio via the Internet.

MPEG Moving Pictures Expert Group – a family of standards used for coding audio and video in a highly compressed digital format.

mpg, mpeg Widely used standard for digital compression of moving images. Files are played locally. Playable with MPEG viewers such as MPEGPlay or Windows Media Player.

MPLS Multi-protocol label switching.

MTA Mail transfer agent.

MUA Mail user agent.

MUD Multi user dungeon.

Multicast A message that is transmitted to selected multiple recipients who have joined the appropriate multicast group. The sender has to generate only a single data stream. A multicast-enabled router will forward a multicast to a particular network only if there are multicast receivers on that network.

MUT Multi-user talk.

MX Mail exchange.

NAPT Network address port translation.

NAT Network address translation – developed as a short-term solution to the problem of public IP address space consumption. The idea is simple: instead of using a large range of public IP addresses, an 'edge' network uses a range of so-called 'private' IP addresses internally.

Network tools A term used for programs that enable a user to to set network parameters, check if they are functioning correctly, test if other hosts can be reached by address and by name, and give a rough idea of possible problems.

NNTP Network News Transfer Protocol.

NREN National Research and Education Network.

NTSC National Television System Committee.

P2P Peer-to-peer is a model of communication between computers where applications do not reside on a server. Hosts communicate and exchange information directly between them.

PAL Phase alternation line.

PC Personal computer.

PCI Peripheral component interconnect.

pdf Portable document format from Adobe – portable across computing platforms. Adobe's Acrobat Reader is needed to read pdf files.

PGP Pretty Good Privacy – a technique for encrypting messages, based on a public key method. The public key is accessible to anyone who wants to send an encrypted message.

PHP A server-side, cross-platform, HTML embedded scripting language that lets you create dynamic Web pages. PHP-enabled Web pages are treated just like regular HTML pages. You can create and edit them the same way that you create regular HTML pages.

PKC Public key certificate.

PKI Public key infrastructure – a system of digital certificates, certificate authorities and other registration authorities that authenticate the validity of each party involved in an Internet transaction.

Plug-ins Software which extends the functionality of the Web browser. Graphical browsers support a range of file types, such as HTML and GIF, as standard. Support for other file types is handled by additional software that works in conjunction with the browser (plug-in) or as a stand-alone application that is launched when the file is downloaded (helper application). Some plug-ins are now provided as part of the browser software, but many more are freely available by downloading from third-party developers.

PNG Portable Network Graphics – a non-proprietary alternative to GIF. PNG offers benefits such as improved image compression (up to 30% smaller than GIFs), variable transparency levels, two-dimensional interlacing and the use of metadata to allow indexing by search engines. PNG is supported in recent versions of Netscape and Internet Explorer.

POP Post Office Protocol – the oldest (and less rich in functionality) access protocol, which allows the recipient program (client) to check the incoming mail on the message store server and retrieve new messages to the local recipient machine (sometimes a copy is left on the POP server). Further processing of retrieved messages occurs on the local machine, e.g. messages are deleted or saved in local mailboxes, also called 'mail folders'.

Port Applications on the host are associated with an address (a number) called a port. This concept gives the ability to run a number of services at the same IP address – the host can run a number of applications (server processes), each 'listening' on its own port. A remote application is thus uniquely identified by the IP address and port number couple.

Portal A starting site for Internet users bringing together lots of disparate information under a single site.

POTS Plain old telephone service.

PRIM Presence and instant messaging.

Protocol A set of rules governing the communication between two entities in a network.

Proxy server A server that operates between a client application (Web browser) and a real server. May be used to provide a gateway between a LAN and the Internet. All outward HTTP requests from the local network pass through the proxy server and similarly all information retrieved comes back in via the proxy server, and is then passed back to the clients. Using the options or preferences, Web browsers can be configured to point to the proxy server. Proxy servers normally maintain a cache of retrieved documents.

ps PostScript file format – includes formatting information primarily for printing to a PostScript printer. May be viewed with GhostScript for Mac, Windows and Unix.

PSTN Public switched telephone network.

QCIF Quarter common intermediate format.

QoS Quality of service – specifies a minimum amount of data transferred from one place to another during a process.

qt QuickTime movie file type from Apple – files are played locally. Playable with QuickTime players.

qt3 QuickTime 3 – advanced compression format for video, audio, MIDI, animation, 3D etc. Playable with QuickTime players.

RA Registration authority.

ra, rm, ram Real audio – pioneering format for streaming audio on the Web, optimized for low-to-medium speed connections. Playable with RealPlayer or Windows Media Player.

RDF Resource Description Framework – a framework for writing metadata, recommended by the World Wide Web Consortium. RDF uses XML to 'wrap' metadata in a standard, interoperable manner. One or more metadata schemes (such as Dublin Core) are contained within the RDF wrapper. The metadata can then be processed by applications.

REP Robot Exclusion Protocol – the use of a file called robots.txt, placed in the root directory of the Web server to indicate parts of the Web site which robots should not index.

RFC Request for comments documents – the specification documents of the Internet protocol suite, as defined by IETF (RFC standards page is available at **http://www.ietf.org/rfc.html**).

RIR Regional internet registry.

Robot See 'crawler'.

Router Connects different networks, forwards IP traffic and determines which path it takes.

RSA Rivest, Shamir and Adelman public key algorithm.

RSVP Resource Reservation Protocol.

RTCP Real-Time Control Protocol.

rtf Rich text format – ASCII rendering of binary wordprocessed documents. Programs such as Microsoft Word will convert to and from rtf files.

RTP Real-Time (Transport) Protocol.

RTSP Real-Time Streaming Protocol.

RTT Round trip time.

rv Real video – format for streaming video on the Web optimized for low-to-medium speed connections. Playable with RealPlayer or Windows Media Player.

S/MIME Secure MIME.

SAML Security Assertion Markup Language – a framework for the exchange of authentication and authorization information, based on XML.

SAP Session Announcement Protocol.

SDK Software development kit.

SDP Session Description Protocol.

Search engine A service that gathers, indexes and provides a searchable interface to Internet sites.

SET Secure electronic transaction.

SG Signalling gateway.

SGML Standard Generalized Markup Language – a standard for organizing the elements of a document. It is used mainly for documents which change frequently and need to be printed in different formats.

SIM Subscriber identity module.

SIMPLE SIP for instant messaging and presence leveraging extensions.

SIP Session Initiation Protocol – a protocol for Internet conferencing.

sit Macintosh archiving and compression format. Use Stuffit on Unix, Stuffit Expander on Mac, Stuffit Expander for Windows on MS Windows.

SMIL Synchronized Multimedia Integration Language – pronounced 'smile', this is a W3C standard for a markup language to allow the synchronization of media including audio, video, images, text and animation. SMIL offers control over layout, sequencing, timing and interactivity to assemble separate media objects into a coherent, time-based presentation. SMIL 1.0 is supported by the Apple QuickTime player and Real player. SMIL 2.0 is supported by the RealOne player. XHTML+TIME is a subset of SMIL 2.0 modules supported in Internet Explorer 5.5 and above.

SMTP Simple Mail Transfer Protocol – the basic e-mail protocol used for transfer of messages from the originator to the destination.

SOAP Simple Object Access Protocol – a lightweight and simple XML/HTTP-based protocol designed to exchange structured and typed information on the Web.

Spider See 'crawler'.

SQCIF Sub-Quarter Common Intermediate Format.

SQL Structured Query Language – a standard language for constructing database queries.

SSH Secure shell – a program to log into a computer over a network, to execute commands remotely. It provides strong authentication.

SSI Server Side Includes – an HTML tag that directs the Web server to generate data dynamically for a Web page when requested.

SSL Secure Sockets Layer – a protocol developed by Netscape for transmitting documents over the Internet in a secure way. SSL creates a secure connection between a client and a server.

Subject gateway Uses humans to select, describe and index Internet resources around a particular subject area.

SVG Scalable vector graphics – a file format that enables two-dimensional images to be displayed in XML pages on the Web.

SVG Scalable vector graphics – a W3C recommendation for creating two-dimensional graphics in XML. SVG drawings can be interactive, dynamic, animated and interactive. SVG is written in plain text and is rendered by the browser or an appropriate plug-in.

swf ShockWave Flash from Macromedia – for delivery of graphics and animation on the Internet. Playable with ShockWave or Flash player.

tar Unix archive format. Tar files may also be compressed. Use tar command on Unix, TAR on Mac, WinZIP on MS Windows.

TCP Transmission Control Protocol.

TCP/IP Basic protocol suite used on the Internet, named by the two most important protocols in the suite – Transmission Control Protocol (TCP) and Internet Protocol (IP).

tiff High-resolution image format. Viewable with common image viewers/browsers.

TLD Top level domain.

TLS Transport layer security.

TSP Telephony service provider.

TTL Time to live.

UA User agent.

UAC User agent client.

UAS User agent server.

UDDI Universal Description Discovery and Integration – the service discovery protocol for Web Services through which companies can find each other.

UDDI Universal Description Discovery and Integration – XML-based worldwide business registration process.

UDP User Datagram Protocol.

URI Uniform resource identifier – defines how an object on the network is named and addressed. URIs are used to 'locate' resources, by providing an abstract identification of the resource location. An example of URI is URL.

URL Uniform resource locator – provides a way of uniquely specifying the address of any document on the Internet. This is the lynchpin of WWW's embedded linking. The URL specifies the method used to access the resource (the protocol), the name of the host computer on which it is located and the path of the resource.

USB Universal serial bus.

uu File converted to text format using the `uuencode` command on Unix. To convert back to original form, use the command `uudecode` on Unix, uuLite on Mac and WinCode on MS Windows. If transferred by e-mail, the mail program may handle conversion automatically.

uue See uu.

Vector graphics Store a description of image properties such as size, shape and colour as mathematical formulae (rather than pixels). Vector graphics tend to be of a significantly smaller file size than bitmaps. In addition, vector graphics can be resized without any loss of image resolution or increase in file size. Vector graphics can be produced by a number of packages including Macromedia Flash and Adobe Illustrator. See also scalable vector graphics (SVG).

viv VIVO format for compression of streaming video, particularly over low bandwidth. Player available at **www.vivo.com**.

VLAN Virtual LAN.

VNC Virtual network computing.

VoIP Voice over IP – voice delivered using the Internet Protocol. This allows sending voice information in digital form in discrete packets rather than in the traditional circuit-committed protocols. The major advantage of this technology is that it provides free telephone calls.

VRML Virtual Reality Modelling Language – an open standard for the definition of 3-dimensional environments used on the WWW. Simple VRML files can be created with a plain text editor but for more complex model building, modelling software will probably be required. VRML files are viewed with a helper application or browser plug-in such as WorldView.

VRVS Virtual Rooms Videoconferencing System.

W3C WWW Consortium (publications are available at **http://www.w3.org/TR/**).

WAI Web accessibility initiative.

WAN Wide area network.

WAP Wireless Application Protocol.

wav MS Windows sound format. Playable with LiveAudio plug-in which comes with Netscape Navigator 3.0 and higher. Playable in Internet Explorer 3.0 and higher or with Windows Media Player.

White Pages Directory services that locate personal information (e-mail addresses, telephone numbers etc.).

Whois A program that will reveal the owner of (any) second-level domain name.

WLAN Wireless LAN.

WML Wireless Markup Language.

WSDL Web Services Description Language – a language in XML format used to describe a Web service's capabilities.

WWW World Wide Web.

WYSIWYG What you see is what you get – a graphical interface to a process which shows how the end result will look as it is being produced. For example, a WYSIWYG HTML editor generates HTML markup and displays the document as if viewed with a Web browser.

X.500 Standard for developing an electronic directory of people in an organization so that it can be part of a global directory.

xDSL Digital subscriber line.

XHMTL Extensible HTML. See also HTML.

XML Extensible Markup Language – a standard for creating markup languages that describe the structure of data. It is not a fixed set of elements, like HTML, but is a meta-language, or a language for describing languages.

XMPP Extensible Messaging and Presence Protocol.

XSL Extensible Stylesheet Language – a style sheet language aimed at activities, such as rearranging a document, that are not supported by CSS, though XSL and CSS share the same underlying concepts. XSL can be used to style XML documents using sets of rules and definitions of actions to be applied.

XSLT Extensible Stylesheet Language Transformations – converts an XML document in another XML-document fragment, following the specifications of the XSL file.

Yellow Pages A standard for building distributed directories.

Z Unix compressed file. To expand, use the command `uncompress` on Unix (if not done automatically by the ftp program), Stuffit Expander with Expander Enhancer on Mac, WinZIP on MSWindows.

INDEX

AAA 102–4
About.com (The Mining Company) 10, 14
Active Directory 21
ActiveX 35
Adobe Acrobat 32
Adobe Illustrator 53, 56–7
Adobe Photoshop 55–6
Adobe Photoshop Elements 56
alltheweb.com (FAST™) 6–7, 10, 11, 12, 18
AltaVista 7, 11, 12, 18
Anna Kournikova macro virus 119
AOL.com 17
AOL Search 14
APOP (Authenticated Post Office Protocol) 98
Apple 134
Application Server 80, 81
APEX (Application Exchange) 128
ASCII 46, 162, 163, 168, 191
ASP (Active Server Pages) 32, 64, 65, 72–3, 79
AskJeeves 10
audioconferencing 132–3
authentication, authorization and accounting (AAA; triple-A) 102–4
authoring 43–5
  assistance/templates 45
  tools 44, 47–8, 49, 54
  WYSIWYG 44, 47, 48

Banca Sella 96
Base64 168–9, 171
BBC 12
BigFoot 24
BinHex 168–9

biometrics 103
bookmarking 31
Boolean algebra 3
broadband 196
browsers 27–30, 33–8
  Internet Explorer 28, 29, 35–6, 110
  Lynx 37
  Mozilla 36–7
  Netscape Communicator 28, 33–5, 48
  Opera 36
  standard functions 28–9
businesses, searching for 22–4
Butler SQL 81

caching 38–9, 65–6
CataList 25
certificate revocation list (CRL) 107, 109
Certificate Store (CS) 110
certification authority (CA) 107, 108
CGI (Common Gateway Interface) 31, 64
chain letters 171
channel 127
chat 125, 127–8
Chernobyl virus 118
CIDR (classless inter-domain routing) 200
CIF (Common Intermediate Format) 133–4
classified directories 2, 13–17
client-side processing 64
CNN 12
Coalition Against Unsolicited Commercial e-mail (CAUCE) 123–4
Code Red worm 120
CODECs 131–4

audio 132–3
  video 133–4
CoffeeCup Image Mapper 59
ColdFusion 45, 79–80
companies, searching for 22–4
CompletePlanet 25
compressed files 169–70
cookies 65, 76–7
CORBA 65
Cosmo Player 63
cracker 91
CSS (Cascading Style Sheets) 33, 35, 66,
    67, 68, 82

Databases 25
  management system 79
  Web 78–81
  Web tools 79–81
DCOM 65
DeBabelizer Pro 57–8
deep web 25
defences 120–2
Development Studio 81
DHCP (Dynamic Host Configuration
      Protocol) 203–4
DHTML 35, 60, 66–9
dictionary attack 92
Differentiated Services (DiffServ) 153
dig 226–9
digital certificates 107–8
Digital Signature Algorithm (DSA) 101
Digital Signature Standard (DSS) 101
digital signatures 104–8
  certificate authorities (CA) 106
  creating 104–6
  verification 110–11
Direct Hit 10
Direct HitSM 8
directory services 20–4
  tools 20–2
Directory System Agent (DSA) 22
Directory User Agent (DUA) 22
distinguished name (DN) 206
distributed object technology 65
Ditto.com 18
DNS (Domain Name System) 207–9
Document Type Definitions 83
Documents, publishing. See Publishing
Dogpile 10–11

Dogpile Web Catalog 10
DOM (Document Object Model) 67
Drumbeat 45
DSA (Digital Signature Algorithm) 101
DSA (Directory System Agent) 22
DSS (Digital Signature Standard) 101
DUA (Directory User Agent) 22
Dublin Core 85
dynamic business Webs 40
Dynamic HTML (DHTML) 35, 60, 66–9

eBAY 12
e-mail 160–72
  addresses 126, 163
  addresses, finding 163–4
  aliases 164
  becoming a user 162–3
  file attachments 168–70
  file transmission 168–70
  mailbox forwarding 164
  message composition 166–7
  MIME 171–2
  MUA configuration parameters 164–5
  receiving 167–8
  security, 96–8
  sending 167
  viruses. See e-mail viruses
e-mail viruses 118–19
  protecting against 121
  transmission 170–1
encryption 99–102
  authentication and 110–11
  digital certificates 107–8
  digital signatures 104–8
  keys 101–2
  methods of 99–101
  single key 99–100
  public key 100–1
  See also Security
Encyclopaedia Britannica 19
Ethernet 196
etiquette (netiquette) 177, 187
Excite 11
Extensible Messaging and Presence
      Protocol (XMPP) 128

FAST 10, 11
Federal Information Processing Standard
    (FIPS) 101

file formats
   compression 169–70
   conversion between 169
   size of 169–70
   transmission of viruses 170–1
file transfer 188–93
   BinHex 168–9
   e-mail 168–70
   FTP. *See* FTP (File Transfer Protocol)
   MIME 162, 166, 171–2
   UUEncode 168–9
   viruses, transmission of 118–19,
      170–1
Filemaker Pro 80, 81
FindWhat 10, 11
firewalls 114–17, 136–7
   Internet 114
   personal 115–17
Fireworks 57
FirstGov 6
Flash (Macromedia) 32, 53, 60, 62
For Your Information (FYI) 197
FQDN (fully qualified domain name) 207
frequently asked questions (FAQ) 186
FrontPage Express (Microsoft) 45, 48
FTP (File Transfer Protocol) 6, 49, 115,
      170
   accessing heavily used sites 193
   examples 191–3
   general aspects 190–1
   retrieving (downloading) files 188–90,
      191, 192–3
   secure (SFTP) 188
   uploading 190, 191, 192–3
fully qualified domain name (FQDN) 207
FYI (For Your Information) 197

gatekeeper, videoconferencing 135,
      140, 144
GDS (Global Dialling Scheme) 144
GIF 30, 54, 60
GIF Construction Set 58
Global Dialling Scheme (GDS) 144
Global System for Mobiles (GSM) cards
      112
Global Yellow Pages 24
GNRT (Guide to Network Resource Tools)
      153
Google 7–8, 10, 14, 18

Graphic Workshop Classic 58
graphics 51–5
   accessibility 55
   Adobe Illustrator 53, 56–7
   Adobe Photoshop 55–6
   Adobe Photoshop Elements 56
   CoffeeCup Image Mapper 59
   DeBabelizer Pro 57–8
   efficient and effective images 53–4
   Fireworks 57
   GIF 52
   GIF Construction Set for Windows 58
   Graphic Workshop Classic 58
   image formats 51
   imagemaps/clickable images 54–5
   JPEG 21, 30, 52, 54
   MapEdit 54, 58–9
   Paint Shop Pro for Windows 56
   Portable Networks Graphics (PNG)
      52–3
   software for 55–9
   vector 53
GRID 91, 159
GSM (Global System for Mobiles) cards
      112

H.320 139–40, 144
H.323 140, 144, 153, 154–5, 158
hacker 91
hash function 105
host 224–6
hostile code 117–22
HotBot 8
HTML 27, 30, 43, 45–6, 47
   dynamic (DHTML) 35, 60, 66–9
   validating 45
HTTP (HyperText Transmission Protocol)
      30, 82, 83
   HTTPS (HyperText Transmission
      Protocol Secure) 93
hypermedia 26–7

Ifconfig 220–1
ImageFinder 18
Imagemaps 54–5
images, searching for 18
IMAP (Internet Message Access Protocol)
      162, 165
IMPP (Instant Messaging and Presence
      Protocol) 128

Infobel.com 23
information, searching for. *See* Searching
InfoSpace 10, 23
Ingenta 25
Inktomi 8, 9, 10, 11
instant messaging (IM) 125, 126
Integrated Services (IntServ) 153
International Telecommunication Union
    (ITU) standards 137–43
Internet Architecture Board (IAB) 197
Internet Engineering Steering Group
    (IESG) 197
Internet Engineering Task Force (IETF)
    128, 197
Internet Explorer (Microsoft) 28, 29,
    35–6, 110
Internet firewall 114
Internet Relay Chat (IRC) 128–9
Internet Streaming Media Alliance (ISMA)
    148
InvisibleWeb 25
IP (Internet Protocol) 195, 197
IP address, networking 198–200
IP telephony 149–50, 152–3
IPSec 202
IPv4 199
IPv6 204
ISDN 135
Ixquick 11–12

Jabber 129–30
Java 33, 35, 80
JavaScript 33, 35
JDBC 79
JISCmail 24
JPEG 21, 30, 52, 54
JScript (Microsoft) 70

KartOO 12
Kerberos 202
keyword spamming 85

LAN (local area network) 195
    firewalls and 114–15
LDAP (Lightweight Directory Access
    Protocol) 20, 21, 23
Listproc 173
LISTSERV 173, 174–5, 177–81
    commands 180

examples 180–1
locating mailing list 179–80
sending commands to 178–9
subscribing/unsubscribing 179
LookSmart 9, 10, 11, 15
love letter worm 119
Lycos 14, 17
Lynx 28, 37

macro viruses 118–19
    protecting against 121
Macromedia Flash 32, 53, 60, 62
Macromedia Shockwave 63
Mail Transfer Agent (MTA) 161, 162
Mail User Agent (MUA) 161–2, 166
    configuration parameters 164–5
Mailbase 173
mailing list managers (MLMs) 173–4,
    176, 177–84
mailing lists 24–5, 172–84
    etiquette 177
    handling correspondence 176–7
    managers 173–4, 176, 177–84
    MLM commands 176
    operation 173–4
    setting up 174–6
    See also LISTSERV; Majordomo
Majordomo 173, 174, 181–4
    commands 183
    examples 183
    locating mailing list 183
    sending commands to 181–2
    subscribing/unsubscribing 182–3
    web and archive tools 184
MapEdit 54, 58–9
MasterCard International 96
MBone 138, 141–3
MCU (multipoint control unit) 136
Melissa macro virus 119
memory-only chips 112
metadata 84–6
meta-search engines 1, 9–13
    pros and cons 9–10
metatags 85
MG (media gateway) 152
MGCP (Media Gateway Control Protocol)
    153
MGC (media gateway controller/call
    agent) 152

Michelangelo virus 118
microprocessor smart cards 112
Microsoft 8
  FrontPage Express 45, 48
  Internet Explorer 28, 29, 35–6, 110
  JScript 70
  Windows Media Player 59, 134
MIME (Multipurpose Internet Mail
      Extensions) 162, 166, 171–2
Mirago 10
mirror sites 193
Mosaic 28
Mozilla 36–7
MP3 6, 59
MPEG family 134
MPLS (Multiprotocol Label Switching)
      153
MSN 12, 18
MSN Search 9
MTA (Mail Transfer Agent) 161, 162
MUA (Mail User Agent) 161–2, 166
  configuration parameters 164–5
multimedia 59–61
  cascading style sheets 33, 35, 66, 67,
      68, 82
  Cosmo Player 63
  distributed object technology 65
  DOM 67
  dynamic content and caching 65–6
  dynamic HTML 66–9
  Flash (Macromedia) 32, 53, 60, 62
  HTTP 30, 82, 83
  MBone 138, 141–3
  media players 148
  media standards 148
  providing 60–1
  QuickTime 61–2
  RealPlayer 62
  resources 148–9
  servers/technologies 149
  Shockwave (Macromedia) 63
  software for 61–4
  streaming 138, 141–3, 145–9
  technology behind 146–8
  WinAmp 63
  Windows Media Player, 59, 62, 134
MySQL 80

NAPT (network address port translation)
      202

NAT (Network Address Translation)
      136–7, 200–3
  dynamic 202
  static 201–2
national research and education
      networks (NREN) 141
netiquette 177, 187
Netscape 18, 191
  Communicator, 28, 33–5, 48
  Media Player 33
  Navigator 28, 33, 109–10
  Personal Security Environment (PSE)
      109
  Search 14
netstat 221–3
network backbone 195–6
network edge 195–6
network tools 211–38
  command line interface (CLI) 212–13
  connectivity testing tools 213–20
    Pathping 218–20
    Ping 214–15
    Traceroute 216–18
  DNS lookup tools 224–31
    dig 226–9
    host 224–6
    nslookup 229–31
  finding contact network managers
      231–2
  host network configuration tools
      220–3
    Ifconfig 220–1
    netstat 221–3
  troubleshooting 211–12
  Whois 232–8
networking
  addressing and routing 198–200
  basic concepts 194–210
  client/server and peer-to-peer model
      197–8
  components and structure 195–7
  DHCP 203–4
  IPv6 204
  naming systems 205–10
    DNS (Domain Name System) 207–9
    network services, ports 206
    URL, URI 209–10
  NAT 136–7, 200–3
  performance and problems 205

protocol layers 198
protocols and standards 197
routing 200
newsgroups 185–7
NNTP (Network News Transfer Protocol)
    185
Northern Light 25
Novell Directory Services 21
NREN (national research and education
    networks) 141
nslookup 229–31
NTE (Network Text Editor) 142
NTSC 133

ODBC (Open DataBase Connectivity) 79
offline reading 29
Open Directory 8, 10, 14–15
Opera 36
Oracle 80, 81
organizations, searching for 22–4
Overture 8, 9, 10, 11

PageRank 7
Paint Shop Pro for Windows 56
PAL 133
passwords 92
Pathping 212, 218–20
PDF (Portable Document Format) 6, 48
Peer-to-Peer (P2P) 91
people, searching for 22–4
personal firewall 115–17
Pervasive.SQL 81
PGP (Pretty Good Privacy) 21, 93, 97,
    167
Photoshop (Adobe) 55–6
PHP 80
PINAKES 17
Ping 214–15
PKC (public key certificate) 94, 109–10
PKI (public key infrastructure) 98, 106,
    108–11
PNG 30
POP (Post Office Protocol) 162, 165
portal services 2, 17–18, 23
ports 206
PRIM (Presence and Instant Messaging
    Protocol) 128
Procmail 168
protocol layers 198

proxy server 38–9
PSTN (public switched telephone
    network) 149, 150
public key certificate (PKC) 94
    obtaining 109–10
public key infrastructure (PKI) 98, 106,
    108–11
publishing. See Web publishing

Qualcomm 98
QuickTime 59, 61

RAT (Robust Audio Tool) 142
RBU (Realtime Blackhole List) 124
RDFs (Resource Description Framework)
    40, 85
RealNetworks 134
RealPlayer 59, 61
reflector 136
RFCs (Requests for Comments) 32, 197
Resource Discovery Network 15–16
RIRs (Regional Internet Registries) 198
robots 86–8
    exclusion protocol 87
    meta tag 87–8
RSA 101
RSVP (Resource Reservation Protocol)
    153
RTP (Real-time Transport Protocol) 138,
    148
RTSP (Real-Time Streaming Protocol)
    148
RTT (round trip time) 205

S/MIME (Secure/Multipurpose Internet
    Mail Extensions) 93, 167
SAML (Security Assertion Markup
    Language) 42
Scirus 6, 19–20
SAP (Session Announcement Protocol)
    138, 142
SCP (Secure CoPy) 188
SDP (Session Description Protocol) 138,
    141, 142, 148
SDR (Session Directory Tool) 142
search engines 1, 5–9, 49–50
    See also under names
searching
    AltaVista 7, 11, 12, 18

AskJeeves 10
case sensitive searching 4
comprehensiveness 5
content, quality of 4–5
control over 2–4
Direct Hit 10
directory services 20–4
Excite 11
FAST 10, 11
Google 7–8, 10, 14, 18
HotBot 10
including/excluding search terms 3
index spamming 5
LDAP 20, 21, 23
Lycos 14, 17
metadata 84–6
meta-search engines 1, 9–13
multiple search terms 2–3
Northern Light 25
for people 22–4
phrase searching 3
proximity searching 3
relevance and ranking, 4–5, 6
results, presentation of 4
search engines 1, 5–9, 49–50
special operators 3
subject gateways 2, 13
tools, choosing 2–5
truncation and stemming 3–4
Whois 20, 22, 23, 198, 232–8
X.500 21–2, 23
Yahoo! 12, 16–17, 50
SECAM 133
Security
  accounting 104
  authentication 103
  authorization 103
  digital signatures 104–8, 110–11
  e-mail 96–8
  encryption 93, 99–102
  for applications 93–8
  maintaining 92
  PGP (Pretty Good Privacy) 21, 93, 97,
    167
  remote system connection 98
  requirements 92–3
  risks 90–3
  S/MIME 93, 167
  SET 93, 96

SSH 93, 98
SSL 93, 94–6, 98
Semantic Web 39–40
SET (Secure Electronic Transaction) 93,
    96
SFTP (Secure FTP) 188
SG (signalling gateway) 152
Shockwave (Macromedia) 63
SIM (subscriber identity module) cards
    111
SIMPLE (SIP for Instant Messaging and
    Presence Leveraging Extensions)
    128
SIP (Session Initiation Protocol) 138,
    141, 156–8
  proxy 135, 141
  user agent 141
smart cards and tokens 111–14
  chips 112
  contact 111
  contactless 112
  types 111–13
SMIL (Sunchronized Multimedia
    Integration Language) 61, 97,
    148
SMTP (Simple Mail Transfer Protocol)
    162
SOAP (Simple Object Access Protocol)
    40, 41
Sorensen Video 134
spamming 122–4
  detection 168
  index 5
  keyword 85
  stopping 123–4
  views of 123
Sprinks 11
SQL Server 79, 81
SSH (Secure Shell) 93, 98
SSI (Server Side Includes) 64, 65, 75
SSL 93, 94–6, 98
SSL/TLS (Secure Sockets Layer/Transport
    Layer Security) protocol 94
streaming 145–9
  MBone 138, 141–3
  media players 148
  media standards 148
  resources 148–9
  servers/technologies 149

technology behind 146–8
subject gateways 2, 13
SVG (scalable vector graphics) 53
synchronous communication 125

T.120 128, 138–9
TechDis initiative 88
telephony
　IP 149–50, 152–3
　standards 153–4
Telnet 29, 98
Teoma 10
Terra Lycos 6, 8
TILE.NET 25
TOPICA 25
Traceroute 212, 216–18
Transmission Control Protocol (TCP) 197
Transmission Control Protocol/Internet
　　Protocol (TCP/IP) 115
Trojan horses 119, 121

UCE (unsolicited commercial e-mail) 168
UDDI (Universal Description Discovery
　　and Integration) 40, 41–2
Unix 28
URLs (Uniform Resource Locators) 5, 27,
　　209–10
　finding specific 29
USB (universal serial bus) tokens 113–14
Usenet News 184–7
　accessing 185
　news coverage 185–7
　newsreader programs 187
UUEncode 168–9

VBScript 35
VIC (videoconferencing tool) 142
ViDeNet 144
videoconferencing 134–45
　multipoint 136
　networks 143–5
　resources 143
　standards 137–43
　use location and address resolution
　　135
viruses 117–18
　e-mail transmission 118–19, 170–1
　macro 118–19
　protecting against 120–1

Visa International 96
Visual Basic Script 118–19
Visual InterDev (Microsoft) 79
Vivisimo 12–13
VMS 28
VoIP 149–52, 153
VRVS (Virtual Rooms Videoconferencing
　　System) 144, 145

WAP protocol 196
WayBack Machine 20
Web databases 78–81
　Active Server Pages 79
　Application Server 80
　ColdFusion 79–80
　database management system 79
　dynamic Web sites 78–9
　Filemaker Pro 80
　MySOL 80
　Oracle 80
　Persuasive.SQL 81
　PHP 80
　SOL Server 81
　tools 79–81
Web design, seven precepts of 88–9
Web publishing 43–89
　accessibility 88–9
　Active Server Pages 65, 72–3
　application program interface 74
　authoring tools 47–8, 49
　Common Gateway Interface 65, 71–2
　cookies 65, 76–7
　dynamic content and caching 65–6
　file upload 49
　graphics. See Graphics
　HTML. See HTML
　interactive Web pages 64–77
　Java 65, 69–70
　JavaScript 65, 70–1
　Microsoft FrontPage 45, 48
　multimedia. See Multimedia
　PHP 74
　Server Side Includes 64, 65, 75
Web services 40–2
Webwhacker 29
White Pages 20, 23
Whois 20, 22, 23, 198, 232–8
WinAmp 63
Windows Media Player (Microsoft) 59,
　　62, 134

World E-mail Directory (WED) 24
World Wide Web 26–32
  access to 27–30
  additional file types 30
  bookmarking 31
  browsers. *See* browers
  caching and caches 38–9, 65–6
  FAQ 32
  hypermedia 26–7
  information, distributed 27
  information, publishing 27
  interactivity 30–1
  offline reading 29
  protocol 29–30
  publishing on. *See* Web publishing
  searching. *See* Searching
  Semantic Web 39–40
  telnet, using 29
  URL, finding a specific 29
World Wide Web Consortium (W3C) 32,
  85
worms 120, 121–2

WSDL (Web Services Description
  Language) 40, 41
WYSIWYG 44, 47, 48

X.500 21–2, 23
X11 202
xDSL 196
XML (eXtensible Markup Language) 35,
  40, 41, 81–4
  browser compatibility 83–4
  Document Type Definitions 83
  implications 83
  XSL (eXtensible Style Language) 82–3
XMPP (Extensible Messaging and
  Presence Protocol) 128
XSL 82–3

Yahoo! 12, 16–17, 50
Yellow Pages 20, 23, 40

zone transfer 224